Denny

God bless you dear brother —
Thanks for the memories

What in the world is God doing?

A verse-by-verse study of Romans

Dr. Dino Pedrone

xulon PRESS

What in the world is God doing?
A verse-by-verse study of Romans
by Dr. Dino Pedrone

Printed in the United States of America

ISBN 978-1-60791-955-1

Unless otherwise indicated, Bible quotations are taken from The King James Version.

www.xulonpress.com

INTRODUCTION

Preaching the Word of God is one of the great joys of my life. I am honored to be a preacher.

In Chambersburg, Pennsylvania, I spent 25 years at the same church preaching week after week the Bible and its message. Since 1995 it has been my privilege to preach God's Word from the pulpit of The Gathering Place at New Testament Baptist Church in South Florida. On Tuesdays I preach at the Presidential chapel of Davis College in Binghamton, New York. I have traveled to nearly 40 states in America and more than 20 countries to preach the Word of God. It is my conviction that preaching God's Word is one of the most important things that needs to happen in our postmodern and post Christian world.

My fear is that there are many people who are called to preach the Word of God but, because of the lack of a challenge to enter the ministry, have not done so. It is my prayer to challenge those who are called to the ministry to accept the call and to be trained in a college of ministry like the one I have the honor to oversee, Davis College. America has historically had the Word of God proclaimed in pulpits throughout rural and urban communities. Today there is a departure from following the authority of the Scriptures as our guide to faith and conduct. Frankly, if I do not have the Scriptures to guide me I have no message to give.

This commentary, the second that this author has produced, is a preaching commentary. The messages are mostly expositional and are in the same basic form that they were given from the pulpit to the wonderful congregation that I have the privilege to speak to every week. In South Florida I have a team of preachers who help me speak in our multiple services. It is my prayer that this commentary will draw men and women to churches that preach God's Word.

The Bible is our book. Preaching is one of the great vehicles to proclaim the truth. This commentary is dedicated to that task.

I want to thank the deacons and trustees of my ministry who make it possible for me to serve the Lord in so many areas. They work laboriously to see that our ministry is fulfilling the God-given vision. I additionally want to thank the trustees of Davis College for their tremendous support of the vision of our ministry that allows me the time to produce these commentaries. I also want to thank my son Jonathan who helped me with this material.

My dear Bobbi, who I met in 1964 and married in 1967, is the greatest wife that a woman can be. All ministry that I do is a team effort. She is truly my soul mate.

PROLOGUE

I often hear people ask the question, "What is God doing in the world today?"

The book of Romans contains volumes of information about who God is and what He is like; therefore, we can learn about what He is doing. He is at work today through His people.

The world today struggles with the question, "Who is God?"

It is this author's prayer to address what the Apostle Paul tells us about God so that we can observe what He is doing.

Chapter 1

DO YOU HEAR THE CALL?

"Paul, a servant of Jesus Christ, called to be an apostle, separated unto the gospel of God, (Which he had promised afore by his prophets in the holy scriptures,) Concerning his Son Jesus Christ our Lord, which was made of the seed of David according to the flesh; And declared to be the Son of God with power, according to the spirit of holiness, by the resurrection from the dead: By whom we have received grace and apostleship, for obedience to the faith among all nations, for his name: Among whom are ye also the called of Jesus Christ: To all that be in Rome, beloved of God, called to be saints: Grace to you and peace from God our Father, and the Lord Jesus Christ." (**Rom. 1:1-7**)

If you were to receive a letter in the mail with the words "The White House" on the outside of the envelope, and that letter contained an invitation for you to spend a day with the President of the United States, you would most likely be delighted. That honor for most Americans transcends political affiliation, and there are very few people who would not respond affirmatively to an invitation from that office.

Now suppose the time has come for your visit and you even get a telephone call from the White House confirming your appointment.

By this point you would be extremely excited. You have been called to meet with the president.

This passage in Romans contains a call from God to every one of us. To understand this call we need to consider some of the background to this epistle.

The Roman Empire at this time was literally a world empire. There have been several world empires in history – the Babylonians, the Medes and Persians, the Greeks. The empire of the Romans was extremely powerful. The ancient Roman civilization that grew from a small agricultural community founded on the Italian peninsula was a powerful force in the world for 12 centuries.

The United States of America is more than 200 years old and probably the strongest nation on the planet. Imagine the U.S. as a world empire that would rule for another thousand years from now. That would be a fair comparison to the Roman Empire.

The Roman government began with a monarchy, then a republic, an oligarchy, a democracy and back to an aristocratic empire. In 5 A.D. a decline began to take place and this great nation became several independent kingdoms. For example, in Eastern Europe it was governed by Constantinople in what was known as the Byzantine government. When the Roman Empire fell, it led to the Middle Ages and the Dark Ages.

The religion of the Roman Empire was organized under a strict system of priestly offices, held by men of senatorial rank. The office of pope was established and Greek influences also came along, including philosophies such as Jupiter, Mars and Neptune. In the second century there was an unusual movement of Christianity throughout Rome. Despite heavy persecution, Christianity eventually became the official religion of Rome.

This was not a good thing. Society cannot organize Christianity as a nation. There must be a born-again experience in an individual soul. If we all decided to make everyone in the United States a Christian, we still could not do that. Only God can make someone a Christian.

In Roman times the home was very patriarchal. The father was in charge. He could divorce his wife at any time or sell his children into slavery. They could make extraordinary claims on family property or even kill other family members. Most fathers began considering prospective husbands for their daughters when the girls were 12-14 years of age.

The educational system in Rome was unique. Children would not attend public schools at an early age, but their parents would teach them to read and write. Young boys would then, starting at around age 12, go to secondary school and start considering agriculture, warfare or public affairs. By 16 many were in law school.

The book "The Decline and Fall of the Roman Empire" was written by Edward Gibbon, and in it the author gives five reasons why Christianity grew throughout the empire: the zeal of the Jewish believers; the teaching of the doctrine of the future life, where people began to believe in a real place called Heaven; miracles that were witnessed by many and fueled the strong belief that God was at work; a level of morality by Christians that was higher than others around them; and the church's role in government, which eventually led to a decline in the church because it became so hierarchal.

A perpetual stream of strangers flooded Rome, and people came from everywhere because the Holy Roman Empire was the world's standard for its time. There is no present-day nation that can compare with that era of world history.

America is a great nation, and I'm glad to be an American. But we are not part of any kind of world empire, although I see some similarities particularly between my home community in South Florida and that of the Romans.

According to media reports in late 2007, seven out of 10 people moving into South Florida were born outside the United States. In my church on a recent Sunday morning, a show of hands indicated that the crowd was split almost 50-50 between those born in this country and those born abroad.

One-third of the residents of South Florida are Hispanic. The area is also getting younger, according to demographic studies. Fifty percent of those who live here move every five years.

We are now home to 1,400 multinational businesses, and the next decade will likely see an increase in the number of Asian businesses operating here. We are truly a cosmopolitan center; we often do not know our neighbors or where our towns begin and end, and we are connected by cell phones, Web sites and satellite communications.

One writer put it this way: "We are in constant movement and change, and people's loyalties, or the relationships about which they feel the most strongly, are not to a physical community. It is culturally, linguistically and religiously the place that they are from and what they connect to." Shortly, all communities will look like this. This statement also reminds us of the importance of the local church. The church, then, must become a family.

The very first verse of Romans carries within it the idea of being called: *"Paul, a servant of Jesus Christ, called to be an apostle, separated unto the gospel of God."* It is repeated in verse 6: *"Among whom are ye also the called of Jesus Christ."* Look at the first part of verse 7: *"To all that be in Rome, beloved of God, called to be saints."*

Three times in the first seven verses we are told about being called. The word *"called"* is a key word. It means to summon, to invite, to be called by name, and there are blessings that await you when you answer the call.

Called Christians are servants

We know that God has called all of us, but to what? Back in verse 1, Paul calls himself a *"servant"* of Christ. Actually he is describing himself as a slave, or bondservant. Why is he a servant? He gives the answer at the end of the verse, *"the gospel of God."* He mentions the Gospel again in verse 9, 15 and 16. Paul is a servant because of the Gospel.

We know that the Gospel is the "Good News" – Jesus died, was buried and rose again. But the Gospel is not just one thing among many; it is THE thing. You cannot connect the Bible without the Gospel.

Some of the other verses in this passage explain this further. Look at verse 3. *"Concerning his Son Jesus Christ our Lord, which was made of the seed of David according to the flesh."* Jesus defines Himself here as a true historical person.

In I Cor. 15:3-7 is often called "the creed of the church." It reads, *"For I delivered unto you first of all that which I also received, how*

To reserve your Free Welcome Gifts you must respond within 7 days!

If you don't reply, your name will be removed from the lineup ...
and replaced with a fan to be named later!

WELCOME TO THE TEAM ...
where the fans are always #1!

RESV A005404

To score a no-risk membership, detach the Membership Acceptance form at right and mail in the postage-paid reply envelope today with "Favorite Team" and "FREE Welcome Gifts" stickers attached.

Please place this card in your wallet immediately

MLB INSIDERS CLUB
NO-RISK
CHARTER MEMBERSHIP
GUARANTEE

Join the team today and send us your Membership Acceptance form now. If you are at all unhappy with your first issue of *MLB Insiders Club Magazine* or your Charter Member Welcome Kit, just write "cancel" on your dues invoice. Nothing more will be said. And you'll owe us nothing. Any free gifts will still be yours to keep.

It doesn't end there. As a Charter Member, if you're unhappy with the benefits of the MLB Insiders Club at any time during your first year, just let us know. Upon your request, you'll receive a full 100% refund of any dues you've paid. You don't risk a single cent.

◀ *Detach and return Membership Acceptance form today.*

that Christ died for our sins according to the scriptures; And that he was buried, and that he rose again the third day according to the scriptures: And that he was seen of Cephas, then of the twelve: After that, he was seen of above five hundred brethren at once; of whom the greater part remain unto this present, but some are fallen asleep. After that, he was seen of James; then of all the apostles."

While Rom. 1:3 shows Jesus Christ in the flesh, verse 4 goes much further: *"And declared to be the Son of God with power, according to the spirit of holiness, by the resurrection from the dead."*

Ten times in the book of Romans Paul refers to Jesus as the Lord Jesus Christ. So as Paul declared himself a servant, all of us who accept Christ as our Saviour should immediately begin making Him the Lord of our lives.

If He is the Lord, than He should be your Lord and my Lord. Whether you agree that He is Lord, it doesn't take away from the fact that He is Lord. When we understand that, we become the servants, or bondservants (slaves), to Him that we should be.

Notice something else about Paul's call in verse 1. He said that he was *"called to be an apostle."* He is referring to the office of an apostle, which in the early church was held by someone who had seen Jesus Christ. But in verse 5, he expands on that qualification: *"By whom we have received grace and apostleship, for obedience to the faith among all nations, for his name."* There he is talking about the function of an apostle, or a missionary.

Christianity in Rome was unusual. It began in the synagogues, as Jews came to Christ, and by about 40 A.D. the Roman government was so upset with Jewish believers that they began to throw them out of Rome. You can read in Acts 18:2 that Aquilla and Priscilla were expelled from Rome, as the majority of Jewish people were, because the Gospel was growing so rapidly.

We usually talk about the book of Romans as a great work of theology, but I believe that if we look at it that way we miss its purpose. It must be taken in its proper context, which is what was happening to Jewish believers at this time.

The book of Romans is referred to as a major theological writing of the Apostle Paul, but there is no reference to the Lord's Supper. The great chapter on the Resurrection is not in Romans, but in

Corinthians. The great subjects relating to Christ are found more in Ephesians than in Romans. Details about the future are found mostly in Revelation.

Called Christians are sent

So what is Paul writing about here? It is a time when the Jews are being cast out, part of a long history of exclusion for them, yet God is saying, "I still have a place for my people."

That is why Rom. 1:16 says, *"For I am not ashamed of the gospel of Christ: for it is the power of God unto salvation to every one that believeth; to the Jew first, and also to the Greek."* What does he mean by *"the Jew first"*? It was the Jews who spread the Gospel first in Rome before they were thrown out.

This does not take away from the fact that Romans is a theological masterpiece. But anyone who looks at solely in that regard will miss out. In fact, in chapters 9-11 God speaks loud and clear about having a place for His people.

A key phrase in Rom. 1:5 is *"among all nations."* God intends for the Gospel to be taken to every known part of the world. The people of my church in South Florida have a unique privilege in that so many nations of the world are represented in our community and we can take the Gospel to them. We have been able to send teams on mission trips to South America and Africa, among other places, but the nations of the world are coming right to our doorstep.

Called Christians are separated

Verse 1 shows that we are not only servants of God and sent by God; we are also separated. That word in this passage means "marked off by bounds." It is the divine action of setting apart men for the Gospel ministry. Paul is saying here, "I belong to God."

A few years ago I sat on an airplane next to a Marine who I was able to lead to Christ. I had a great time talking to him. He was so proud of being a Marine. When I mentioned the other branches of military service, he said, "Those are all right, but I am a Marine." When I asked him what a Marine did, it was 10 minutes before I got another word in because he loved to tell me what he did. He was set apart for a special group.

God has called us in a similar fashion to be part of something very special, to be separated unto Himself. The word *"nations"* in verse 5 is *"ethos."* It refers to the idea of guiding beliefs, standards and ideals that characterize or pervade a group; the spirit that motivates the ideas, customs and practices of a people. It is the idea of being called unto God.

From that we can look at the first part of verse 7. *"To all that be in Rome, beloved of God, called to be saints."* That means we are called to be holy. You might think you're not very holy, but when you are saved by Jesus Christ, you stand before God as if you had never committed a sin. So, because of our position in Christ, you and I are holy.

Let's look again at who is calling us. Verse 6 says, *"Among whom are ye also the called of Jesus Christ."* It is interesting that, in verses 1-7, Christ is referred to as *"his Son," "Jesus Christ," "our Lord," "the seed of David," "the Son of God"* and *"the Lord Jesus Christ."*

The word "lord" is a very powerful word. It can be used to simply mean "sir." But that is not the way it is used here. Often when used in the Bible, it is not merely a title of respect but also a reference to mastery and ownership.

In the Greek version of the New Testament, the Septuagent (which was well-known to the Jewish community), the word translated here would be *Yahweh.* That word in the Old Testament shows divinity. Here it simply shows us that Jesus is God.

You may recall the story of Jesus appearing to His disciples after His resurrection, when Thomas was absent. When Thomas saw Him the next week, he saw the scars in Christ's hands and side before falling down and crying out, "My Lord and my God." The word used for "Lord" in that instance is the same one used here, to show Christ's divinity. It is the word *kurios*, meaning "master."

Note the following scriptures. *"As concerning therefore the eating of those things that are offered in sacrifice unto idols, we know that an idol is nothing in the world, and that there is none other God but one. For though there be that are called gods, whether in heaven or in earth, (as there be gods many, and lords many,) But to us there is but one God, the Father, of whom are all things, and we in him; and one Lord Jesus Christ, by whom are all things, and we by him."* (I Cor. 8:4-6)

> *"Let this mind be in you, which was also in Christ Jesus: Who, being in the form of God, thought it not robbery to be equal with God: But made himself of no reputation, and took upon him the form of a servant, and was made in the likeness of men: And being found in fashion as a man, he humbled himself, and became obedient unto death, even the death of the cross. Wherefore God also hath highly exalted him, and given him a name which is above every name: That at the name of Jesus every knee should bow, of things in heaven, and things in earth, and things under the earth; And that every tongue should confess that Jesus Christ is Lord, to the glory of God the Father."* (Phil. 2:5-11)

There are those who state, "Let's get saved and become believers, but we won't make a big deal out of it." You have to understand that when living under the Roman government when these epistles were written, if you had Jesus then you had something very near and dear to your heart. The Caesars wanted themselves declared lord by everyone under their rule, meaning that no one else could be lord of one's life but Caesar. To say, "Jesus is Lord," is the same as saying, "Caesar is not Lord."

The 86-year-old Polycarp was the chief pastor in Smyrna. When the Roman leaders wanted him to proclaim that Caesar is lord, he said, "I can't do that. Jesus is Lord." His best friends encouraged him to just say it, even if it didn't mean it, so he could live, but he wouldn't do it. Here are his words just before he was put to death: "For 86 years I have been Christ's slave and He has done me no wrong. How can I blaspheme my King who saved me?"

The title of "Lord" is a symbol of Christ's victory over the forces of evil. If Jesus has been exalted over all principalities and powers of evil, as He has, it is because all of these powers are under His feet. He has conquered them on the cross, and our very salvation – our rescue from sin, Satan, fear and death – is due to His victory. Jesus

Christ is Lord, and we are called to recognize His Lordship in our lives.

What is the evidence of our calling? It is shown in verse 7: "*To all that be in Rome, beloved of God, called to be saints: Grace to you and peace from God our Father, and the Lord Jesus Christ.*" Aren't you glad for God's grace?

In the sports world in late 2007, when Atlanta Falcons quarterback Michael Vick went to prison for his part in a dogfighting operation, he became a sad figure and even a national punch line when he said that he had "found Jesus" as a result of his ordeal. We cannot know for certain if he has come to Christ, but each of us needs grace from time to time just like Vick does.

When impeachment proceedings were conducted for President Bill Clinton after his affair with Monica Lewinsky was made public, there was no doubt among most of the American public about the wrong he had done. But is there grace to cover something like that?

The ESPN series "The Bronx is Burning" retold the story of the 1977 New York Yankees and their march to the World Series amid so much unrest in New York City as the "Son of Sam" murders were also taking place. David Berkowitz then talked of how Christ gloriously saved him from a life as an avowed atheist, and his testimony has been published around the country. Is there grace for the Son of Sam?

In the 1987 film "Ironweed," starring Jack Nicholson and Meryl Streep and based on a popular novel of the same name, Nicholson's character is talking about an Eskimo woman and asking, "Is she a drunk or a bum?" Other people speculate as to whether she was a prostitute or worse, and eventually they conclude that at one time she was a little girl.

"A little girl is something," Nicholson's character says, "A little girl is not a bum. Let's take her in."

That is what grace is all about. It is when God takes you in despite what He knows about you.

It is easy to go through the book of Romans, read about some of the sins listed there and say, "I'm glad I'm not like that." But as the Apostle Paul points out in chapter 2, when you do that you are just as bad as the people you are judging.

For this important calling of God that we have been considering, we need grace. No one comes to God except through grace. The result of that grace, as verse 7 indicates, is the peace we receive from the Lord Jesus Christ.

Humorist Erma Bombeck told a story of a boy sitting in church smiling. He wasn't doing anything else, just smiling. His mother leaned over and said to him, "You shouldn't be smiling. We're in church!"

Bombeck said that she was stunned at that and even began to get angry. "Doesn't God ever smile?" she thought.

The Bible says that God gives us peace. It doesn't matter if we are young or old; God says that we need grace and He will give us peace.

God is calling. He is ringing our number. The message He is sending to us is that we need to make Jesus Christ our Lord in everything we do.

Called Christians are servants and sent.

Chapter 2

A THANKFUL HEART LEADS TO A LIFE OF PRAYER

"First, I thank my God through Jesus Christ for you all, that your faith is spoken of throughout the whole world. For God is my witness, whom I serve with my spirit in the gospel of his Son, that without ceasing I make mention of you always in my prayers; Making request, if by any means now at length I might have a prosperous journey by the will of God to come unto you. For I long to see you, that I may impart unto you some spiritual gift, to the end ye may be established; That is, that I may be comforted together with you by the mutual faith both of you and me. Now I would not have you igno-rant, brethren, that oftentimes I purposed to come unto you, (but was let hitherto,) that I might have some fruit among you also, even as among other Gentiles. I am debtor both to the Greeks, and to the Barbarians; both to the wise, and to the unwise. So, as much as in me is, I am ready to preach the gospel to you that are at Rome also." **(Rom. 1:8-15)**

Television producer Richard Eyer studied the religious quest for meaning. In his quest he went to all of the inhabited continents of the globe to study what the various religions taught.

He concluded that all of the great religions attack the same problem, but they do it in a variety of ways. "Human beings want to be whole," he said. "Everyone is trying to find a way to have whole-ness in life. Yet in the struggle for wholeness, there is a constant war going on."

For example, a Jew will come to you and say, "Shalom," while a Muslim will say, "Saloma." Both of those words mean "peace," but those two groups of people are regularly at war with each other.

So the question remains, what makes someone whole? In his studies, Eyer found six basic things that religion teaches. Some teach that if you have the right rituals, sacrifices, festivals and ceremonies, or if you remain on a pilgrimage in your life, you can find whole-ness. Another prescription he found was that the suppression of all desires would allow you to find your way to God.

Then there is the philosophy that salvation is achieved by behaving the right way, by not hurting people. The fourth method is that which includes deep meditation and intense concentration, while another way involves the pursuit of pleasure. The sixth cate-gory includes those whose primary goal is to obey the law.

So goes the world of religion. Religion, however, does not deal with the wholeness of the human being. The Christian faith has the unique symbol of the cross. In looking at this portion of Romans 1 where the Apostle Paul addresses some things he is thankful for and praying about, we should understand that the cross is the key symbol in all of this.

In the first chapter of this book, we looked at the numerous refer-ences Paul made to the Gospel. In nearly all of his letters in the New Testament, he writes about how we should live the Christian life because of the Gospel.

In non-Christian religions, sin is always regarded as an act. If sin is an act, then the issue is how we can avoid it. There are many sins listed in the first chapter of Romans, such as idolatry, sexual immo-rality, envy and covetousness. Looking at that entire list reveals something that you struggle with in your life.

Let me illustrate it this way. You have a neighbor whom you like, but your neighbor always seems to have more than you do. One day you look outside and see a Hummer parked in their driveway. "Wow," you say. "How did they afford that?"

A few months later you see a Jaguar parked there. You've always wanted one, so you tell your spouse that you are getting a Jaguar, no matter what it costs, because you are not going to let your neighbor outdo you. You are envying and coveting, and if you don't stop you will be bankrupt as well.

Those are sins. But our problem is not the specific sins in our lives. We are taught from our early youth that sin is the act of doing something wrong. But Christianity teaches us that we have a nature of sin, and that is why we sin.

I have a 20-foot swimming pool at my home. It is no problem for me to swim from one end of that pool to the other. But if you drop me in the Atlantic Ocean about 10 miles off the coast of Fort Lauderdale and tell me that my salvation depends upon whether I can swim to shore, I am going to drown – no matter how good my intentions or my effort. I will need someone to come out and save me.

The reason that Christianity is the only thing that makes sense is that you and I cannot save ourselves. We have a multitude of sins, and no matter how much we determine that we're not going to sin, we will eventually sin anyway.

That is why we recognize the symbol of the cross. It is not for us to worship; if you have a cross set up for worship, you should take it down. The important thing for us about the cross is what it symbolizes, and the Bible speaks of this often:

> *"For Christ sent me not to baptize, but to preach the gospel: not with wisdom of words, lest the cross of Christ should be made of none effect. For the preaching of the cross is to them that perish foolishness; but unto us which are saved it is the power of God."* (I Cor. 1:17-18)
>
> *"But God forbid that I should glory, save in the cross of our Lord Jesus Christ, by whom the world is crucified unto me, and I unto the world."* (Gal. 6:14)
>
> *"And that he might reconcile both unto God in one body by the cross, having slain the enmity thereby."* (Eph. 2:16)

"And being found in fashion as a man, he humbled himself, and became obedient unto death, even the death of the cross." (Phil. 2:8)

"For many walk, of whom I have told you often, and now tell you even weeping, that they are the enemies of the cross of Christ." (Phil. 3:18)

"And, having made peace through the blood of his cross, by him to reconcile all things unto himself; by him, I say, whether they be things in earth, or things in heaven." (Col.1:20)

"Looking unto Jesus the author and finisher of our faith; who for the joy that was set before him endured the cross, despising the shame, and is set down at the right hand of the throne of God." (Heb. 12:2)

Thank God for the cross. As these repeated references in Scripture demonstrate, we cannot understate its importance.

Look at 2 Cor. 5:21. *"For he hath made him to be sin for us, who knew no sin; that we might be made the righteousness of God in him."*

God made Jesus to be our sin-bearer. In the Christian faith, it is not about our efforts to attain to God but about what God did for us through Jesus Christ. That is the Gospel.

With this in mind, we can look back at our text in Romans 1 about what Paul is thankful for and how it leads to prayer. Look again at verse 8. *"First, I thank my God through Jesus Christ for you all, that your faith is spoken of throughout the whole world."*

Notice how Paul personalized God here. When we accept Christ as our Saviour, God becomes "our" God. He also refers to the reader's faith, which in verse 12 he calls a *"mutual faith,"* demonstrating that it is one faith which draws us together as believers.

There are many things that draw people together. One of those things is a bloodline. We all have relatives that we care for a great deal (and some we may not care for as much).

A momentous event can unite people. I attended Game 7 of the 1997 World Series, when the Florida Marlins defeated the Cleveland Indians in the 11th inning to win the championship. I was giving high-fives and hugging people I had never seen before in my life, and most of them I have probably never seen since. But that one night drew us together.

You may be a Republican or a Democrat, and you attend a meeting on behalf of someone you want to see elected. All of you at that meeting are working together for a candidate or a cause.

But there is nothing that draws us together like the Gospel. We are living in a generation that is trying to "dumb down" the Gospel. People today laugh at others who read and study the Word of God. They think we should just lay the Bible aside.

How does God speak to us? A recent article in Time magazine about Mother Teresa addressed the question of whether God had really spoken to her. There really is no mystery concerning how God speaks to any of us. He does it through the Bible.

Occasionally you will hear someone who wants to see a great miracle that will prove to them the existence of God. I was witnessing one day to a man who said, "If God would just come down and talk to me, I would believe in Him." He has already done that, and we have a Book to prove it.

God has ways of speaking to us in all kinds of circumstances, but ultimately it comes back to the Bible. When Paul spoke of his thankfulness for his fellow Christians, it was because of their unity in faithfulness to their God and their obedience to His Word.

There is an all-out war in our culture today over the Bible, but I am delighted to remind you that the final chapter is the winning chapter, and God's final victory was won when Jesus Christ died on the cross, was buried and rose again.

Now look at verse 9. *"For God is my witness, whom I serve with my spirit in the gospel of his Son, that without ceasing I make mention of you always in my prayers."*

Paul had not yet been to Rome when he wrote this, yet he constantly included the Romans in his prayers. This verse demonstrates his exceptional prayer life.

Have you ever stopped to pray and, within two minutes, forgotten what you were praying about? Perhaps you prayed five minutes or so and then fell asleep. You read about people who pray for a half-hour or an hour and you wonder how in the world they can do that.

Buy yourself a notebook and keep a prayer journal. Write down your prayer requests on the left side of the page so you can read and remember them as you pray. When God answer a prayer, record the date on the right side of the page. When you begin to see how God answers prayer, it will make you want to pray even more.

If you come to me and give me a thousand dollars, I will be very appreciative (and I will gladly take it). But if you tell me that you are praying for me every day and you mean it, that is much more valuable than your money. If Paul could pray continually for these people he had never met, we can certainly pray for one another.

He wrote in verse 11 of the anticipation he felt toward his friends, because of the opportunities he knew would be there. *"For I long to see you, that I may impart unto you some spiritual gift, to the end ye may be established."* This is the reasoning behind his desire concerning them in verse 10: *"Making request, if by any means now at length I might have a prosperous journey by the will of God to come unto you."*

People often wonder if the will of God is a place. Well, it is in this passage. When you and I realize that we are here for a purpose, and God has a reason for our lives, it is exciting to know that He also has a location for us.

Paul was a unique human being. When he went to Jerusalem, the religious center, they mobbed him. When he went to Athens, the intellectual center, they mocked him. When he went to Rome, the legislative center, they martyred him. His life is a continual reminder to us that we should not live simply for ourselves.

We notice in verse 13 that, while he had a burden to see souls saved and to bear fruit, he speaks in verse 14 of being a debtor, and once again it is in reference to his responsibility concerning the Gospel.

Look at verse 14. *"I am debtor both to the Greeks, and to the Barbarians; both to the wise, and to the unwise."* In Rome at this time there were Jewish Christians who were on fire for God. But Paul made it clear that he was also ministering to non-Jewish people. We hear people today talk about tailoring a ministry to a specific market, but Paul never did that. He was always after whoever he could reach.

It is interesting to note, at this writing, how many prominent Christian leaders have recently gone on to Heaven: Ruth Graham, Jerry Falwell, D. James Kennedy, and Lee Roberson, just to name a few. But this is our day. It is your day to serve the Lord.

Notice Paul's boldness in verse 15. *"So, as much as in me is, I am ready to preach the gospel to you that are at Rome also."* He was prepared for whatever might be awaiting him.

This is because of the belief expressed in verse 16. *"For I am not ashamed of the gospel of Christ: for it is the power of God unto salvation to every one that s believeth; to the Jew first, and also to the Greek."* He believed in the supremacy of the Gospel, and it is still the most important thing we can impart to people today.

He expounds on the basis for this in verse 17. *"For therein is the righteousness of God revealed from faith to faith: as it is written, The just shall live by faith."* Conformity to righteousness is through Christ, going from the initial act of faith to our continued daily walk with Him.

But it always comes back to the Gospel. I was flying home from a meeting and sat behind a handsome couple with a beautiful girl who looked to be about two years of age. She leaned over the back of her seat and waved at me, so I waved back at her. Then she winked at me, and I returned the gesture. She made a face at me, but I didn't do that, so she sat down.

About halfway through the flight, she began screaming because she was tired and wanted to get off the plane. I wondered how the father would deal with this problem. As he took her out into the aisle she kept fussing. Then he put her hand in his and began to squeeze. The child's expression changed, and you could tell that she was thinking, "Daddy means business." I could relate to that, as I used to squeeze the hand of whichever one of my children was causing embarrassment when we were out in public.

When you come to Christ, you are literally in the palm of the Lord's hand and He is helping you all the way through the rest of your life. Do not renege on the Gospel.

There is something in all of us that makes us think we somehow have to please God. The Bible says that when we are saved we have an innate desire to please Him, but if you are trying to please Him for salvation it will never happen. The only way we can please God is through Christ.

John Wesley was considered the greatest evangelist of his era. In fact, there are churches all over the world started by John Wesley. For years he was a missionary though he was unsaved, and he tried to work his way to God. In his testimony he said that as a discouraged missionary he went unwillingly to a meeting in London, where he said a miracle took place.

It was about a quarter to nine, he wrote later in his journal, that "I felt my heart become strangely warm, as I had trusted Christ and Him alone for my salvation." The speaker at that meeting was speaking from the first chapter of Romans.

The book of Romans can thrill your heart and change your life, but it has to be applied to your life for that to happen. The way to live out your faith is not by trying to earn brownie points with God, or earn His acceptance through your own merits, but because of what Christ has done for us. Jesus Christ is the righteousness of God.

Aren't you glad to be a child of God and part of the family of God? We should be thankful for that. Paul was thankful for those fellow believers he had not even seen.

We often have a misunderstanding about Christianity that goes back to other religions. We come to church and evaluate the worship service to decide if we like it. That's not what it's about. The important thing is whether your life is changed by the power of the Gospel, and that you become an agent of change of other people's lives as they come to the Lord.

The Gospel is the Good News – that Jesus died, was buried and rose again. That is the greatest message people can hear.

Build a prayer life and do it with thanksgiving, and you will be surprised at how God works in and through you.

Chapter 3

THE GREAT DIFFERENCE

"For I am not ashamed of the gospel of Christ: for it is the power of God unto salvation to every one that believeth; to the Jew first, and also to the Greek. For therein is the righteousness of God revealed from faith to faith: as it is written, The just shall live by faith." (**Rom. 1:16-17**)

The Apostle Paul wrote, *"For I am not ashamed of the Gospel of Christ."* The shame he refers to is a type of shame or fear that would prevent someone from carrying out a specific task.

When God saves us He gives us Jesus Christ, and we should not be ashamed. God does not ask us to behave to be saved, but only to believe to be saved.

The city of Rome was a very proud city, in contrast with the humble city of Jerusalem from which the Gospel had come. Christians in Rome were often considered among the elite, while the Christians in Jerusalem were usually counted among the commoners.

Origination

So among the great philosophers and philosophies of the day, Paul announced that he was not ashamed of the Gospel. Warren Wiersbe put it so well when he wrote that there are four elements to what Paul is saying here. First, he is speaking about the **origination** of the Gospel; it is a message that deserves immediate attention. It is a message about the Son of God.

If you have a message that needs to be told, then it stands to reason that there are people who need to hear it. Some of us are old enough to remember when President John F. Kennedy was assassinated by Lee Harvey Oswald. You likely remember where you were and what you were doing when that took place, because it was such an incredible event.

I was a student at North High School in Binghamton, New York, when I heard about it. I was in history class and my teacher was Nate George. A young girl came into the classroom and interrupted the class with the news that President Kennedy was dead. What right did a student have to disrupt the class? It was because of the message she carried.

Operation

Paul is telling us in this passage that he has a message, and that message is a powerful one for all who hear it. He also talks about the **operation** of the Gospel and how it is the power of God.

Rome had become a wicked city at this time. The philosopher Seneca once said it was a "cesspool of iniquity." Another philosopher said that it was like "a filthy sewer into which the dregs of the Empire were flooding through."

So here comes Paul with his presentation of the Gospel that changes lives. It's one thing to talk about the Gospel or speak well of it; it's another thing to say that there is only one Gospel. But the Gospel is meaningless until it changes your life.

Outcome

Paul also speaks here about the **outcome** of the Gospel, which is salvation. That word here literally means deliverance. People in Rome looked to the emperor Caesar as their savior, and to come along and say that someone else is a savior was pretty remarkable.

Notice in Rom. 10:1 how the Bible emphasizes the concept of having a savior. *"Brethren, my heart's desire and prayer to God for Israel is, that they might be saved."*

This thought is continued in verses 9, 10 and 13. *"That if thou shalt confess with thy mouth the Lord Jesus, and shalt believe in thine heart that God hath raised him from the dead, thou shalt be saved. For with the heart man believeth unto righteousness; and with the mouth confession is made unto salvation. For whosoever shall call upon the name of the Lord shall be saved."*

This salvation is in Jesus and Him alone. There is no other salvation.

Outreach

Now look at the **outreach** of the Gospel. As Rom. 1:16 says, it is *"to the Jew first, and also to the Greek."* Paul preached in the synagogues about the Messiah, and many came to the Lord.

Does this mean that the Jew is better than the Gentile? Not at all. Rom. 2:6-11 points this out: *"Who will render to every man according to his deeds: To them who by patient continuance in well doing seek for glory and honour and immortality, eternal life: But unto them that are contentious, and do not obey the truth, but obey unrighteousness, indignation and wrath, Tribulation and anguish, upon every soul of man that doeth evil, of the Jew first, and also of the Gentile; But glory, honour, and peace, to every man that worketh good, to the Jew first, and also to the Gentile: For there is no respect of persons with God."*

The Gospel is for anyone and everyone who wants it, and it is all in the name of Jesus. There really is something about that name.

In Rom. 1:17 you will find a thought that is as powerful as any thought in all of God's Word. *"For therein is the righteousness of God revealed from faith to faith: as it is written, The just shall live by faith."*

What is righteousness? How is it ever possible for any of us to become righteous? The word "righteous" is seen more than 60 times in various forms in the book of Romans. Righteousness and justice go hand in hand.

Righteousness is the character and quality of being right. It's the gracious gift of God whereby everyone is brought into the right relationship with Him.

When we talk to a husband and wife who are not getting along but seem to be fussing all the time, we find out that each of them wants to prove that he or she is right. She may say, "He always thinks he's right," while he is thinking the same about her.

The only One who is always right is Almighty God. His gracious gift of a right relationship with Him needs to be brought into every person's life, but the only way to do that is by faith. *"The just shall live by faith."*

So we see here the **revelation** of righteousness. How can a holy God forgive people and remain holy? Consider in Rom. 4:16-17 these words about the Old Testament leader Abraham. *"Therefore it is of faith, that it might be by grace; to the end the promise might be sure to all the seed; not to that only which is of the law, but to that also which is of the faith of Abraham; who is the father of us all, (As it is written, I have made thee a father of many nations,) before him whom he believed, even God, who quickeneth the dead, and calleth those things which be not as though they were."* These verses refer to Abraham's saving faith.

I believe that there are many people who come to church, who make professions of faith in Christ, but who may not truly be saved. The Bible says it is by faith. Saving faith is more than mentally saying, "I believe that Jesus died, was buried and rose again." You can believe that and not be saved.

You may claim to believe that Christ exists and you are not an atheist, but you want to be called a Christian. Yet there is not much evidence in your life that what is important to God is important to you. You have a mental understanding but you missed out on the most important area, which is faith.

D. James Kennedy, who passed away in the fall of 2007, was a great Christian leader in south Florida and around the world. It has been said that as many as six million people are in Heaven today because of his ministry. He made the following statement: "So many people are saved mentally, but they're 18 inches away. It's in the head but not in the heart."

You will know if you are a child of God by the desires that you have, because of certain things in your heart that are important to you. Today in the United States of America we have a very watered-down form of Christianity. One-third of Americans claim to be Christians, but it that were true and we were living for God there would be a sweeping revival in this country. We would be living in a very different world today.

There has to be not only a receiving of grace that is issued, but also an appropriation of faith. So to return to the question of how a holy God can forgive sinners and remain holy, the first reason is that He punished sin. Rom. 1:18 says, *"For the wrath of God is revealed from heaven against all ungodliness and unrighteousness of men, who hold the truth in unrighteousness."*

You look at the sins listed in Romans and think to yourself, "I'm glad I don't do all of that." Well, you are probably doing at least some of it.

Look at Rom. 3:24. *"Being justified freely by his grace through the redemption that is in Christ Jesus."* So He punished sin, He died for sinners and He rose again. But that doesn't do anything for you until you appropriate that by faith into your life.

When the Bible says in II Cor. 5:17, *"Therefore if any man be in Christ, he is a new creature: old things are passed away; behold, all things are become new,"* it is true because of the revelation of the grace of God. It is true that only Jesus can save us, wash away our sins and take us to Heaven, but it means nothing to any of us until, by faith, we have appropriated that.

Saying that Jesus is the Saviour, or even that He is the only Saviour, is not enough. You have to say, "Jesus is my Saviour."

Also found in Rom. 1:17 is the **response** to righteousness. It is in the last six words of that verse: *"The just shall live by faith."*

Three other times in Scripture we see this phrase:

"Behold, his soul which is lifted up is not upright in him: but the just shall live by his faith." (Hab. 2:4)
"But that no man is justified by the law in the sight of God, it is evident: for, The just shall live by faith." (Gal. 3:11)
"Now the just shall live by faith: but if any man draw back, my soul shall have no pleasure in him." (Heb. 10:38)

Faith is not a work. But faith is believing God.

Look at Rom. 3:21-31 and notice eight references to faith. *"But now the righteousness of God without the law is manifested, being witnessed by the law and the prophets; Even the righteousness of God which is by faith of Jesus Christ unto all and upon all them that believe: for there is no difference: For all have sinned, and come short of the glory of God; Being justified freely by his grace through the redemption that is in Christ Jesus: Whom God hath set forth to be a propitiation through faith in his blood, to declare his righteousness for the remission of sins that are past, through the forbearance of God; To declare, I say, at this time his righteousness: that he might be just, and the justifier of him which believeth in Jesus. Where is boasting then? It is excluded. By what law? of works? Nay: but by the law of faith. Therefore we conclude that a man is justified by faith without the deeds of the law. Is he the God of the Jews only? is he not also of the Gentiles? Yes, of the Gentiles also: Seeing it is one God, which shall justify the circumcision by faith, and uncircumcision through faith. Do we then make void the law through faith? God forbid: yea, we establish the law."*

Some people talk about faith as some superfluous idea in the edge of your imagination. No, faith is in the knowledge of God. It is not just an attitude, but it is the belief that Jesus died, was buried and rose again, and I am trusting Him for my salvation.

Faith is a heart response, not just to a principle but to a Person – the Lord Jesus Christ. Faith is a commitment that Jesus alone is my Saviour.

Charles Spurgeon put it this way: "Faith is not a blind thing, for faith begins with knowledge. It is not a speculative thing, for faith believes facts of which it is sure. It is not an impractical or dreamy thing, for faith states its destiny upon the truth of revelation. Faith is the eye that looks, the hand that grasps, the mouth that feeds upon Christ."

As the old hymn says, "Nothing in my hand I bring; simply to the cross I cling."

Assume for a moment that I am in a room with only one exit door. There are two glasses of juice on a table in the middle of the room. If I drink from the correct glass, the door will open and I can leave. If I pick the wrong glass, I will drink juice laced with arsenic and die.

You walk by and, acting as my friend, say, "Pastor, I think that the glass on the left is the correct glass." I would then say, "Thank you for your friendship, but now is not the time for what you think. I have to know."

Someone else might say, "That glass on the left looks funny. There's something not right about it. I believe you should pick the one on the right."

My response would be, "I am not interested in your belief system. I need to know for certain which glass is safe."

Now suppose my wife comes in and says, "I know which one it is. Drink this one; I tasted it."

She says that she knows, and I believe her because she loves me and I know she would want me to drink the right one and besides, she has tasted it.

Faith is when you say, "I am trusting Jesus – not for my spouse or my children, not because my pastor said so, not because I walked down the aisle at a church with my friend. I understand that this is for me." That is how the just live by faith.

Now consider the **experience** of righteousness. It is as if we are in a courtroom and we need someone to come alongside and do something for us.

As you study the book of Romans, you see some interesting things. In the latter part of chapter 1 you see the wrath of God revealed and you learn that we are all lost. To prove His own righteousness God shows us just how lost we really are.

At first you might think, "I'm glad God pointed this out because I know some people who really need it." But in chapter 2 the Lord shows us that those who think they are moral and good, the ones who go around judging other people, are just as lost as everyone else. He concludes this thought in one of the most well-known verses of the entire Bible: "*For all have sinned, and come short of the glory of God.*" (Rom. 3:23)

James Montgomery Boice, a great Bible teacher, said that Rom. 1:16-17 are perhaps the most important words not only in Scripture, but in all of literature. These verses speak to us about something very intense because in Christ there is victory, liberty and security.

Dr. Martyn Lloyd-Jones put it this way: "There are at least eight reasons why we should not be ashamed: the Gospel is good news; it is the way of salvation; it is God's way of salvation; salvation reveals that we are sinners; the Gospel is the power of God for everybody; salvation reaches to the sinner, and righteousness is from God, so it is from first to last, from beginning to end."

This is the heart of God.

Martin Luther was a young man who began his academic life by studying law. His dad wanted him to be lawyer so he could make a good living. He excelled in his legal studies but he was troubled in his soul.

Luther was convinced that there was a God and was concerned about the idea of meeting God. He would go to his church in Mansfield, Germany, and look at the stained glass windows with the pictures of Jesus in a sad posture. "Maybe He is sad because of me," Luther thought.

On August 17, 1505, he left the university and went to the Augustinian hermits at Hereford, Germany, where he decided he would become a monk and find God. He was told to fast, pray, and devote himself to the menial tasks that surrounded him. He did all of that and began the sacrament of penance and confessing his sins for hours and hours – every sin he could think of.

His piety led him to a reputation as a most exemplary monk. He wrote, "I was indeed a pious monk and followed the rules of my order more strictly than I can express. If ever a monk could obtain Heaven by his monkish works, I was that monk. Of this all the friars who have ever known me can testify that if I had continued much longer, I might have died because I was so mortified by the way I had lived."

So he kept thinking that he must do something about his soul. Can you sense the agony that must have been within him? If we look far enough within ourselves we will find that same kind of agony.

In his continuing search for God, Martin Luther met John Stopitz, the vice-general of the congregation where he was. "Martin," Stopitz said one day, "you always look so sad."

"I don't know what will become of me," Luther replied.

"What you must do is look at the promises of God and the wounds of Jesus Christ, and see what He did for you."

Luther listened to that but he couldn't grasp it, so he began to study the first chapter of Romans. He read verses 16 and 17 over and over, and he heard a sermon by a man named Borham who described a famous man whose life had been changed by the Word of God and drew a picture of the dawn shining through a lattice to illuminate a Bible.

All Luther could think about was the words, *"The just shall live by faith."* "But how do you do that?" he thought.

For five years he struggled. After two years as a monk he began teaching the Bible at a university, and he was then ordered to go to Rome. He became very ill during the journey, and as he stopped his soul began to mourn again as he contemplated how to find God. When he reached Rome, he was turned off by the sacraments and rituals that were emphasized but he could not find any help from priests or anyone else.

In Rome there is a set of stairs that, according to tradition, were brought from Pilate's house in Jerusalem and were called "the holy stairs." I was there in the summer of 1997 when a display was set up for a Gianni Versace fashion show but he had been murdered in Miami Beach the day before. Luther knew that he was supposed to take the stairs one at a time and on those steps would be the blood of Christ. He was supposed to say penance but all he could think of was, *"The just shall live by faith."*

According to his own story, as Luther walked those steps he thought, "This is nonsense." He came back down the stairs as Rom. 1:16-17 set his soul ablaze, and after a long journey of wondering and wandering he gave himself to Christ.

He returned to his homeland and put on the doors of the church the Ninety-Five Theses that caused many to turn against him. Eventually he was brought to the Diet of Worms as leaders tried to decide what to do with him for his rebellion against the church. He was asked to recant, and this is what he said:

"Since Your Most Serene Majesty and Your Most Mightiness require from me a simple and clear, precise answer, I will give you this. I cannot submit my faith to the Pope nor to the councils, because it is clear to me as the day that they have frequently erred and contradicted each other, unless I am convinced therefore by the testimony of Scripture or the clearest reasoning, unless I am persuaded by means of the passages I have quoted, and unless they thus render my conscience bound by the Word of God, I cannot and I will not recant. Here I stand; I can do no other. May God help me."

He was thrown out of the church, and from that beginning came what we know as the Reformation. Shortly after this happened, he told his congregation, "If God be for us, who then can be against us?"

When you allow the truth of justification by faith into your life, you will be reformed. Your whole outlook will be different. That is what Paul meant when he wrote, *"From faith to faith."*

These verses are like the Magna Carta of the Christian faith. They are the Bill of Rights for what we believe. This is our Constitution; it is where we stand.

You begin with your faith in Christ, and in a short time you are living out that faith. It is who you are.

It is what causes a teacher to instruct a child not only in an academic subject, but a Christian worldview.

It is what promotes a mission trip so that people sacrifice their time and their money to be able to go.

It is what encourages a 70-year-old man I met recently, who is going back to school to earn a Ph.D. in Old Testament theology.

It is what causes a man to pick up his family, leave behind everything else and go to another city in this country or on the other side of the world and start a church.

It is what causes someone like George Mueller, when his mission board told him at 80 years of age that he was too old to continue his work with his great orphanages, to move on and become a missionary.

It is what causes people to come to church to worship God, to the point that they can't wait to arrive and they hate to leave. It makes them give their tithes and offerings, and go out on Saturday mornings to help feed the homeless and visit children's homes.

Until you understand that the faith life is the fulfillment of the law and love of God, and that it can be yours, you are missing out on what life is really all about.

When you live the faith life, you are more interested in the kingdom of God than the economy, politics or your 401(k). You are more interested in souls saved than sports championships. You have put Christ ahead of all other causes.

Faith takes a man from Internet pornography to a PC study Bible. Faith takes a prostitute and makes her life pure so that she can have her own children someday. Faith leads single people to take a "hands-off" approach until marriage. Faith lets a person prize the Bible more than the television.

Faith stands at a grave and does not say, "Goodbye," but instead says, "I'll see you again."

A young man who was martyred for the cause of Christ wrote these words which were found in his cell in Africa: "I am part of the fellowship of the unashamed. The die has been cast, and I have stepped over the line. The decision has been made and I am a disciple of Jesus Christ. I won't look back, let up, slow down, back away or be still. My past is redeemed, my present makes sense, and my future is secure. I am finished and done with low living, sight-walking, small planning, smooth knees, colorless dreams, chintzy giving and dwarfed goals. I no longer need preeminence, prosperity, position, promotions, plaudits or popularity, because I now live by His presence, learning by faith, loving by patience, lifting by prayer and laboring by power. My pace is set; my gait is fast. My goal is Heaven; my road is narrow. My way is rough; sometimes the companions may be few. But my guide and mission are clear. I cannot be bought, compromised, deterred, lured away, turned back, deluded or delayed. I will not flinch in the face of sacrifice, hesitate in the presence of adversity, negotiate at the table of the enemy, ponder at the pool of popularity or meander in the maze of mediocrity, for I am a soldier of Jesus Christ. I must go until Heaven calls, give until I drop, preach all I know and work until He comes. And when He comes to take His own, you'll have no problem recognizing me because my colors will be clear. I am a soldier of Jesus Christ."

There are people who go to church and even read their Bibles but have never really been saved. The way you know you are saved is when this faith life gets a hold of you.

You don't have to try to turn people off, and you can be kind and gracious, but if Jesus loves you and died for you, and you have accepted Him, then you should live out the faith life. It will dictate the rest of your life, one step of faith at a time.

Chapter 4

DO YOU AGREE WITH GOD?

"For the wrath of God is revealed from heaven against all ungodliness and unrighteousness of men, who hold the truth in unrighteousness; Because that which may be known of God is manifest in them; for God hath shewed it unto them. For the invisible things of him from the creation of the world are clearly seen, being understood by the things that are made, even his eternal power and Godhead; so that they are without excuse: Because that, when they knew God, they glorified him not as God, neither were thankful; but became vain in their imaginations, and their foolish heart was darkened. Professing themselves to be wise, they became fools, And changed the glory of the uncorruptible God into an image made like to corruptible man, and to birds, and four-footed beasts, and creeping things. Wherefore God also gave them up to uncleanness through the lusts of their own hearts, to dishonour their own bodies between themselves: Who changed the truth of God into a lie, and worshipped and served the creature more than the Creator, who is blessed for ever. Amen. For this cause God gave them up unto vile affections: for even their women did change the natural use into that which is against nature: And likewise also the men, leaving the natural use of the woman, burned in their lust one toward another; men with men working that which is

unseemly, and receiving in themselves that recompence of their error which was meet. And even as they did not like to retain God in their knowledge, God gave them over to a reprobate mind, to do those things which are not convenient; Being filled with all unrighteousness, fornication, wicked-ness, covetousness, maliciousness; full of envy, murder, debate, deceit, malignity; whisperers, Backbiters, haters of God, despiteful, proud, boasters, inventors of evil things, disobedient to parents, Without understanding, covenant-breakers, without natural affection, implacable, unmerciful: Who knowing the judgment of God, that they which commit such things are worthy of death, not only do the same, but have pleasure in them that do them." **(Rom. 1:18-32)**

This passage contains virtually every vile and sinful thing a person can think of. As you read it, you might be thinking that you fit in here somewhere.

Sometimes we think that it would be a wonderful world if everyone agreed with us, but we know that is impossible because of human frailty. We should all be asking ourselves instead if we agree with God.

Imagine for a moment a courtroom scene where someone is about to be put on trial – only in this case, it is God who is on trial. God gets blamed for many things, and we often try to make up our own god in our minds, to fit into our circumstances and needs. Sometimes we don't like what God says and we struggle with Him.

When my family and I moved to south Florida in the mid-1990s, some friends came to visit us from the northeastern United States. They stayed in a hotel, rented a car to drive around in and had a wonderful time with us. One day they were driving through Hollywood, a small city between Miami and Fort Lauderdale, and came through a school zone too fast. A police officer stopped them and gave them a ticket.

The lady of the family was very upset when they arrived our house. "With all the crime in south Florida, why can't they leave the tourists alone?" she complained. "What's this all about?"

It wasn't until they returned home that they learned the amount of the fine, which was $135. This really made her mad. She wrote a lengthy letter to the police department that she enclosed with the check. A few days later she told me over the phone what she had written and said, "What do you think?"

"I think they threw the letter in the trash without even reading it and just took your money," I replied.

It reminded me of an episode in Pennsylvania, where we used to live. I was driving to a Penn State-Indiana University basketball game. It was a two-hour drive and I was running late as I passed through the small town of Mount Union. Yes, I was speeding, but there was no one around.

When the police officer pulled me over, I explained to him that I was going to a game and had to get there before the opening tip-off. He was not at all impressed with my excuse and wrote me a ticket. I got home that night and griped to my wife about the ticket and the fine I had to pay.

I didn't know exactly what the speed limit was in that spot. There was no one else around. I had every excuse you could imagine. I wanted my own law, just as my friend did.

That's what we do sometimes with God. As we look at this passage in Romans and put God on trial, we see God for what He really is and not just what we want Him to be. You and I have a way of trying to fit God into our own little mold.

Consider verse 18, especially the issue of His wrath. *"For the wrath of God is revealed from heaven against all ungodliness and unrighteousness of men, who hold the truth in unrighteousness."*

The wrath of God is a dominant Bible teaching. We go to the Bible for our own needs to be met, or for God's promises, or even for our own prosperity and success. We don't like to talk about wrath or think about God in this way. But here it is in this verse, as plain as it can be.

There are three words that are translated as wrath or anger in the New Testament. One word means to have the heat of a battle and become quickly violent. You may know someone of whom you say, "Here comes So-and-so. Watch what you say; they get mad very easily."

Are there times when God just zaps us to get us in line? There is a word in Revelation that talks about that, but most of the time it is not that way.

A second word describes passion, and the third word used is one that means to grow ripe for something. When I think of my father, I remember a Godly man who seldom got angry. But when he did get mad, it was time to leave because I didn't want to be around. Something had been brewing in him for a while until it finally set him off.

That is the kind of wrath talked about in Romans 1:18. Bible teacher Arthur Pink wrote, "A study of the concordance will show that there are many more references in Scripture to the anger, fury and wrath of God than there are to His love and tenderness."

In the Old Testament there are more than 20 different Hebrew words that refer to wrath or anger in some 600 passages. You and I learn about the heart of God when we begin to understand the wrath of God.

For example, in the book of Exodus God said in wrath that the people were not to take advantage of a widow or an orphan. That is a great admonishment that we would all agree with – but regardless of whether we agree, God said it.

John Murray wrote, "Wrath is the holy revulsion of God's being against that which is the contradiction to His holiness."

There are a number of references to wrath in the book of Romans, and many of them are the same root word:

> "*But after thy hardness and impenitent heart treasurest up unto thyself wrath against the day of wrath and revelation of the righteous judgment of God.*" (Rom. 2:5)
>
> "*Because the law worketh wrath: for where no law is, there is no transgression.*" (Rom. 4:15)
>
> "*Much more then, being now justified by his blood, we shall be saved from wrath through him.*" (Rom. 5:9)
>
> "*What if God, willing to shew his wrath, and to make his power known, endured with much longsuffering the vessels of wrath fitted to destruction.*" (Rom. 9:22)

"Dearly beloved, avenge not yourselves, but rather give place unto wrath: for it is written, Vengeance is mine; I will repay, saith the Lord." (Rom. 12:19)

"For he is the minister of God to thee for good. But if thou do that which is evil, be afraid; for he beareth not the sword in vain: for he is the minister of God, a revenger to execute wrath upon him that doeth evil. Wherefore ye must needs be subject, not only for wrath, but also for conscience sake." (Rom. 13:4-5)

In every one of these verses, it is the Greek word *orge* that is used, demonstrating that God has compassion and love but will also show wrath when it is appropriate. Leon Morris put it this way: "The Biblical writers habitually used a word for divine wrath that denotes not so much a sudden flaring up of passion, which is soon over, as it does a strong and subtle opposition to all that is evil rising up out of God's very nature."

The first chapter of Romans does not teach the evolution of man, but rather the degeneration of man. These verses are saying to us that there is a God in Heaven who has wrath because He is a holy God, and in a gradual way that wrath will come out.

Did you ever have someone hurt you, and you knew you were right, so you prayed for God to "get" them? We ask God why He allows certain things to happen, and in reality we want to take God's place ourselves and make decisions for Him. We want His wrath to come down on those who deserve it, but never on us.

Now let's look at the evidence of God in verse 19. *"Because that which may be known of God is manifest in them; for God hath shewed it unto them."* God is saying, "Here is the proof of My existence – as if I needed to prove it to you."

If you were dropped down onto this planet today at your present age, and you got in a car and drove out on the nearest highway, you would not assume for a moment that the road you were on or the cars passing by just happened by accident. The same goes for the clothes on your back or the possessions in your home. All of it had to be made by someone.

If it is true that God made each of us and created the air we breathe and the food we eat, then we must consider the words of theologian R.C. Sproul: "If there is a God, then why are there atheists?"

The word *"manifest"* in verse 19 means it is exhibited. Remember our courtroom where God is on trial. Here is Exhibit #1: the understanding that there must be something or Someone out there.

You might say, "Well, I'm not really sure that God exists." That does not change the fact of His existence. Whether you like how God does certain things does not matter.

If I brought an auto mechanic onto the platform at my church and began debating the details of a car engine, it would take about 30 seconds before the congregation started encouraging me to sit down, since I barely know where to find the engine in a car. Yet we have this naïve feeling that we can question certain details about God.

It's not a matter of whether God exists; the problem is that sometimes we don't like what God does or even like Him. But God is sovereign. It's His way or no way. Our opinions are of no more value than the excuses we make to the police officer who writes us a speeding ticket.

Even though you might hire a lawyer, go to court and beat that speeding ticket, you can't do an end run around God's law. If you don't want to come through Christ to get to God, that's too bad. It's the only way you can.

Imagine you get a phone call from the principal who wants to talk to you about your child. Judging from the tone in the principal's voice, it's probably not your child's straight A's that will be the topic of conversation. Once in the principal's office, your attitude is expressed this way: "Change the teacher. Change the principal. Change the school or the school district. Change something – but don't do anything to my child."

We all have a tendency to go against authority, so it's with that kind of attitude that we bring up our excuses about God. "He's not fair. He doesn't love me. He's not just." Who are we to question God?

Verse 20 is powerful. *"For the invisible things of him from the creation of the world are clearly seen, being understood by the things that are made, even his eternal power and Godhead; so that they are without excuse."*

Nature itself is evidence of God. We have often heard the statement, "If God is just, why are there people in the world who have not heard about Him?"

Leif Samuel of Intervarsity Fellowship wrote, "Many missionaries point out that the heathen know more than we think. They know that there is a God. There are no atheists among heathen tribes."

Isn't that interesting? We have plenty of atheists in the United States of America.

He continues: "There has never been discovered on Earth a tribe of people, no matter how small or depraved, that does not believe in some kind of God or have some system of worship. The heathen found in so-called primitive tribes know that they have sinned, and when a Christian comes to talk to them about sin he often finds ready acknowledgement that this is true. They seem to know that their sins must be punished; they seem afraid or punishment and of death, as are most people everywhere. They know their sins must be atoned for, and they seek ways of appeasing their angry deities."

The issue is not whether God is unjust, but whether we will be concerned enough to send missionaries and whatever support they need so that the heathen can hear the Gospel. The justice of God is not in question.

Job lost so much – his children, his possessions, and his health. To top it all off, he had a wife who doubted God. Very few of us could ever have gone through what he did. But he did at some point begin to wonder and question God concerning his situation. Look at what God said to him in Job 38:1-11.

"Then the LORD answered Job out of the whirlwind, and said, Who is this that darkeneth counsel by words without knowledge? Gird up now thy loins like a man; for I will demand of thee, and answer thou me. Where wast thou when I laid the foundations of the earth? declare, if thou hast understanding. Who hath laid the measures thereof, if thou knowest? or who hath stretched the line upon it? Whereupon are the foundations thereof fastened? or who laid the corner

stone thereof; When the morning stars sang together, and all the sons of God shouted for joy? Or who shut up the sea with doors, when it brake forth, as if it had issued out of the womb? When I made the cloud the garment thereof, and thick darkness a swaddlingband for it, And brake up for it my decreed place, and set bars and doors, And said, Hitherto shalt thou come, but no further: and here shall thy proud waves be stayed?"

God wants to know where Job was when all of this glorious creation was coming about, since Job seemed to know so much about God.

Ps. 19:1-6 says, *"The heavens declare the glory of God; and the firmament sheweth his handywork. Day unto day uttereth speech, and night unto night sheweth knowledge. There is no speech nor language, where their voice is not heard. Their line is gone out through all the earth, and their words to the end of the world. In them hath he set a tabernacle for the sun, Which is as a bridegroom coming out of his chamber, and rejoiceth as a strong man to run a race. His going forth is from the end of the heaven, and his circuit unto the ends of it: and there is nothing hid from the heat thereof."*

God made it all. He spoke the word and it happened. We have no right to question Him.

The other important facet of the evidence of God is the evidence from within. People do not know God because they don't want to know Him.

Some of the attributes of God are His sovereignty, holiness and love. His holiness addresses His majesty – that He is the God of all gods.

From all of this we find the conclusion in verse 20: *"So that they are without excuse."* Don't think that you can go to God and say, "I didn't see the speed limit sign." That's not going to work.

The issue is who is going to get glory and be worshipped. Look at verses 21-25. *"Because that, when they knew God, they glorified him not as God, neither were thankful; but became vain in their imaginations, and their foolish heart was darkened. Professing themselves to be wise, they became fools, And changed the glory of*

*the uncorruptible God into an image made like to corruptible man,
and to birds, and fourfooted beasts, and creeping things. Wherefore
God also gave them up to uncleanness through the lusts of their
own hearts, to dishonour their own bodies between themselves: Who
changed the truth of God into a lie, and worshipped and served the
creature more than the Creator, who is blessed for ever. Amen."*

Instead of being thankful for all that God has given to us, and
giving Him the glory, and worshipping Him, we decide to make our
own gods. You see them everywhere. A person will put so much
dependence upon a spouse when that person should be depending
upon God.

Author Warren Wiersbe says that verses 21-23 show how we are
without excuse due to our ignorance, while verses 24-27 reflect that
we are without excuse because of our indulgence.

Notice in verse 24 how God *"gave them up."* According to the
Greek text, He permits them to go on in their sins and reap the sad
consequences. It's as if God said, "OK, if that's the way you want to
go, just go. But you will pay for it one day."

I remember when I was in seventh or eighth grade I sat in a history
class with a friend of mine who was always goofing off. Finally the
teacher was fed up and shouted at him, "I've had it! You're on your
own. From now on, you get no more help from me."

"Wow," I thought. "We can barely make it through this class
with the teacher's help. How will he get by without it?"

In a sense, God is telling the wicked in this verse that they are on
their own and they had better enjoy it while they can, because they
will reap what they sow.

Verse 25 talks about how they *"changed the truth of God into
a lie."* Satan always wants you to believe the lie. He makes the lie
look good.

Paul writes in the following verses about homosexuality, which
was rampant in Roman times. Look at verses 26-27. *"For this cause
God gave them up unto vile affections: for even their women did
change the natural use into that which is against nature: And likewise also the men, leaving the natural use of the woman, burned in
their lust one toward another; men with men working that which*

is unseemly, and receiving in themselves that recompence of their error which was meet."

In Genesis 18 and I Corinthians 6, along with Jude 7 and these passages in Romans, God condemns this sin. It all begins when we try to make ourselves like God. So He abandons these wicked people to their sinful ways, knowing that His wrath will soon come. As the old saying goes, "He who excuses himself accuses himself."

Someone may say, "I just don't agree with God or the Bible." It doesn't change anything. Someone may need to discipline their children at various times when they didn't agree. It didn't matter to you, did it? All children go through the "why" stage at some point, and you finally just have to tell them, "Because I said so."

God is saying here that when we start worshipping the flesh (and there is flesh to worship all around us today), He will give us up and let us go do our own thing. But a day of reckoning will come.

Notice in verses 28-32 that we are also without excuse because of impenitence. Verse 28 says, "And even as they did not like to retain God in their knowledge, God gave them over to a reprobate mind, to do those things which are not convenient." The word "reprobate" here means a depraved mind, or a mind that does not form correct judgments.

In verses 29-31 the writer lists 24 sins. *"Being filled with all unrighteousness, fornication, wickedness, covetousness, maliciousness; full of envy, murder, debate, deceit, malignity; whisperers, Backbiters, haters of God, despiteful, proud, boasters, inventors of evil things, disobedient to parents, Without understanding, covenantbreakers, without natural affection, implacable, unmerciful."*

Sometimes we can feel pretty good about ourselves because we're not into something as vile as homosexuality, but when God introduces this list we want to hide under the rug in shame.

The word *"fornication"* in verse 29 refers to any kind of sexual immorality. Simply put, God ordained sex for use by a man and a woman in marriage and nowhere else. You may not agree with it, but that is God's law.

The same goes for *"covetousness"* (wanting that fancy car your neighbor has and ruining your finances to get it) and *"malicious-*

ness" (saying, "I'll get back at him – and God, you get him for me too").

Who among us has not been deceitful or a gossip? Violent, proud, undiscerning, untrusting, unloving, unforgiving, unmerciful – it's no wonder that God considers us to be without excuse. Dan Crawford of the British Missionary Society wrote, "The heathen are sinning against a flood of light."

We have been looking at this passage as if God is on trial. Some might say that God is guilty because they don't like Him this way. But someone's personal feelings do not change the fact that He is God.

We were created in the image of God, and we rejected Him in the sin of Adam. So we make excuses and put God on trial.

"What about the people who have never heard the Gospel?"

"Isn't the Bible full of contradictions?"

"Why does God tolerate evil?"

"Why do bad things happen to good people?"

It's as if God has to answer us. But we must learn that we do depraved things because we are sinners.

I am really concerned about the Western world and our country. There was a time when adultery was looked down upon, and now prostitution is legal in some areas. Pornography used to be seen only in the sleaziest joints around, and now it is available on your home computer. Abortion is running rampant.

You say, "Whatever two consenting adults want to do is fine with me." But what if consenting adults decide that child prostitution is OK? Where do we draw the line?

That is the question being asked in the first chapter of Romans. I really believe that as we look at God on trial, we must realize that we are the ones who belong there, not Him.

Rom. 3:24 says, "*Being justified freely by his grace through the redemption that is in Christ Jesus.*"

Suppose I get ready to pay my traffic fine and I chew out the police officer, only to find out that he paid the fine for me – not because I deserved it, but simply because he took the penalty in my place.

The sins that you and I have committed, every single one of them, have been put upon Jesus. All of the sins listed in Romans l were put on Him. That is why Paul wrote in Gal. 6:14, *"But God forbid that I should glory, save in the cross of our Lord Jesus Christ, by whom the world is crucified unto me, and I unto the world."*

Imagine for a moment that you and I are walking through a neighborhood that we knew to be very religious. We walk by an elaborate Hindu temple with beautiful painted images of gods and goddesses.

"Wow," we say. "What do we do now?"

"Take these gods as your own and follow them," the leaders of the temple reply.

Then we pass by a Muslim temple with a towering spire and are told to adapt the teachings of Islam, that Allah is the true God and Mohammad is his prophet. "Maybe that is the answer," we think.

Just past that spot is a Buddhist temple with monks praying before a statue of Buddha. We ask for guidance there as well.

Then we come upon a church, and in the corner is a cross – a symbol of rejection and a picture of humiliation. You wonder if perhaps the church should put that old cross away and find a better symbol.

But it is precisely that cross to which the Apostle Paul was refer- ring in Galatians, because it was upon that cross that Jesus took on Himself all of the sins of the world. Every sin you can name was placed on that cross, which is why the poet said, "Well might the son in darkness hide and shut her glories in, when Christ the mighty Maker died for man the creature's sin."

A hymn writer said, "I'll never know how much it cost to see my sin upon that cross, so here I am to worship, here I am to bow down, here I am to say that you are my God."

When you look at who your God is, there is not one of us who can stand before Him unless His son takes every one of our sins. And if you allow Christ to do that, then you had better agree with what He says in Romans and every other book of the Bible.

What you believe means nothing unless you believe Him. And if you believe Him, you have all you need because of Jesus, who will never leave you nor forsake you. So why would go another way?

Chapter 5

WHO IS THE JUDGE?

"Therefore thou art inexcusable, O man, whosoever thou art that judgest: for wherein thou judgest another, thou condemnest thyself; for thou that judgest doest the same things. But we are sure that the judgment of God is according to truth against them which commit such things. And thinkest thou this, O man, that judgest them which do such things, and doest the same, that thou shalt escape the judgment of God? Or despisest thou the riches of his goodness and forbearance and longsuffering; not knowing that the goodness of God leadeth thee to repentance? But after thy hardness and impenitent heart treasurest up unto thyself wrath against the day of wrath and revelation of the righteous judgment of God; Who will render to every man according to his deeds: To them who by patient continuance in well doing seek for glory and honour and immortality, eternal life: But unto them that are contentious, and do not obey the truth, but obey unrighteousness, indignation and wrath, Tribulation and anguish, upon every soul of man that doeth evil, of the Jew first, and also of the Gentile; But glory, honour, and peace, to every man that worketh good, to the Jew first, and also to the Gentile: For there is no respect of persons with God. For as many as have sinned without law shall also perish without law: and as many as have sinned in the law shall be

judged by the law; (For not the hearers of the law are just before God, but the doers of the law shall be justified. For when the Gentiles, which have not the law, do by nature the things contained in the law, these, having not the law, are a law unto themselves: Which shew the work of the law written in their hearts, their conscience also bearing witness, and their thoughts the mean while accusing or else excusing one another;) In the day when God shall judge the secrets of men by Jesus Christ according to my gospel." **(Rom. 2:1-16)**

Occasionally we will receive word about one of our church members who is going to court, and one of our pastors or I will accompany that person. We will usually meet with the attorney ahead of time, and the attorney will often say that the case depends a great deal upon the judge who is hearing it, and how that judge typically rules in such matters. The judge is obviously of great importance in any criminal or civil case in the United States.

In the last chapter we looked at what God says about the wickedness of the world. Now we will see in these pages that God is actually the Judge and we will consider how he speaks to those who think that they are moral people.

We find in verse 17 that Romans 2 is written specifically to the Jew, and traditional Jewish teaching tells us that moral Jews did not want to confess their disobedience. In fact, all moral people feel that same reluctance.

In this passage there are two excuses given for man-made righteousness. One excuse is morality, and the other is religion.

Some people think that they are good enough to stand before God because they did not commit the sins that are mentioned in the first chapter of Romans. It's the standard "I'm a good person" type of thinking. Moral people usually applaud the kind of condemnation found in Rom. 1:18-32. But in Romans 2 they are brought face to face with the One who is considered the Judge.

The problem is that we like ourselves and tend to think highly of ourselves. You might have noticed that even when we pray, it is often about issues that pertain to ourselves. Even when thinking about our relationship with God, we tend to talk more about ourselves than about His kingdom. You and I are essentially selfish people. We want to do our own thing in our own way, and our Christian life is often tied to our own agenda.

Our church has a main campus in Miami-Dade County and another in Broward County (Fort Lauderdale). When I am driving from my home to the Dade campus on a weekday, the traffic is fairly light if I leave between 6 and 7 a.m. But if I leave after 7 a.m. there are hundreds of cars on the road with an agenda against me. Often I will say aloud to the motorists in front of me, "Get out of the way. Why don't you get moving?" But there is no one who can hear me. If someone pulls in front of me, I might ask aloud, "What are you doing?" There is still no one who can hear me.

Simply put, I like a quick commute to work and I want everyone to get out of my way so I can accomplish this. I am a selfish person.

If you say that you are not selfish, then the easiest and nicest thing I can think to say is, "Yes, you are." We are all selfish people. We often look at people and judge them by the way they are dressed or how they look. So many times we have our own agenda, and as we discussed in a previous chapter, we often want God to fit into what we want Him to be. But in the second chapter of Romans we find a very different view of God.

It starts right away in verse 1, where the word "judge" is found three times. *"Therefore thou art inexcusable, O man, whosoever thou art that judgest: for wherein thou judgest another, thou condemnest thyself; for thou that judgest doest the same things."*

This theme of judgment is found throughout the chapter – verses 2, 3, 5 and 16 have specific references to judging.

The word "judge" or "judgment" refers to a decision that is made or someone who makes that decision. A case is brought before a judge who rules on it. In that ruling, the judge essentially is saying, "This is my decision."

In verse 5 of chapter 2, as well as Rom. 1:22, we find the words *"righteous judgment."* Those two words in the Greek text are talking about a righteous act or a right decision.

Is it possible that a human judge can make a wrong decision and send an innocent person away to prison for years? The answer is yes. It is also possible that a jury can make a wrong decision with the same result.

But can God make such a decision? No, because He is God.

The first nine verses of Romans 2 give us the standard for His judgment, starting with verses 2-3. *"But we are sure that the judgment of God is according to truth against them which commit such things. And thinkest thou this, O man, that judgest them which do such things, and doest the same, that thou shalt escape the judgment of God?"*

The Jewish moralist in Roman times looked at the Gentiles and agreed with the conclusions made in Romans 1 about all of the sins listed there. Historians tell us that these Jews often referred to Gentiles as the "dogs of the land." But they were practicing the very same things they were condemning. The Jewish people considered themselves God's elect because He had given them the Scriptures. But we see here in Romans 2 that they are accountable and responsible to God for their actions, and they will be judged according to the truth.

Jesus gave a great illustration of this that is described in Matt. 7:3-5. *"And why beholdest thou the mote that is in thy brother's eye, but considerest not the beam that is in thine own eye? Or how wilt thou say to thy brother, Let me pull out the mote out of thine eye; and, behold, a beam is in thine own eye? Thou hypocrite, first cast out the beam out of thine own eye; and then shalt thou see clearly to cast out the mote out of thy brother's eye."*

The truth that we are judged by in Rom. 2:2 is an impartial truth. It does not judge Jews one way and Gentiles another way. It is the same regardless of your gender, race, color or cultural background. We are all judged according to the truth.

The problem that sometimes arises is that certain people believe they have a monopoly on truth. Have you ever talked to someone who thinks he knows a great deal about the Bible and doesn't want your opinion on any of it? But truth is God's standard, not ours.

When I was pastor of the Open Door Church in Chambersburg, Pennsylvania, we started Cumberland Valley Christian School. Those first few years we were desperate to find good teachers because we were a brand-new school. One of those we hired was a beautiful young lady. She was head and shoulders above most of her peers in the classroom and also a very moral person who sat near the front in church and always carried her Bible. When you spoke to her, she seemed impeccable in so many ways.

I will never forget one day when I gave an invitation during a church service. I was standing in front to receive anyone who wished to come, and she came forward to take my hand. Her eyes were full of tears as she looked straight at me and said, "Pastor, I am not saved."

After the service in my office, she explained to me how she had gone down the aisle as a young girl to make a profession of faith and get baptized solely because her parents said so. She wanted to please people and do all the right things, but there was never a time when she received Christ. "I know I look the part," she said. "But I'm not."

It's one thing to look at someone who is living in open sin, but what about the person who lives a moral life? It's all the same before God, who judges according to the truth. John 14:6 says, "*Jesus saith unto him, I am the way, the truth, and the life: no man cometh unto the Father, but by me.*"

Pilate asked in John 18 what truth is, and Paul wrote about teaching the Gentiles in faith and truth (I Tim. 2:7) and speaking the truth in love (Eph. 4:15). Jesus said in John 8:32, "*And ye shall know the truth, and the truth shall make you free.*"

Truth is not even what some Christians think it is. Two people will occasionally have a disagreement over theology, and each one will claim that he has the truth.

But truth, as written in the Bible, comes from a Greek word that means "unconcealed; manifested; true to the fact; genuine; the ideal." Truth is found in Christ.

The book of Romans lays out a great treatise of the truth, but the only way that you can know this Judge is to understand that you must approach Him in truth, as He is always right.

Verse 4 shows us the source of His judgment. "*Or despisest thou the riches of his goodness and forbearance and longsuffering; not knowing that the goodness of God leadeth thee to repentance?*"

What brings someone to truth? Some would say that it is the fear of God, and this is not the only thing. In this verse it is the goodness of God.

Nahum 1:7 says, *"The Lord is good."* Sometimes we just need to stop whatever we are doing and think about that. You cannot over-state how good God is.

The children of Israel had been given great spiritual riches – the temple, the law, the priesthood, and the providence of God. Yet they sinned against Him over and over again on their way to the prom-ised land.

On one occasion, according to Numbers 21, the people were continually speaking out against God and Moses, so the Lord sent snakes that bit and killed many of them. Moses cried out to God and asked what could be done to save the people, and God told him to erect a brazen serpent so that whoever looked upon it would live. It was a picture of Someone who would be raised on a cross one day, and whoever looked upon Him would also live. It's all about the goodness of God. God is good.

Assume for a moment that you gave me a gift of $10,000. If you did this on a couple of occasions and I never thanked you, you would start to wonder why. We should have such gratitude with God because it is not our own morality that will carry us through when we stand before Him, but it is His goodness. If we truly believe that He is a good God, then saving faith will lead to obedience and Godly living.

Look at verses 5-6. *"But after thy hardness and impenitent heart treasurest up unto thyself wrath against the day of wrath and revela-tion of the righteous judgment of God; Who will render to every man according to his deeds."* God's wrath is backing up here like a dam holds back water, as we suppress His moral law while passing judg-ment on others.

God is showing us two paths in these verses. First, if we are expecting to get by according to our morality, we will have to be extremely moral to enter His kingdom. Second, we can recognize for ourselves what we really are in His sight and deal with it according to His Word.

He speaks of a holy heart in verse 7. *"To them who by patient continuance in well doing seek for glory and honour and immortality, eternal life."* A holy heart is a changed heart, a transformed heart.

My wife and I traveled to upstate New York one time to celebrate a milestone at the college of which I am now president, and we saw many dear friends from years gone by. A missionary friend of mine who had done a great work in Africa had returned home to stay because of cancer. A dear lady we knew had lost so much weight in just a few months because of health problems that we did not recognize her at first. Another man moved around with the help of a walker.

As I visited with each one of these people, I noticed right away that all of them talked about the goodness of God. Isn't that amazing? When you have a heart that follows after the things of God, it isn't the events of our lives or the things we have that make the greatest impression. There's something about Him that is special.

There are many references in the Bible to the glory of God. Rom. 5:2 says, *"By whom also we have access by faith into this grace wherein we stand, and rejoice in hope of the glory of God."*

Consider also Rom. 8:18. *"For I reckon that the sufferings of this present time are not worthy to be compared with the glory which shall be revealed in us."* Verse 30 of that same chapter says, *"Moreover whom he did predestinate, them he also called: and whom he called, them he also justified: and whom he justified, them he also glorified."*

This is an ongoing theme in the book of Romans, and we see it again in Rom. 9:23. *"And that he might make known the riches of his glory on the vessels of mercy, which he had afore prepared unto glory."*

Now look at II Cor. 3:12-18. *"Seeing then that we have such hope, we use great plainness of speech: And not as Moses, which put a veil over his face, that the children of Israel could not stedfastly look to the end of that which is abolished: But their minds were blinded: for until this day remaineth the same vail untaken away in the reading of the old testament; which vail is done away in Christ. But even unto this day, when Moses is read, the vail is upon their heart. Nevertheless when it shall turn to the Lord, the vail shall be taken away. Now the Lord is that Spirit: and where the Spirit of the Lord is, there is liberty. But we all, with open face beholding as in a glass the glory of the Lord, are changed into the same image from glory to glory, even as by the Spirit of the Lord."*

This explains how we give all honor back to God. There is no glory in ourselves; it is all in Him. When we grasp what we are before a holy God, and that He is giving us His holiness, it is an awesome thing to consider.

No one reading this book is perfect. Each of us may know one of two others whom we consider really good people, but none of them are perfect.

I had a few heroes while growing up and one of them was my pastor. One day I saw him get very angry and yell at some people, and this made quite an impression on me because I thought he was perfect. My first thought was, "Those people must have done something really wrong. Whatever he is telling them, I'm sure they deserve it."

I found out later that he was actually wrong. But it reminded me that our holiness is not in ourselves. It is His holiness.

If you stand before that almighty Judge and are accepted into His kingdom, you must understand that it is all because of what He has done as a holy and righteous God. It has nothing to do with your morality. All of this is pointing back to Him and what He is.

Going back to Romans 2, we see in verses 8-9 the results of a heavy heart, or one that is not holy. *"But unto them that are contentious, and do not obey the truth, but obey unrighteousness, indignation and wrath, Tribulation and anguish, upon every soul of man that doeth evil, of the Jew first, and also of the Gentile."*

The fruits of an honored heart are portrayed in verses 10-11. *"But glory, honour, and peace, to every man that worketh good, to the Jew first, and also to the Gentile: For there is no respect of persons with God."*

All of us live our own lives wanting our own way, but that morality will never be sufficient in the eyes of a holy God.

Watch your own life in the next few days and notice how absolutely selfish you really are. It's the same for all of us; we just need
to accept it.

I remember the many delicious meals my wife prepared over
the years for us and our four children. When the kids were small we
taught them to pass around the food, but every one of them would
take his or her portion and leave the dish where it was. When it got
to me, I usually did the same thing. That is simply a reflection of our
sinful attitude that leads us to look out for ourselves before anyone
else. We have our own agendas, whether it be the food on our plates
or something else.

But you cannot have your own agenda when dealing with God.
You cannot say, "God, here is my morality, and it is good." That
doesn't work with Him.

The phrase "worketh good" in Rom. 2:10 can give the impression to some readers that God is putting emphasis on good works
for salvation. But when you read the succeeding verses you see a
different picture.

Look at verses 12-15. *"For as many as have sinned without
law shall also perish without law: and as many as have sinned in
the law shall be judged by the law; (For not the hearers of the law
are just before God, but the doers of the law shall be justified. For
when the Gentiles, which have not the law, do by nature the things
contained in the law, these, having not the law, are a law unto themselves: Which shew the work of the law written in their hearts, their
conscience also bearing witness, and their thoughts the mean while
accusing or else excusing one another.)"*

The Jew of this era would often boast of the law. "I know the
law and I keep it," he might say. "The Gentiles don't even have the
law. They don't know any better, so how could they ever come to
God?"

Various passages in Romans 2 show that the judgment of man is
"according to truth" (verse 2), *"according to his deeds"* (verse 6),
and it considers *"the secrets of men by Jesus Christ according to my
gospel"* (verse 16). Would you want your secret thoughts brought out
in front of anyone, let alone God? I don't know a soul who would

want that, and you could say the same for our deeds or actions that no one knows about.

So what is God saying here? He is also telling us that we have the laws of nature, our conscience, knowledge of right and wrong, and our own memories to help guide us. The message here from God is this: If you are depending upon your morality as the way to God, you had better be perfect.

Verse 16 is powerful. It is a verse of deliverance. *"In the day when God shall judge the secrets of men by Jesus Christ according to my gospel."* You and I should be extremely thankful that those secrets are judged by the atoning work of Christ on the cross.

So if you're going down the path of morality, you have to be perfect. We know that none of us are perfect. That's the wrong path.

Have you ever been driving around lost but you refuse to ask for directions? I've done that. I just keep going and sometimes I end up way off course. In these verses, God is telling us that we're on the wrong track and we need to get ourselves turned around. You have to get off the path of morality or religion and recognize that our judgment is based upon what Christ did on the cross for us. It couldn't be more clear than in the last four words of verse 16: *"according to my gospel."*

For our 25th wedding anniversary my wife and I took a trip to Europe. Returning home on British Airways, my wife and I were separated, with my wife sitting in the front and me in the back of the airplane. I was pretty upset about the fact that we couldn't even sit together on the final leg of this special trip.

I sat next to an elderly man from Brooklyn, New York. I thought that God had likely put me here to witness to him. His brother sitting next to him wore an oxygen mask the entire time. I had a phenomenal conversation with the man.

When I asked him if he would like to know that he's going to Heaven, he said he would and I began to share the plan of salvation.

"Do you know that you're a sinner?" I asked.

He bristled. "I am not."

I told him that everyone was a sinner, and I was a sinner also. "No, you're not," he replied.

"Yes, I am."

"No, you're not." (He almost convinced me.)

I couldn't get him to realize he was lost. He claimed that he was as good as the next guy, and he probably was. He told me about all of the good things he had done in his life. But he had to realize that when God comes knocking, we had better let him in.

Charles Spurgeon, in the book "All of Grace," tells the story of a woman in his church who needed money and, when the church took up an offering for her, he went personally to deliver it to her at her home in a poor section of town. He walked up to her door and knocked but no one answered, so he left.

He saw her at church a few weeks later and told her he had some money for her. "I came to your house and knocked on the door, but no one answered," he said.

"When did this happen?" she asked.

He told her what day and that it was around noon. She nodded and said, "I heard you knock, but I thought it was the man coming for the rent so I didn't answer the door."

She could have had the money that day, but she didn't respond to his knock at the door. We need to recognize when God is knocking at the door of our heart, and we had better be ready to answer.

I really believe that there are people in my own church and hundreds of other churches across the nation who, despite their morality or good intentions, do not know Jesus Christ as their personal Saviour. They are trying to find their own way through life.

Horatio Spafford, when he lost his children at sea in the 1800s, later rode over that same spot where their bodies lay and penned the words to that famous hymn, "It Is Well With My Soul." One verse of that song contains these words:

My sin, oh the bliss of this glorious thought;
My sin, not in part but the whole,
Is nailed to His cross and I bear it no more:
Praise the Lord, praise the Lord, oh my soul.

Our morality takes us nowhere. By the same token, to think that as born-again people we can live however we like is insanely wrong. Becoming a part of the family of God brings with it a desire and a thirst to live for Him. A child of God will never be completely happy until he understands that is what it's all about.

Our God is a great and wonderful God. The second chapter of Romans tells us how deplorable and bad we really are as it reminds us how good He is.

A popular philosophy in the world today says, "I'm OK. You're OK. We're all OK." The book of Romans shows us that we are not OK, especially when compared to a holy God.

When we stand before Him in our own works, we won't go very far. But if you go before God in the righteous of Jesus Christ, He gives you His righteousness and you are in His family. So make it your goal to live that way.

Look at Rom. 3:24. *"Being justified freely by his grace through the redemption that is in Christ Jesus."* Christ should be all that we want or need. It was His sacrifice that made salvation possible for us. We have a great King and a great Saviour.

Chapter 6

RELIGION OR RELATIONSHIP?

"Behold, thou art called a Jew, and restest in the law, and makest thy boast of God, And knowest his will, and approvest the things that are more excellent, being instructed out of the law; And art confident that thou thyself art a guide of the blind, a light of them which are in darkness, An instructor of the foolish, a teacher of babes, which hast the form of knowledge and of the truth in the law. Thou therefore which teachest another, teachest thou not thyself? thou that preachest a man should not steal, dost thou steal? Thou that sayest a man should not commit adultery, dost thou commit adultery? thou that abhorrest idols, dost thou commit sacrilege? Thou that makest thy boast of the law, through breaking the law dishonourest thou God? For the name of God is blasphemed among the Gentiles through you, as it is written. For circumcision verily profiteth, if thou keep the law: but if thou be a breaker of the law, thy circumcision is made uncircumcision. Therefore if the uncircumcision keep the righteousness of the law, shall not his uncircumcision be counted for circumcision? And shall not uncircumcision which is by nature, if it fulfil the law, judge thee, who by the letter and circumcision dost transgress the law? For he is not a Jew, which is one outwardly; neither is that circumcision, which is outward in the flesh: But he is a Jew, which is one inwardly; and circum-

cision is that of the heart, in the spirit, and not in the letter; whose praise is not of men, but of God." (**Rom. 2:17-29**)

As we look at the latter portion of Romans 2, it is helpful for us to put the book of Romans in context so we know what Paul is talking about.

Written in 55-57 A.D., Romans is one of the first books written by Paul. In fact, it was probably written before the Gospels or nearly any other book in the New Testament.

The Jews were expelled from Rome on two occasions. The first time was in 19 A.D. by the emperor Tiberius, and then it happened again in the 40s by the emperor Claudius. Christians were not looked upon very highly at this time, and one of the main reasons for the second Jewish expulsion was that a lot of people were supposedly causing trouble as followers of a man called "Chreestus," a name that sounds a lot like Christ. In the 60s under the emperor Nero there was the great fire of Rome, and Nero blamed that event on the Christians.

But at the time of the writing of Romans many Jews had been able to return to the city, so there was a healthy mix of Jews and Gentiles. It is this mixed group, which is greatly segregated, that is Paul's target audience with this epistle. The situation is similar to the racial segregation that has taken place in the United States at various times in its history. Jews and Gentiles did not mix and mingle because they did not like each other, as the Jews thought they were far superior to the Gentiles.

So in Romans 2 Paul is speaking to the Jewish people as a nation, telling them why their Judaism is no longer an automatic way to get to God. What we need to understand now is exactly what the Jews believe.

Judaism was not just a system of beliefs; it was a way of life. If you go to a Baptist church for the first time and ask what makes a Baptist distinctive from other faiths or denominations, you would be shown a doctrinal statement and perhaps some other items related to what Baptist believe. But if you asked a Jewish person at this time what Judaism was all about, you would not get just a list of beliefs. They didn't look at it that way. Their attitude was more like, "This is who I am and how I live in the world based upon what God has done for me."

This is an important comparison because when Jesus came along, He radically redefined what it meant to be Jewish. This was continued with Paul beginning with his dramatic conversion on the road to Damascus. Before that he was a Pharisee, a very important Jew who killed Christians not just because he was mean, but because he thought that by doing so he was being faithful to God and doing His will. So after his conversion and throughout his ministry, Paul made Jews take a completely different look at how they viewed their religious lives and how they looked at the Torah and the Bible.

The Jewish people believed in creational monotheism, which essentially means that there is one true God who created the world. They also believed that God didn't just leave the world alone and go away, but He remained actively involved in their daily lives, as illustrated so often during their time in the wilderness with Moses are they were led by the pillar of fire and fed by manna from Heaven. For these people, the presence of God was right there and they felt as though they could almost touch it.

Covenantal monotheism was another primary Jewish belief, which means that God had made a covenant with His people. After Adam and Eve fell in sin, God named the children of Israel as His chosen people and made a solemn promise to Abraham in Gen. 12:3. "And I will bless them that bless thee, and curse him that curseth thee: and in thee shall all families of the earth be blessed."

God made Abraham the father of this great nation because He wanted every descendant of Abraham to be a part of the family of God – His representatives on Earth. In essence, God was telling the Israelites, "I am going to bless you, and you are then to bless everyone else."

God gave them the Torah, or their covenant charter, so that they would be able to know about Him. One of His desires was that the Israelites use this to bless the rest of the world, just as we are blessed today with the Word of God and He has charged us to take its message to everyone we meet in our community and elsewhere.

Jewish scholars have put it this way: "I will make Adam first, and if he goes astray I will send Abraham to sort it out." That is a fairly accurate description of how the Jews viewed their world.

The final major point in the Jewish worldview is their eschatology, which is what they believe about the future. The Jews believe that one day God will come back to rescue and restore His chosen people, and at that point they will be the holy ones who are in charge and who are esteemed highly by God.

As you read the Old Testament you see that the children of Israel endured many hardships during that portion of their history. They were exiled and sold into slavery, among other things. A passage in the book of Nehemiah portrays the Jews returning to their homeland while still feeling as though they are enslaved or exiled. They look forward to the day when God will come back and restore them, setting things right by judging those who have oppressed them for so long.

Neh. 9:36-37 says, *"Behold, we are servants this day, and for the land that thou gavest unto our fathers to eat the fruit thereof and the good thereof, behold, we are servants in it: And it yieldeth much increase unto the kings whom thou hast set over us because of our sins: also they have dominion over our bodies, and over our cattle, at their pleasure, and we are in great distress."*

They looked forward to the Lord's return as something more than just how it would affect their individual lives. You might often look upon your salvation solely as it pertains to you, and that is important. But the Jewish people were looking forward to how their entire families and communities would be restored.

Paul tells them in the first chapter of Romans that what they have been waiting for all this time has actually happened, but not in the way they expected. The events surrounding the death, burial and resurrection of Jesus Christ changed everything, Paul contends, and this is the fulfillment of what the Jews had longed for.

Look at Rom. 1:1-5. *"Paul, a servant of Jesus Christ, called to be an apostle, separated unto the gospel of God, (Which he had promised afore by his prophets in the holy scriptures,) Concerning his Son Jesus Christ our Lord, which was made of the seed of David according to the flesh; And declared to be the Son of God with power, according to the spirit of holiness, by the resurrection from the dead: By whom we have received grace and apostleship, for obedience to the faith among all nations, for his name."*

This sums up everything that has happened to the Jews so far. After the fall of Adam, God selected Abraham to be the father of His chosen people, to take His truth and be a light to the Gentiles. Abraham and his descendants failed at this, as we see from dozens of examples in the Old Testament.

When the Israelites couldn't be that light to the Gentiles, God sent His Son to take that role upon Himself. Gal. 3:13-14 says, *"Christ hath redeemed us from the curse of the law, being made a curse for us: for it is written, Cursed is every one that hangeth on a tree: That the blessing of Abraham might come on the Gentiles through Jesus Christ; that we might receive the promise of the Spirit through faith."*

Christ's death on the cross was most important because of His atonement for our sins, but it was also a way to fulfill the role of the nation of Israel. It was as if Jesus said, "Now all nations through me will be blessed."

This came at a time of supreme arrogance among the Jewish people, particularly the men. They were known for prayers that included such words as, "Lord, thank you that I am not a Gentile or a woman." Gentiles were considered wicked, evil, nasty people who were no better than dogs while the Jews thought of themselves as a special group that was closest to God.

"That's not right," Paul told the Jews. "Being Jewish does not give you exclusive privileges where God is concerned. We as a people are just as messed up as the Gentiles or anyone else. In some ways they are better off than we are. We have some real problems."

The climax of this discussion is reached beginning with Rom. 2:17. *"Behold, thou art called a Jew, and restest in the law, and makest thy boast of God."* The Jews understood that following the law was not by itself a way to salvation, but they followed all of these rules because they considered it a response to their position as the covenant people of God. They considered themselves separated from other races in this regard. Obedience to the law, even its minutiae, was their standard that divided the good Jews from the bad ones.

Paul further illustrated this piety, and the pride that resulted from it, in verses 18-20. *"And knowest his will, and approvest the things that are more excellent, being instructed out of the law; And art confident that thou thyself art a guide of the blind, a light of them which are in darkness, An instructor of the foolish, a teacher of babes, which hast the form of knowledge and of the truth in the law."*

The Jews thought they were pretty hot stuff, but Paul showed them that they were supposed to be a light to the very people they constantly ridiculed and denigrated for being inferior. Their job was to be a witness to the Gentiles, and they didn't do it.

God told the Israelites in Isa. 42:6-7, *"I the LORD have called thee in righteousness, and will hold thine hand, and will keep thee, and give thee for a covenant of the people, for a light of the Gentiles; To open the blind eyes, to bring out the prisoners from the prison, and them that sit in darkness out of the prison house."*

Instead of following this mandate, the Jews kept it to themselves and formed their own holy clique. They looked down upon those who were not like them instead of sharing God's light with them. On top of that, they rejected the Lord and followed other gods at various times in the Old Testament.

This is a recurring theme in Isaiah 40-55. As the prophet writes to the Jews about these issues, he weaves in repeated references to Jesus and His coming as the Messiah. Where Israel failed, Christ will succeed.

Paul continues to attack the Jews for their religious arrogance in Rom. 2:21-24. *"Thou therefore which teachest another, teachest thou not thyself? thou that preachest a man should not steal, dost thou steal? Thou that sayest a man should not commit adultery, dost thou commit adultery? thou that abhorrest idols, dost thou commit sacrilege? Thou that makest thy boast of the law, through breaking the law dishonourest thou God? For the name of God is blasphemed among the Gentiles through you, as it is written."*

Blasphemy is a serious offense to the Jews. Even speaking the name of God is sometimes considered blasphemous. I have known

Jewish people today in the United States, who are not what one would consider strict practicing Jews, refusing to say the name of Yahweh aloud.

In the original Hebrew, that name is often written as a longer title that is nearly unpronounceable. Many people state that this was done intentionally so that God's name would not be repeated orally, to prevent blasphemy.

So for a Jewish person to read verse 24, in which the Jews are accused of blasphemy for their actions, it is like a knife in the back or a punch in the mouth. They have prided themselves on their own holiness, and now they are being told that their words and deeds have prevented Gentiles from coming to God.

Isa. 52:5 says, *"My name continually every day is blasphemed."* Interestingly, that indictment of the Jews comes just one chapter before a more well-known passage that talks of the coming Messiah. It is one more illustration of how Christ will come and do what the nation of Israel was unable to do.

After attacking the Jews for their hypocritical stance regarding the Torah, Paul takes aim at the practice of circumcision in Rom. 2:25-29. *"For circumcision verily profiteth, if thou keep the law: but if thou be a breaker of the law, thy circumcision is made uncircumcision. Therefore if the uncircumcision keep the righteousness of the law, shall not his uncircumcision be counted for circumcision? And shall not uncircumcision which is by nature, if it fulfil the law, judge thee, who by the letter and circumcision dost transgress the law?"*

One of the key questions in the early church was whether Gentiles who came to Christ had to be circumcised. Some Jews would not have communion with those who were not circumcised or even let them join their churches.

Paul pointed out that circumcision meant nothing without obedience to God. In essence, Paul created a new category of those who followed the law yet were not circumcised, and he asked which group was better off: Those who were circumcised yet disobedient, or those who obeyed God and His law. One relied on an outward symbol of holiness, while the other reflected a true change of heart.

Notice how the chapter is concluded in verses 28-29. *"For he is not a Jew, which is one outwardly; neither is that circumcision, which is outward in the flesh: But he is a Jew, which is one inwardly; and circumcision is that of the heart, in the spirit, and not in the letter; whose praise is not of men, but of God."*

What matters now, Paul writes, is not the outward badges of Judaism, but the emergence of Jesus as the One who kept the covenant the Jews failed to keep. The emphasis is now placed on a Spirit-filled life that spreads the light of God to all people and doesn't focus inwardly on a particular people group. Because of the role Christ fulfilled, the Gentiles were able to receive the Gospel.

What is the relevance of this lesson for us in the 21st century? It is a sad fact that we can sometimes do exactly as the Jews in the early church did by focusing on ourselves – we go to church, we are fed spiritually, we meet and worship with others in our little circle – and forgetting what we have been called to do. We have been brought into the family of God not just to enjoy its benefits by ourselves, but to share His love and His message with the world around us.

We believe in a God that is triune, or three in one. Before the world or even the angels were created, the Father, Son and Holy Spirit communed among themselves. God is a social God and a God of love. Before Adam even existed, there was a giving and receiving of love between the Father, Son and Holy Spirit.

That triune model is one for us to follow today. The Father sent the Son into the world so we could be saved. The Son sent the Holy Spirit into the world to guide and direct us. Now the Father, Son and Holy Spirit send us – the church – into the world to be a light for the lost.

Coming to church every Sunday is important, but it is not the only thing. We come to encourage each other so we can have an impact on the outside world the remainder of the week. We don't gather just so we can think highly of ourselves and forget everyone else. Our mission is to spread the Gospel to those we come in contact with every day of our lives.

Suppose you took a tour of an oil refinery and were shown all of the intricacies of the refining process. At the end of the tour someone asked, "We have seen everything except the shipping department. A refinery this size is equipped to handle huge amounts of oil and gas. Where do you take it so it can be shipped out around the world?"

"Well," said the tour guide, "we don't have a shipping department. All of the oil we produce is used as energy to keep the refinery going."

An operation like that serves no purpose whatsoever. But it is a similar idea to that of the Jews who had the Word of God and His blessings but chose to keep it all to themselves. We can have the same attitude if we are not careful.

Jesus had twelve disciples. After He ascended to Heaven, if they had not continued His work by telling others about Him there would have been a serious problem. Our mission today is the same. We must go out and be a light to the world by sharing what God has done for us.

Chapter 7

A GUILTY WORLD

"What advantage then hath the Jew? or what profit is there of circumcision? Much every way: chiefly, because that unto them were committed the oracles of God. For what if some did not believe? shall their unbelief make the faith of God without effect? God forbid: yea, let God be true, but every man a liar; as it is written, That thou mightest be justified in thy sayings, and mightest overcome when thou art judged. But if our unrighteousness commend the righteousness of God, what shall we say? Is God unrighteous who taketh vengeance? (I speak as a man) God forbid: for then how shall God judge the world? For if the truth of God hath more abounded through my lie unto his glory; why yet am I also judged as a sinner? And not rather, (as we be slanderously reported, and as some affirm that we say,) Let us do evil, that good may come? whose damnation is just. What then? are we better than they? No, in no wise: for we have before proved both Jews and Gentiles, that they are all under sin; As it is written, There is none righteous, no, not one: There is none that understandeth, there is none that seeketh after God. They are all gone out of the way, they are together become unprofitable; there is none that doeth good, no, not one. Their throat is an open sepulchre; with their tongues they have used deceit; the poison of asps is under their lips:

Whose mouth is full of cursing and bitterness: Their feet are swift to shed blood: Destruction and misery are in their ways: And the way of peace have they not known: There is no fear of God before their eyes. Now we know that what things soever the law saith, it saith to them who are under the law: that every mouth may be stopped, and all the world may become guilty before God. Therefore by the deeds of the law there shall no flesh be justified in his sight: for by the law is the knowledge of sin. But now the righteousness of God without the law is manifested, being witnessed by the law and the prophets; Even the righteousness of God which is by faith of Jesus Christ unto all and upon all them that believe: for there is no difference: For all have sinned, and come short of the glory of God; Being justified freely by his grace through the redemption that is in Christ Jesus."
(Rom. 3:1-24)

Imagine for a moment a row of chairs on the platform in your church sanctuary. These chairs are filled with people like you and me who have come to church with a need to be a part of the family of God.

Sitting in the first chair is a businessman. He is well-dressed, looks good and has a great deal of money. He sits on a number of boards of various organizations in the area and has been known to contribute to a number of charitable and philanthropic causes. All of this makes him well-respected in the community. No one knows he cheated the IRS a few years ago. When you see him at church, you make sure you greet him and he gets to know you because it might be beneficial to you somewhere down the road.

Next to him sit a husband and wife with their children. Together they look like the all-American family, and everyone wishes their family could make such an impression. Their appearance at church does not give away the fact that the husband and wife had an argument that nearly turned into a brawl just a couple of hours before the service. They are conscious to put up the appropriate front for their fellow church members, and they know that they can always pick up the fight where they left off when they get back home.

In the next chair is a young lady who is a prostitute. No one wants anything to do with her. She has earrings in all kinds of places and her body odor is less than desirable. She sits all alone, looking at the businessman and the family next to her with disdain and resentment, and she wonders if anyone even notices her.

The all-American family looks at her and thinks that people like her are one of the reasons this country is going downhill. They cringe at the thought of her going to the same altar that they use when they come forward to pray, and they wonder what kind of embarrassment she might be to the entire church.

The next seat is occupied by a man who has embezzled from his company. No one knows it yet but it will hit the front page of the local paper within a week. As so many people greet him warmly every Sunday he wonders what they will think of him once the news of his demise becomes public.

As his luck would have it, Ms. Tell-it-all sits in the chair next to him. She can't help herself; she blabs everything she hears to whoever will listen. If she doesn't know, she will make something up so she can keep yakking to everyone.

In another chair is a man who is adulterer and has been married several times. He wonders if the people there accept him. He knows he needs something, even if he's not sure what that something is.

So this is our cross-section of attendees in a Sunday morning church service. It is interesting that as our study of Romans has progressed, we have gone from putting God on trial to seeing ourselves in that same spot. If God were to walk into a service this week with our fictitious characters or a church that any of us attend, He would say, "All of you are guilty."

The businessman might claim that he is not as guilty as the prostitute, and the family may argue that its members are in pretty good standing compared to the rest of the crowd. Meanwhile, the adulterer and the prostitute are likely to confirm their own guilt while wondering if anyone else even cares about them.

This scenario is an appropriate background as we begin to look at Romans 3. If these people were on trial, the summation of the prosecution could be found beginning in verses 1-2. "*What advantage then hath the Jew? or what profit is there of circumcision?*

Much every way: chiefly, because that unto them were committed the oracles of God."

Our row of church characters could also include the religious leader who is verse thoroughly in the Bible. He knows Hebrew and Greek, and he is quick to pounce when the preacher makes a mistake. His knowledge and adherence to the Scriptures give him the upper hand, at least in his eyes.

It singles him out in God's eyes as well, but not in the way he might think. God considers him more accountable because of what he knows.

The discussion continues in verses 3-4. *"For what if some did not believe? shall their unbelief make the faith of God without effect? God forbid: yea, let God be true, but every man a liar; as it is written, That thou mightest be justified in thy sayings, and mightest overcome when thou are judged."*

Since the Jewish people are the called and chosen of God, would their unfaithfulness change the way God looks at things? Absolutely not. In fact, it further establishes God's view.

Another point is made in verses 5-8. *"But if our unrighteousness commend the righteousness of God, what shall we say? Is God unrighteous who taketh vengeance? (I speak as a man) God forbid: for then how shall God judge the world? For if the truth of God hath more abounded through my lie unto his glory; why yet am I also judged as a sinner? And not rather, (as we be slanderously reported, and as some affirm that we say,) Let us do evil, that good may come? whose damnation is just."*

This addressed the argument made by some that, since our sin shows the righteousness of God, perhaps we should all sin just to show how righteous God is. Of course, as this passage shows, that is not a good idea at all.

Then we come to the most important question. It is aimed squarely at the church member who looks down the pew and sighs, "Thank God that I am not like all of these other people." As we saw in the last chapter of this book, it is the same way the Jews viewed the Gentiles in the early church.

Verse 9 poses the question: *"What then? are we better than they? No, in no wise: for we have before proved both Jews and Gentiles, that they are all under sin."*

The answer comes in the remainder of Romans 3, beginning with verse 10, one of the best-known verse in the Bible. *"As it is written, There is none righteous, no, not one."*

This is the ultimate statement for everyone who sits satisfied in the fact that he or she dresses up nicely for church, sits with Bible open as the pastor speaks, and otherwise thinks, "I'm OK. I'm doing pretty good."

The verdict is in. You're guilty.

Verse 10 begins a list of the evidence against us, using a series of quotations from the Old Testament. According to verses 11-12, *"There is none that understandeth, there is none that seeketh after God. They are all gone out of the way, they are together become unprofitable; there is none that doeth good, no, not one."*

Now compare those verses to Ps. 14:1-3. *"The fool hath said in his heart, There is no God. They are corrupt, they have done abominable works, there is none that doeth good. The LORD looked down from heaven upon the children of men, to see if there were any that did understand, and seek God. They are all gone aside, they are all together become filthy: there is none that doeth good, no, not one."*

But we look at ourselves in relation to others and think that we're pretty good. The word *"understandeth"* in verse 11 indicates that this passage is speaking about the mind, while *"seeketh"* refers to the heart. If you are seeking God in your religion, you will never find anything.

Go back to our imaginary row of church attendees. A viewing screen is being lowered, and now they are going to see just how bad things really are. It's as if God is performing an X-ray from top to bottom.

The results of our X-ray begin with verse 13. *"Their throat is an open sepulchre; with their tongues they have used deceit; the poison of asps is under their lips."* That is a combination of quotations from Ps. 5:9 and Ps. 140:3.

Verse 14 says, *"Whose mouth is full of cursing and bitterness."* Those words are taken from Ps. 10:7.

77

We find in verses 15-17, *"Their feet are swift to shed blood: Destruction and misery are in their ways: And the way of peace have they not known."* A similar charge is found in Is. 59:7-8.

Verse 18 says, *"There is no fear of God before their eyes."*

Are you glad you're not on display for everyone to see what you've done in your life? We are now coming face to face with how we look before a holy and righteous God.

Have you ever watched "Perry Mason" on television? I prefer a bit more action in my shows, but my wife enjoys that series immensely. Think about how the attorney Mason closes in on the guilty party in the witness chair as he does in nearly every episode. The man or woman in question will begin to squirm in the seat and nervously adjust an article of clothing, perhaps due to perspiration. Maybe the collar is getting a bit tight. The subject avoids eye contact with Mason, knowing the game is up.

Guilty.

That is what we are dealing with in these verses. We must recognize that we are lost, we are condemned, and we have nothing to offer to God.

The prosecution rests its case in verses 19-20. *"Now we know that what things soever the law saith, it saith to them who are under the law: that every mouth may be stopped, and all the world may become guilty before God. Therefore by the deeds of the law there shall no flesh be justified in his sight: for by the law is the knowledge of sin."*

Now it's time for the defense to present its case. What could possibly be said to stem the tide of these overwhelming charges that have been brought?

I am a member of a leadership group in Miami that meets once a month. We are given regular reading assignments, and one recent selection was "The Purchase of a Soul" by Victor Hugo, author of "Les Miserables."

In "The Purchase of a Soul," a man comes to a pastor or bishop with absolutely nothing and looking for help. Here is what the man of God says to him:

"You don't have to tell me who you are. This is not my house; it is Christ's. He does not ask any guest his name, but only whether he has an affliction. If you are suffering, or hungry, or thirsty, you are always welcome. Don't thank me as if I am taking you to my house, for this is the house of no man except him who needs refuge. You as a traveler are more at home here than I. Whatever is here is yours. Why would I have to know your name; besides, before you told me I knew it."

That is what happens when you stand before a holy God and you need a defense attorney.

Some of the greatest theology and Biblical truth is found in the latter part of Romans 3. Let's start with verses 21-25.

> *"But now the righteousness of God without the law is manifested, being witnessed by the law and the prophets; Even the righteousness of God which is by faith of Jesus Christ unto all and upon all them that believe: for there is no difference: For all have sinned, and come short of the glory of God; Being justified freely by his grace through the redemption that is in Christ Jesus: Whom God hath set forth to be a propitiation through faith in his blood, to declare his righteousness for the remission of sins that are past, through the forbearance of God."*

In verse 24, being "*justified*" means you are given a new standard before God. "*Grace*" is what we are given that we most certainly do not deserve. Our "*redemption*" is the manner in which we were purchased by Christ from the slave market of sin. The "*propitiation*" referred to in verse 25 is mercy.

What does this means? All of you – the respected businessman, the proud family, the pastors and church members who think so much of themselves – can repent and be forgiven. It is the same for the prostitute or anyone else whose body and mind are warped by sin. It is the same for everyone.

You may think that you have an important position in your church, but you can always be replaced. To qualify for the role I am talking about now, you must repent and see yourself as you really are. The hymn writer put it like this: "Nothing in my hands I bring; simply to the cross I cling."

Now read verse 26. *"To declare, I say, at this time his righteousness: that he might be just, and the justifier of him which believeth in Jesus."*

We talk a lot in our churches about revival, and we all want to see it. We revive ourselves each morning from our sleep as we reach for that first cup of coffee and prepare to face the day. If we are going to have revival in our spiritual lives and our churches we must have an understanding of the great truths contained in these verses from Romans 3.

Many years ago as a young preacher, I was traveling with the great evangelist B.R. Lakin and he said to me, "What do you think is the most important doctrine in the entire Bible?"

Wanting to impress him with my brilliance, I immediately replied, "The doctrine of Christ."

"No," he said. "That's not it."

I went through a half-dozen other possibilities and he rejected them all. Finally I asked him what it was, and he said, "The most important doctrine in the Bible is the doctrine of sin. It is the knowledge that we are sinners."

Why does a businessman cheat on his taxes, or a family be overcome with pride, or a woman sell her body? The answer is always the same. It is sin.

Suppose a man slips into the church service late and sits in the back, and the person sitting next to you leans over and whispers, "That guy is a homosexual. What is he doing here?"

You might think the same thing, so let me ask you a question. Who did Jesus die for? Was His death for all sinners, or just a few who think they are living right?

The message of this chapter of Romans is this: The God who says, "Guilty," is the same God who says, "Forgiven." What a wonderful thought.

He is the same God who sees one of His children go astray and squander everything, but when that child returns He says, "Welcome home."

One of Billy Graham's daughters told a story publicly about how she had done some pretty awful things in her life and developed a great amount of guilt and remorse over her actions and what had become of her life. She wondered what it would be like to go back home to Dad. As she pulled up in the driveway of that North Carolina house, she found her father standing outside waiting for her and saying, "Come on home." That is redemption.

If Jesus behaves like this toward us, shouldn't we as a body of believers do the same toward each other? If we sit around too long thinking about how good we are, God will show us exactly how good we are. When we realize what we truly are, we recognize that everyone's sin is the same in God's eyes and His redemption is for us all.

When was the last time you had a real repentant heart that cared about others knowing Jesus? When was the last time you started to look at someone else with a judgmental eye but stopped in the realization that we are all in the same category as sinners?

There is an old poem that states:

My eyes are dry, my faith is cold,
My heart is hard, my prayers are cold.
I know how I ought to be –
Alive to you and dead to me.
What can be done to an old heart like mine?
Soften it up; cleanse me, I cry.
Let my heart break, let tears flow again
Down my face for the souls of lost men.

We have a ministry in our church that feeds homeless people. I will never forget the first time that as a young preacher I spoke to such a group. I got up and gave what I thought was a fantastic sermon, but no one seemed to care about that.

My attitude changed when I met them one-on-one and began talking to them. One had been a lawyer and another was once a preacher. They were people just like me until something in their lives happened.

We began to understand something that day about sin and guilt. But let me remind you now that there is always the cross of Jesus Christ, and redemption can always be found there. When Christ died, everything – one man's scandal, a woman's impurity, another man's perversion, all of our pride – was put upon Him. Every single thing we have done was taken by Him, and that is why our redemption is through Christ and Him alone.

The devil doesn't like that, which is why he tries to discourage people from using the name of Jesus. But we know, as Phil. 2:10 says, "That at the name of Jesus every knee should bow, of things in heaven, and things in earth, and things under the earth."

So when we think about His redemption, we should be ever so thankful that we are forgiven, and we need to stop and think about those who also need that forgiveness. When you encounter those people in need, share the Gospel with them and hit your knees in prayer for them.

All of us could be in that row of people we discussed at the beginning of this chapter. We are all guilty. But there is a Redeemer. From Rom. 3:24 through the end of Romans 8 we see all the things that this Redeemer is – what He has done, how we can live for Him, how He works in our lives. But until we understand how to get beyond our place among the guilty and without hope, we cannot get to where we need to be.

You can be forgiven, born again and children of God but still live with guilt. You can lapse into sin and begin to question yourself. That is the natural thing to do, but instead of questioning yourself you need to question Him so He can remind you what was done at the cross and how it was all put under the blood. The sooner we understand that, the better off we are in living the rest of our lives for God.

Chapter 8

A NEW STANDING BEFORE GOD

"What shall we say then that Abraham our father, as pertaining to the flesh, hath found? For if Abraham were justified by works, he hath whereof to glory; but not before God. For what saith the scripture? Abraham believed God, and it was counted unto him for righteousness. Now to him that worketh is the reward not reckoned of grace, but of debt. But to him that worketh not, but believeth on him that justifieth the ungodly, his faith is counted for righteousness. Even as David also describeth the blessedness of the man, unto whom God imputeth righteousness without works, Saying, Blessed are they whose iniquities are forgiven, and whose sins are covered. Blessed is the man to whom the Lord will not impute sin. Cometh this blessedness then upon the circumcision only, or upon the uncircumcision also? for we say that faith was reckoned to Abraham for righteousness. How was it then reckoned? when he was in circumcision, or in uncircumcision? Not in circumcision, but in uncircumcision. And he received the sign of circumcision, a seal of the righteousness of the faith which he had yet being uncircumcised: that he might be the father of all them that believe, though they be not circumcised; that righteousness might be imputed unto them also: And the father of circumcision to them who are not of the circumcision only, but who also walk

in the steps of that faith of our father Abraham, which he had being yet uncircumcised." (**Rom. 4:1-12**)

For more than a year in the mid-1990s this nation was riveted by the "trial of the century" when O.J. Simpson was charged with the murder of his ex-wife Nicole as well as Ron Goldman. The events surrounding that case and the ensuing trial captured the minds of America. I remember occasionally coming home from work and turning on the television to catch up on what was happening with the trial that particular day.

As we all know, Simpson was acquitted at the end of that trial. After that there was a second trial that did not captivate the country nearly as much, and in that civil trial it was ruled that Simpson was responsible for those deaths to the tune of a $33 million judgment.

Was he innocent or guilty? It depends upon who you ask. The evidence and circumstances surrounding the murders were the same for both trials, yet one resulted in acquittal and the other in a finding of guilt. In the eyes of the law, Simpson was justified from a criminal standpoint but not in the civil realm.

In the most important legal issues of our day, even with the best legal minds being involved, we are confused sometimes about what our standing really is. Only in the defendant's own mind is it known for certain whether he or she is truly guilty.

But as the book of Romans declares, there is a Judge we know as the God of Heaven. And when He issues a decree, you can mark it down that it is absolutely correct every single time. He makes no mistakes.

As we have been going through Romans we have seen a number of questions answered, but one that has not yet been answered is this: How were people in the Old Testament – who lived before the death, burial and resurrection of Jesus Christ – actually saved?

Go back for a moment to Gen. 15:6 and look at what happened to Abraham. *"And he believed in the LORD; and he counted it to him for righteousness."* That is how faith in God led to salvation during that time. The same thought is expressed in Romans 4, Galatians 3 and James 2. The Bible tells us that Abraham was justified in the Old Testament the same way that we are justified today.

People in the Old Testament were waiting for and looking forward to a Messiah. We believe as Christians that the Messiah has already come in the Person of Jesus Christ, so we are looking back. So all who have been saved, from Adam up to now, have received that salvation though faith in Christ, whether they looked forward to His coming or are looking back from today.

Our study of the first three chapters of Romans have shown us the extent of our sinful condition and the fact that our works do not satisfy a holy God. Peter on the day of Pentecost used the Old Testament scriptures, as did Paul in these writings, to emphasize the fact that we are all lost without a savior.

In Romans 4 we find a new term for this discussion, and that is justification. As we know from the legal system in the United States, acquittal does not necessarily mean innocence. But in the eyes of God, justification is righteousness.

The Father looks at us and sees us as lost sinners without anything good that we can bring before Him in and of ourselves. But when He looks at us and sees Jesus Christ standing between us and Him, the Father pronounces us righteous and we stand before Him as if we had never committed a sin.

Justification is the word that best describes our new standing before God. The example used here in Romans 4 is Abraham, the acknowledged father of the Jewish nation who is referred to several times in the Bible as God's friend.

It is amazing to consider that those of us who are born again can stand before God as if we had never sinned. That is what justification is all about.

There is a very important word mentioned throughout this chapter. In fact, it is seen 11 times and translated three different ways – as "*counted*," "*reckoned*" or "*imputed*." Put simply, it is an accounting term used by God.

Let's say that you come to church this Sunday and you have no money in your wallet. Someone comes up to you and gives you a check which you put in your wallet immediately. You can't wait until you get outside and look at how much the check is for.

Once you are in your car, you take a peek and see that the check is in the amount of $10,000. You are so happy. God has answered your prayers, and you are on your way the first thing Monday morning to put that money in the bank.

There's one problem. Eventually you are going to use up that money.

Suppose someone offers to give you $20,000 every single week, but you must spend each installment within a week before you get the next one. As good as that deal sounds, there will come a time when you are unable to fulfill that requirement.

God says, "I have put on your account all that you ever want in righteousness, and no matter what happens it is always available to you."

I had a friend who, as a teenager, was told by his father about a cookie jar in their house. That jar did not contain cookies, the father explained, but would always have money that was to be used only if the son really needed it.

"You'd be surprised how often I thought I needed that money," my friend said. "Sometimes I would take too much and the jar would eventually sit empty for a while."

When God gives you righteousness, there is always plenty for you to have throughout your life. You can go to His source over and over again, and it never runs dry or empty.

Look again at verse 3, where the word "*counted*" first appears. God put righteousness in Abraham's account upon his belief in Him.

In verse 4 we see the word "*debt.*" If you are depending upon your works for favor with God, you are operating at a deficit. It will never work that way.

The ensuing verses continue to build upon this thought, with the repeated mention of an accounting for righteousness (verse 5) and the idea that God accounts for this righteousness apart from works (verse 6).

In verse 8 we see the blessing that results when sin is not added to one's account, followed in verse 9 by another mention of faith resulting in an accounting of righteousness. Verses 10 and 11 use the practice of circumcision to illustrate how this righteousness is a result of faith and not works.

These truths are emphasized throughout Romans 4, concluding with verses 21-25. "And being fully persuaded that, what he had promised, he was able also to perform. And therefore it was imputed to him for righteousness. Now it was not written for his sake alone, that it was imputed to him; But for us also, to whom it shall be imputed, if we believe on him that raised up Jesus our Lord from the dead; Who was delivered for our offences, and was raised again for our justification."

So the word translated as *"counted,"* *"reckoned"* or *"imputed"* is used 11 times in this chapter, referring to the fact that our sins are placed upon Christ and His righteousness is added to our accounts. This allows you to stand in absolute righteousness before a holy God, as if there had never been a sin committed in your life. We don't always live that way, but our position in Him is one of righteousness.

One of the biggest problems we have today, that keeps us from a revived spirit at times, is our failure to grasp that we are considered righteous through the finished work of Jesus Christ. As Romans 4 points out, God justifies the ungodly and not the godly, because there are no godly people to justify.

Look again at Rom. 4:7-8. *"Saying, Blessed are they whose iniquities are forgiven, and whose sins are covered. Blessed is the man to whom the Lord will not impute sin."*

Here is the issue we face. Every one of us has a conscience that reminds us of the things we have done. I have learned in 40 years as a pastor that people who seek counseling are often burdened heavily about these kinds of things.

The late Donald Barnhouse told the story of a woman who came to talk to him one day, and he could tell that she was deeply troubled. This was a fine woman who was a member of his church. When he asked her to come to the point of her visit, she said, "I hate to tell you this, pastor, but 40 years ago I murdered a man and no one knows about it."

Can you imagine laying something like that on your pastor, or anyone else for that matter? The woman went on to explain that a man came into her family's home as a boarder when she was young, and he raped her. Seething with intense hatred for her attacker, she waited until one day she found him lying in his room asleep. She turned up the gas on the old heater next to his bed and left the room. When the gas filled the room, it killed him.

"The police came and ruled that it was an accident," she told her pastor. "What should I do?"

No one knew about this incident for 40 years, but her conscience would not let her forget it. People often bring up long-hidden secrets in this manner, and their minds are filled with all types of thoughts. "How do I get this out of my head?" they wonder.

Although the law of the land has rules or subjects such as this, I think we often fail to understand the incredible depth of the redemptive work of Jesus Christ. When He justified us before the Father, we were forgiven of every single sin we had ever committed. Can you grasp that?

You may be wondering, "How can God forgive me?" You might have done something that no one else can forgive, but that's not the point. The holy God of Heaven will forgive you, and He has proven that in the life of Abraham.

The second illustration used in this passage is that of David. We all know the story of how he agreed to meet Goliath when no one else would, and the stone from his sling sent the giant tumbling to the ground. God used David to become king of Israel, and great things happened in his life.

But one day he saw Bathsheba and fell into sin. To cover up his adultery with Bathsheba he commissioned a heinous crime by sending her husband Uriah to a certain death on the battlefield. How can God justify something like that?

It is explained in verses 6-8, which show that God will count us as righteous apart from our works and He will not count our sin against us when we are justified. As born-again believers our record contains Christ's perfect righteousness and can never again contain our sin.

With that in mind, look at Abraham's testimony in verses 9-12. According to verse 9, "*faith was reckoned to Abraham for righteousness.*" Verse 11 refers to "*a seal of the righteousness of the faith which he had.*" The latter part of verse 12 shows us "*the steps of that faith of our father Abraham, which he had being yet uncircumcised.*"

The question for us is this: How is your faith? I have heard people say, "It's hard to have faith in someone you can't see." The Bible describes several different ways our faith operates.

I Cor. 15:14-17 speaks of a vain faith that questions the resurrection of Christ. "*And if Christ be not risen, then is our preaching vain, and your faith is also vain. Yea, and we are found false witnesses of God; because we have testified of God that he raised up Christ: whom he raised not up, if so be that the dead rise not. For if the dead rise not, then is not Christ raised: And if Christ be not raised, your faith is vain; ye are yet in your sins.*"

Do you believe that Jesus died and rose again, visibly and victoriously? If that is the case, then our faith is not a dead faith.

Our works cannot get us where we need to be. Our works cannot help us be justified. The only One who can justify us is our Heavenly Father through Jesus Christ. Our faith sometimes has dead works attached to it, not showing what God has done in our lives, and the Bible teaches that "*faith without works is dead*" (James 2:20). If you ever see someone working constantly in an attempt to become right with God, that person is working toward a dead end.

I once sat across the aisle on an airplane from a man who was leaving South Florida to return home from a conference. This man wore a large hearing aid, and when he saw my Bible he asked if I was a Christian. That led to a conversation about God during which he spoke loudly because of his hearing deficiency, and people who sat nearby began to notice us.

Finally a tiny woman came and sat beside me. She was so slight that she was able to cross her legs easily in front of her despite the cramped conditions so common on today's airliners. As she heard the other man talking, she said, "That's what I need."

"What do you need?" I asked.

"I need God."

The man looked over and nearly shouted, "What did she say?"

"She said she needs God."

"Well, tell her about God," he shouted.

I said that I would, and as I began to talk to this lady I heard her story about her broken marriage to a doctor that left her alone with a great deal of money. She had decided to give it all to the poor, and as we spoke she was actually returning from a trip to India where she had given money to Mother Teresa. She had very little left for herself.

"I still feel empty inside," the woman confessed.

I then had the privilege of leading her to Christ, after which the man across the aisle asked loudly, "What did she say?" When I told him, he got excited and began talking to everyone around him.

This episode once again emphasizes the very important point that our salvation cannot be earned. I am convinced that there are people in churches all over our country who are not saved, although they may appear to be born again because of what they do or how they act.

The Bible speaks about many different types of faith, such as a believing faith (Mark 16), a small faith (Mark 7) or a weak faith (Romans 14). The kind of faith God wants us to have can only be achieved when we realize that it is a gift from Him.

Eph. 2:8-9 says, *"For by grace are ye saved through faith; and that not of yourselves: it is the gift of God: Not of works, lest any man should boast."*

Look at Rom. 5:1. *"Therefore being justified by faith, we have peace with God through our Lord Jesus Christ."*

You go to the airport to catch a plane. Going through security, you take off your shoes and belt as your belongings are searched by people you don't even know. As you board the plane, you have no idea who the pilot is. That giant metal vehicle bounces down the runway a bit as it creeps into the sky, and all the while you have faith in that unknown pilot to steer you safely.

You may be reading this and thinking about a miracle you need in your life. You may feel empty inside or be struggling with something you don't think you can handle. If you can trust an airplane pilot you don't even know, you can also trust a sovereign and holy God in Heaven to take care of you. If anyone is worth trusting, He is.

When Peter walked on water, he began looking at what was happening around him and began to sink. We do the same thing in our lives. We look at our circumstances and we start to sink. It doesn't have to be that way.

Many years ago a man walked on a tightrope across Niagara Falls from the Canadian side to the New York side. People were aghast as they watched him cross those raging waters, but they cheered wildly when he reached land.

"How many of you think I can do that again?" the man asked the crowd, and nearly all of them raised their hands in affirmation.

"All right, then," he said. "Who wants to climb on my shoulders and go with me?"

I would never do something like that. But someone actually did get on his shoulders that day, and both of them crossed Niagara Falls. If someone can do that, can't we trust in the God of Heaven today for whatever burdens we are carrying?

Justification is one of the greatest words in the entire Bible. It reminds us of our standing with God, and that what He did for you and me is all that is needed. He is worth trusting.

Chapter 9

WHAT GOD PROMISES,
HE PERFORMS

"For the promise, that he should be the heir of the world, was not to Abraham, or to his seed, through the law, but through the righteousness of faith. For if they which are of the law be heirs, faith is made void, and the promise made of none effect: Because the law worketh wrath: for where no law is, there is no transgression. Therefore it is of faith, that it might be by grace; to the end the promise might be sure to all the seed; not to that only which is of the law, but to that also which is of the faith of Abraham; who is the father of us all, (As it is written, I have made thee a father of many nations,) before him whom he believed, even God, who quickeneth the dead, and calleth those things which be not as though they were. Who against hope believed in hope, that he might become the father of many nations, according to that which was spoken, So shall thy seed be. And being not weak in faith, he considered not his own body now dead, when he was about an hundred years old, neither yet the deadness of Sarah's womb: He staggered not at the promise of God through unbelief; but was strong in faith, giving glory to God; And being fully persuaded that, what he had promised, he was able also to perform. And therefore it was imputed to him for righteousness. Now it was not written for

his sake alone, that it was imputed to him; But for us also, to whom it shall be imputed, if we believe on him that raised up Jesus our Lord from the dead; Who was delivered for our offences, and was raised again for our justification." (**Rom. 4:13-25**)

It is amazing to think that God will do everything He promises. But for that to happen in our lives, we have to live by faith. We must believe God and follow Him.

Our future begins today. A lot of things in the past are good and helpful to us. God has given us a **promise** through the death, burial and resurrection of Jesus Christ. He has given us a **purpose**, every one of us, from the moment we were brought into this world. We have been given **power** in the form of the Holy Spirit, who enters our lives at the moment of salvation. God also has told us about our **potential**, and there is a great **proof** of what we believe in the fact that Christ arose from the grave.

All of those things are from the past, but we have to live out our faith now and into the future. So my future begins today, and so does yours.

Abraham was called by God to go and look for a land. But for that to happen, God had to offer another promise, which was that Abraham would be given a child who would grow up to become the son of promise. Abraham had to follow that path by faith.

We believe that the land of Israel has been promised to the Jewish people, and it belongs to them and should be secured by them. But God's promise to Abraham did not concern a specific piece of land as much as it did to a child being born.

If you are to believe a promise someone makes to you, then you have to believe in the character of the person making that promise, which indicates that person's ability to perform the promised act. Likewise, the ability of God to perform what He promises is based upon the character and the very nature of God.

With that in mind, let's look at some key words in this passage from Romans 4. The first word is *"faith,"* which appears no less than five times in these verses. It means to believe something with a firm persuasion; you believe in something and are persuaded that it is so.

In this portion of Scripture the words *"faith"* and *"belief"* come from the same Greek root word and mean exactly the same thing. God is telling us here that we should have faith and belief in a few important things, not the least of which is His own character.

The next key word is *"hope,"* found beginning in verse 18: *"Who against hope believed in hope, that he might become the father of many nations, according to that which was spoken, So shall thy seed be."* This word speaks about confidence and expectation.

When you and I talk about hope, it is often accompanied by the thought, "I want this to happen." When the Bible speaks about hope, it is saying, "This is going to happen." It is based upon God's promises.

The other key word, perhaps the most important, is the word *"promise."* It appears three times in verses 13-16. *"For the promise, that he should be the heir of the world, was not to Abraham, or to his seed, through the law, but through the righteousness of faith. For if they which are of the law be heirs, faith is made void, and the promise made of none effect: Because the law worketh wrath: for where no law is, there is no transgression. Therefore it is of faith, that it might be by grace; to the end the promise might be sure to all the seed; not to that only which is of the law, but to that also which is of the faith of Abraham; who is the father of us all."*

We see it again in verses 20-21. *"He staggered not at the promise of God through unbelief; but was strong in faith, giving glory to God; And being fully persuaded that, what he had promised, he was able also to perform."*

In these verses the word is a legal term comparable to a summons, and it is based upon a solemn commitment. It goes hand in hand with the words *"justified,"* *"counted"* and *"imputed"* that we discussed in the last chapter as accounting terms that refer to our standing with God.

If we are to accept a promise, we are doing so based upon the character of the person making that promise.

Recently before a birthday party at our house, my wife told me that she was going to pick up the balloons. I was glad she said that since I have trouble picking them out, putting them in the car and getting them out of the car. "You go get the cake at four o'clock," she told me.

So everything went smoothly from there. She brought the balloons back, and they were beautiful. I picked up the cake, brought it home and set it on the table in time for the party.

Now what would have happened if she had forgotten to get the balloons or I had forgotten the cake? The party would have been in serious trouble. But we worked together based upon our promises to each other that we would do what we said we would do.

All of us have made promises that we have failed to fulfill. On the other hand, God has never failed to keep a promise, and He is worthy of our belief in Him whenever He makes a promise.

But when we pray to God about something, it usually goes something like this: "Lord, I am asking you today for such-and-such. Here is how you can do it, this is the time I want it, and here are the other details you will need."

We tell God exactly how, when and where we want our prayer answered, and if it doesn't go according to our plan we wonder if God is listening to us. But when you look back at the circumstances of your life, you will find that God usually does a much better job according to His plan than if He had performed precisely to your own specifications. The wonderful promises we are studying in Romans are based upon God's character as well as His timing.

Our faith leads to familiarity with God. The more you trust someone, the more familiar you become with that person.

Look at verse 16. *"Therefore it is of faith, that it might be by grace; to the end the promise might be sure to all the seed; not to that only which is of the law, but to that also which is of the faith of Abraham; who is the father of us all."*

Our faith links us to His grace. We cannot be saved without grace. Faith makes the spiritual world real and tangible, and it helps us appreciate the blessings of God.

The Bible says in Heb. 11:1, *"Now faith is the substance of things hoped for, the evidence of things not seen."* Our salvation depends upon the mighty hand of God.

This portion of Scripture is not talking about the land promise made to Abraham, but the offspring that are compared in number to the stars in the sky, as God explained to him one night while he was gazing at the heavens. Abraham thought that was a pretty good deal, but for it to come to pass he must have a male child through whom this could be fulfilled. As Abraham progresses in age from his 50s to his 90s, he wonders if this will happen.

His wife Sarah was convinced that it wouldn't happen, so she brought out her handmaid Hagar who bore Ishmael for Abraham. Untold wars have since taken place and continue to this day because of that birth.

Abraham and Sarah soon realized that Ishmael was not the son of promise. It wasn't until Sarah was 90 and Abraham was nearly 100 that Isaac was born, fulfilling God's promise. It happened just as He said it would.

Is God worth trusting? I believe He is, and so should you.

Suppose you buy a piece of land for $1 million. After you pay it off, you want to build a house on that site and it will cost you $3 million, so you go to the bank to borrow the money. The bank takes a look at your land and agrees to loan you the money, thinking that it is a good risk. But the land is encumbered in the deal. If you make the payments on the loan, everything is fine. But if you don't, the bank will take the land and whatever you have built on it.

As you and I live a life of faith, according to His promises, God is the guarantee that those promises will be kept, much like the land is a guarantee on the loan for the house. We live, then, upon the promises of God. He is worth trusting.

Faith also brings us to the future. The first part of verse 17 says, *"As it is written, I have made thee a father of many nations."* The Arabs were descended from Ishmael, while the Jews descended from Isaac. We as Gentiles are grafted in because of Christ. So as we look back at Abraham as the father of Christians, Jews and Arabs. God's promise has come true.

Look at verse 18. *"Who against hope believed in hope, that he might become the father of many nations, according to that which was spoken, So shall thy seed be."* Abraham had hope in Christ that was based upon the standard God had given to him.

The miracle of it all is considered in verse 19: *"And being not weak in faith, he considered not his own body now dead, when he was about an hundred years old, neither yet the deadness of Sarah's womb.*" Abraham realized that God was going to do something impossible, and He did.

Perhaps there is something in your life right now that needs God's attention. Do you need Him to perform a miracle for you? We have the same God today that Abraham had, and He can do far above anything we hope and pray for. He tells us in His Word that just as He opened Sarah's womb and gave Abraham a son in his old age, He can do great things for us. He does not change.

Abraham's great faith is demonstrated in verse 20. "*He staggered not at the promise of God through unbelief; but was strong in faith, giving glory to God.*" He looked at the stars and was reminded of God's promise, and we can look back at the cross of Calvary in the same way, seeing Christ and our salvation.

Verse 21 continues this thought. "*And being fully persuaded that, what he had promised, he was able also to perform.*" Abraham took God at His word. The outstanding feature of Abraham's faith was that it was a God-centered faith, not just a breezy optimism. God received prominence throughout Abraham's life, and he recognized the obstacles of his life as opportunities for God to prove His power and sovereignty.

We need to believe God. You and I need to continue growing in our faith, taking God for what He says. If you were asked today for a testimony of what God is doing in your life, would you have to go back five or 10 years into the archives of your life to find something, or is God working dynamically in your life today?

The fundamental sin in all of our lives is our failure to believe God will do what He says. Genuine faith adheres to God's promises despite the whirlwind of external circumstances that seem so real.

Abraham believed God and the result is seen in verse 22: "*And therefore it was imputed to him for righteousness.*"

Faith is an experience. Just as Abraham had faith in God, we must have the same faith for the same purposes.

A few months ago I received a phone call from my former pastorate in Pennsylvania. A van carrying a group of teenage boys after a soccer match was involved in an auto accident and two 16-

year-old passengers from that church were killed. Especially in a large church, that can happen a couple of times every year.

What can you possibly say in a situation like that? You have to return to the promises of God. *"Let not your heart be troubled: ye believe in God, believe also in me. In my Father's house are many mansions: if it were not so, I would have told you. I go to prepare a place for you. And if I go and prepare a place for you, I will come again, and receive you unto myself; that where I am, there ye may be also"* (John 14:1-3).

You get a report from your doctor about a mass that is growing inside your body. You pray for healing and wonder what will happen next. What is God's promise? *"I will never leave thee, nor forsake thee"* (Heb. 13:5).

We say, "But, that's not the way we had it planned, God."

Then God reminds us, "It's my plans that are important, not yours."

A lot of times people speculate about when they get to Heaven, God will explain to them why certain things happened the way they did. I'm not so sure that, once we get to Heaven, we'll even care about it anymore. Once we get to Heaven we will only be thinking about how happy we are that we are there.

Just as Abraham had faith, we also need to have faith that God is always in the process of growing our lives. Whatever we are going through in life right now is an opportunity for God to build character in us. Just as we trust in the character of God for our own blessings, we must allow God to build character in us so that we can be a blessing to others.

That brings us to the central principle that this passage is all about, which is the fact that we have to live our lives by faith. As the Bible says in several places, including Rom. 1:17, *"The just shall live by faith."* If you are justified by Him, you have to live a life of faith.

So what are some of the promises of God? You can't just make up your own and claim that they are from Him. But there are hundreds of His promises in the Bible.

Look at Rom. 5:1-2. *"Therefore being justified by faith, we have peace with God through our Lord Jesus Christ: By whom also we have access by faith into this grace wherein we stand, and rejoice in hope of the glory of God."*

If you are justified, you have peace with God. It doesn't matter whether you feel particularly good about yourself or what you think God may think about you at any particular time. You are in the family of God, and because of that you can rejoice about what God has in store for you. It is a promise of God.

If you stop and think about it, every one of us has reasons to be discouraged. Life is very discouraging at times. We all know people who constantly talk about how bad things are, so much so that you don't even want to be in the same room with them.

Life is full of heartache. As long as we look only at our life down here and never at what awaits us with Him one day, we will be discouraged. But when we *"rejoice in hope of the glory of God,"* we eliminate discouragement.

Another important promise of God is found in Rom. 8:31. *"What shall we then say to these things? If God be for us, who can be against us?"* That is powerful. We as children of God, when facing all that the world throws at us, have the greatest ally we could possibly have.

Continue reading in verse 32. *"He that spared not his own Son, but delivered him up for us all, how shall he not with him also freely give us all things?"* If He could send Christ to take our place, we cannot imagine how He could possibly spare us anything that is for our good.

What God has shown you in secret through prayer and His Word, all He has promised you – don't ever let anyone take that away from you in public.

Through all that we may be going through in life, we can rest assured in what God has promised in verse 35. *"Who shall separate us from the love of Christ? shall tribulation, or distress, or persecution, or famine, or nakedness, or peril, or sword?"*

Many of us are going through trials or perhaps being persecuted in the workplace for our testimony. Around the world, there are more people being martyred for their Christian faith than at any time in human history. But nothing can stop Christ from loving us.

More of His promises are evident in verses 38-39. *"For I am persuaded, that neither death, nor life, nor angels, nor principalities, nor powers, nor things present, nor things to come, Nor height, nor depth, nor any other creature, shall be able to separate us from the love of God, which is in Christ Jesus our Lord."*

I remember my father's death partly because it was the first major death to affect my life. My dad and I were best friends; we had a ball together. I remember reaching into the casket and touching his cold hand, and it was as if God said to me right then, "That's not your dad. He's in Heaven with Me." There is something about the comfort God gives even in death.

Jesus loves you because He has chosen to love you. That is a promise from God.

God told Abraham that He wanted him to be a man of faith. I don't think Abraham ever comprehended how people would write about him and preach about him all over the world some 4,000 years later. I believe he was just being obedient to God, but because he chose to be a man of faith we are using him as our role model so many centuries later.

Abraham was not a perfect man, and neither was David. We see obvious examples of this from the Biblical accounts of their lives. But God chose to use them as He did despite that, and I believe that it was because of their hearts. Both of them were men after the heart of God.

You might be thinking about how rough your life has been, and how many times you have sinned before God. I'm so glad there is redemption in Christ, and God can bring us back out of the slave market of sin to the place we need to be. But you have to choose to live the life of faith.

I read a great story about a man called Telemachus. Very little is known about him from history, but he lived in Rome during the time of the gladiators. The Colosseum would host fights between men, and it was a form of entertainment for the Roman people to watch these warriors battle to the death.

Telemachus thought it was tragic to have this kind of entertainment, but he came to the Colosseum once to watch an event. As

101

he saw the spectacle played out before his eyes, he was sickened. Finally he stood and shouted, "In the name of Christ, stop!"

No one listened to him because of the roar of the crowd, so he ran down onto the floor of the arena, stood between the combatants and repeated that cry. The men looked at him with shock and one of them accidentally ran his spear through Telemachus, causing his death. Here is how history records this event:

"The gladiators stood looking at the tiny figure of a man. Slowly, everyone left the Colosseum. The year was 391 A.D. Never again would they witness men killing each other for the sake of a crowd. The last battle to the death between gladiators was changed by one small voice."

We need men and women of God who will be that one small voice of faith. Do you realize that when you go to your job you are the only Jesus some of your coworkers ever see?

We have to learn to get away from our own personal problems, however many there may be, and focus instead upon "*the author and finisher of our faith*" (Heb. 12:2). The Christian life must be a faith life.

You're going to have problems in life. There will be some days that you don't even want to get out of bed because of what you know you must face that day. But our eyes need to be centered on what awaits us above, not down here on Earth. We should be more concerned with how God is working in our hearts and lives than whatever else may be going on.

Notice the application to our lives in verses 23-25. "*Now it was not written for his sake alone, that it was imputed to him; But for us also, to whom it shall be imputed, if we believe on him that raised up Jesus our Lord from the dead; Who was delivered for our offences, and was raised again for our justification.*"

Corrie Ten Boom was a great Christian woman. For years she was a prisoner in concentration camps during World War II and she was abused physically as well as sexually.

When she was released, God used her life in an incredible way. She saw many souls saved through her speaking and writing. But she knew that what had happened to her in the past would be difficult to get over.

One day she was shaking hands after giving a speech. She looked up and saw one of the guards who had heaped abuse upon here, now standing before her asking for her forgiveness. From a human standpoint, this is unforgiveable.

She struggled with her reaction to this situation. How would you react? To demand his death would seem almost justified. But God spoke to her heart and she forgave him.

That can happen because of the promises of God, who tells us that we have His guarantee of forgiveness, but we must also be forgiving to others.

The promises of God are amazing and they are sure. What God promises, He performs.

He has promised us that Jesus Christ is coming again. There are a number of other things that He has promised us will take place. He never goes back on His promises.

Chapter 10

LIVE LIKE A KING OR QUEEN

"Therefore being justified by faith, we have peace with God through our Lord Jesus Christ: By whom also we have access by faith into this grace wherein we stand, and rejoice in hope of the glory of God. And not only so, but we glory in tribulations also: knowing that tribulation worketh patience; And patience, experience; and experience, hope: And hope maketh not ashamed; because the love of God is shed abroad in our hearts by the Holy Ghost which is given unto us. For when we were yet without strength, in due time Christ died for the ungodly. For scarcely for a righteous man will one die: yet peradventure for a good man some would even dare to die. But God commendeth his love toward us, in that, while we were yet sinners, Christ died for us. Much more then, being now justified by his blood, we shall be saved from wrath through him. For if, when we were enemies, we were reconciled to God by the death of his Son, much more, being reconciled, we shall be saved by his life. And not only so, but we also joy in God through our Lord Jesus Christ, by whom we have now received the atonement." **(Rom. 5:1-11)**

You might say, "I'm not a member of royalty, and I don't have a lot of money. How could I ever be considered royal?"

But this passage speaks about a unique relationship that we have with God. Perhaps it can be best described through a story told by John Phillips, a native of Wales who is now an outstanding Bible teacher in America.

A little boy came to Buckingham Palace one day and walked up to one of the imposing soldiers at the gate. "I want to see the king," he said.

"Go away," the soldier answered. "You cannot see the king."

Overwhelmed by that response, the boy walked away and began to cry. A tall, handsome man in a fine suit saw him and walked over. "Why are you crying?" he asked.

"I've always wanted to see the king, but the soldier won't let me in."

The man smiled. "Take my hand."

As they walked together toward the gate, the soldiers all snapped to attention. The boy was amazed, and he saw the same reaction from the soldiers inside the magnificent building, along with comments like, "Good morning, sir."

They walked from room to room and finally came into the room where the king would be. The boy had always seen pictures of the king but was mesmerized now that he saw him in person. As he was led by the hand to the throne he heard this comment from the king to his escort:

"Son, who have you brought to see me today?"

The distinguished gentleman who made that boy's dream come true that day was the Prince of Wales, the son of the king.

"I've brought this boy for a visit," the prince said. "He has always wanted to meet you."

The fifth chapter of Romans tells us about One who brings us to the king of the universe. It is our Saviour, the Lord Jesus Christ, who brings us into the presence of God the Father. Christ is the only way by which we can gain an audience with God.

Two of the saddest words in human history are, "No hope." But when we have Christ, we have a wonderful expectation and hope in the Lord, and He will take us straight into the presence of the Father.

You may notice that this chapter of Romans begins with the word, *"Therefore."* This word is often used in Romans to denote a change from one section of the book to another. Some people have said, "When you see a 'therefore' in the Bible, you need to find out what it is 'there for.'"

Look at how chapter 4 ends, with verse 25. *"Who was delivered for our offences, and was raised again for our justification."* As we have previously discussed, that is a reference to our new standing with God. From there, the first portion of Romans 5 goes on to talk about the blessings that come from our justification. Isn't it wonderful to be a child of God?

There are at least seven blessings mentioned in the first 11 verses of Romans. These are promises of God that He will never take back.

I remember a small boy who used to attend one of our Christian schools, the Master's Academy. Whenever he would see me, he acted as if he were in awe. When I said hello, he would just nod at me. I didn't really know what he thought about me.

One day as I came by he had a candy bar in his hand. When he saw me he reached out and handed me the candy. "Thank you," I said as I took it.

Within moments, his eyes went from me to the candy bar. He took it back, opened it up, took a bite, rolled the wrapper around what was left and gave it back to me.

God has said in these verses that He is giving us some things, but He will never take them back. What He gives is given willingly and permanently.

The first blessing in this passage is **peace.** Verse 1 says, *"Therefore being justified by faith, we have peace with God through our Lord Jesus Christ."*

The unsaved person is at odds with God today. According to Is. 48:22, *"There is no peace, saith the LORD, unto the wicked."* It cannot be plainer than that.

According to Rom. 8:1, *"There is therefore now no condemnation to them which are in Christ Jesus, who walk not after the flesh, but after the Spirit."* The word *"condemnation"* is a pretty strong word that carries with it the idea of a declaration of war, as it were. God says that, apart from Christ, we are condemned.

Justification, on the other hand, is where God declares us to be righteous. It is a declaration of peace rather than war, made possible by Christ's death on the cross.

It is interesting to note the justification reference in Rom. 5:1. In the Greek text it is the *aorist* tense, which indicates the actual time that each individual, upon the exercise of faith, was justified in the sight of God. When you accepted Christ and made Him your Saviour, you were automatically justified at that moment before God.

That boy was able to see the king because the prince took him in. We see God because of Christ, but it gets even better: Christ stands before God in our stead. You are accepted into the family of God because He sees you through Jesus, and you are never taken out of the family.

Sometimes a mistake can be made in the distinction between one's standing before God and his state, or relationship with God. A person can go through times where he doesn't feel saved, but once you have accepted Christ and are depending upon Him for your salvation, that will never change.

I have probably officiated at several hundred weddings during my ministry. Typically the event culminates in a lavish reception at which the bride and groom appear utterly exhausted because of everything that has gone into the wedding and the days leading up to it.

But I often notice something very interesting. Almost without exception, the bride will attempt to impress the groom's family and the groom will try to impress the bride's family. The newly married couple goes around the room trying to connect everyone and make sure all are comfortable and happy with the proceedings. Despite their efforts, each family usually goes off about halfway through the reception and gathers in separate groups anyway.

When you accept God by faith, you are automatically accepted into His family. You can look around your church auditorium Sunday morning and see a crowd of several hundred people, some of whom you may have never met. But in Christ you are all as one in that blessed and wonderful family.

In verse 2 we find that we are given a **path** to God. *"By whom also we have access by faith into this grace wherein we stand, and rejoice in hope of the glory of God."* The word *"access"* suggests a path; it is the process of gaining entrance to the king through the favor of another.

In Bible times, the priest would go once a year into the tabernacle and behind the large curtain known as a veil to offer a sacrifice to God for the sins of the people. The children of Israel would stand outside and wait. The Gentiles, meanwhile, had to wait in the Gentile court; any of them caught going past that area could be killed.

When Jesus died, that veil in the temple was torn and came down, as did the wall of the Gentiles mentioned in Eph. 2:14. So we are drawn to God by the riches of His grace, and we have direct access to God because of what Christ did for us. We can talk to Him and give our burdens over to Him.

You might be loaded down with burdens right now. All of us experience that at one time or another. Preacher Phillips Brooks said that on every single row of every single church on a given Sunday morning, there is someone with a burden that is huge. I think that is probably true.

We come to church and enjoy the worship and fellowship, thinking to ourselves, "Why can't it be this good all the time?" The fact is, you have direct access to God 24 hours a day, seven days a week. You don't have to come to a pastor or a priest. You can go directly to God.

I am fairly certain that someone reading this book right now needs a miracle from God. Did you ever notice that we pray more often when we have trouble? Our prayer lives often slack off when things are going well, but when problems arise we run to God.

He is OK with that. God is not particularly happy when your prayer life suffers, but He wants to be the One you run to when you need something. He wants you to come to Him. When a child has a problem and the last one to know is the parent, that parent is not very happy. God wants us to come to Him first.

The third blessing in this passage is **hope**. We find it mentioned in the latter part of verse 2 and also in the beginning of verse 5. This hope is defined as a confident expectation that does not disappoint.

The word *"rejoice"* as used in verse 2 means that we literally boast in the hope of God. There is always a better day coming for the child of God.

That burden you are carrying is going to get better. You can unload it if you want to.

The fourth blessing is **tribulation**. It is probably the most difficult to understand. Look at verses 3-4. *"And not only so, but we glory in tribulations also: knowing that tribulation worketh patience; And patience, experience; and experience, hope."*

God has told us that we as Christians will all experience tribulation in this world. That is an interesting word, coming from a root word speaks of a piece of timber with spikes in it on the threshing floor, used to separate the wheat from the chaff. The idea being expressed here is that tribulation helps get the chaff out of your life and eventually brings you to a new level in your character. Hard times in our lives, that we do not want to go through and did not sign up for, have a way of building our character.

One of the greatest preachers at the beginning of the 20th century was George W. Truett, pastor of the First Baptist Church of Dallas, Texas. God used him in an incredible way. One day there was a horrific accident where he shot and killed one of his best friends. People said that he was never quite the same after that.

Charles Weigle was a great preacher, singer and songwriter. One day his wife told him, "I don't want to be a pastor's wife anymore." She left him and it broke his heart. He went on to write the timeless song "No One Ever Cared For Me Like Jesus." He wrote it out of his heartbreak.

Tribulation is an opportunity to build character. Most of us like to tell God, "I don't need the tribulation, Lord. I'll just figure out the character part on my own." It doesn't work that way. God knows what we need, and He knows it a lot better than we do.

Many times when tribulation comes we get embarrassed. We hide from the church and from our friends. It's tempting to get a cabin out in the woods and go spend the rest of life there. You want to escape, but escape is not the answer. But God is showing us that, just as Jesus was nailed to a cross and we are all eternally better for it, our tribulations will make each of us better for having endured them.

Do we look at these events as blessings? From our tribulations come some of the greatest blessing of life.

One of the greatest men I have ever known was one of my college professors. One day I said to him, "I don't want to embarrass you, but you are one of the Godliest men I know. How did you get that way?"

He looked at me and said, "By going through trouble."

None of us really wants to hear that answer. But God has a way of working through our lives, and this is one of those ways.

That leads us to the fifth blessing in this passage, which is **patience** to grow. Read verses 5-8. *"And hope maketh not ashamed; because the love of God is shed abroad in our hearts by the Holy Ghost which is given unto us. For when we were yet without strength, in due time Christ died for the ungodly. For scarcely for a righteous man will one die: yet peradventure for a good man some would even dare to die. But God commendeth his love toward us, in that, while we were yet sinners, Christ died for us."*

The Holy Spirit lives in the heart of every child of God. Patience makes it possible for believers to grow in character and become mature in Christ.

The first three fruits of the Spirit are love, joy and peace. It is interesting to note that all three are named in this passage. We just read about love in verse 5, while joy is expressed through the word *"rejoice"* in verse 2 and peace is cited in verse 1.

God gives us patience to grow and it makes us more understanding of the people around us, so that we try to win them and not condemn them. It's easy for us to condemn people who are not like we are, but Jesus did not come to condemn people; He came to save people. Too often we like to have our little cliques at church like the Pharisees, but we lose sight of the fact that Jesus came for the unrighteous, not the righteous.

As we grow, we get a better understanding of who God really is and or our walk and relationship with Him. From that, we understand what it is like to win someone to Jesus Christ. We all need to be aware of this so that we don't let someone go to Hell when we can step in front of him and tell him about Jesus. If you are glad that you have a great God and a great Saviour, tell someone what He is doing in your life.

The sixth blessing is a **provision**, found in verses 9-10. "*Much more then, being now justified by his blood, we shall be saved from wrath through him. For if, when we were enemies, we were reconciled to God by the death of his Son, much more, being reconciled, we shall be saved by his life.*"

In the Old Testament there was an offering called the trespass offering. To make good on the loss suffered by the victim, the trespasser would have to add one-fifth to the restitution.

Before Adam sinned he lived in what is known as the age of innocence. If Adam had never sinned and sin had not entered the world, we would still be living in that age. We would not have had the sacrifice of Christ on the cross. But because of the cross we have in Christ and His blood a direct link to the Father, and we can triumph in any problems of life because of the provision God has given to us.

Wherever you go, He goes with you. Whatever you do, He knows about it. When you bring glory to Him, He is well-pleased.

Verse 11 shows us the **peacemaker** that Christ has become in bringing us to God the Father. "*And not only so, but we also joy in God through our Lord Jesus Christ, by whom we have now received the atonement.*"

There was an old poem written, actually a wicked poem, about an evil woman who demanded from a man who loved her the heart of a woman. As the man was taking it to her, he fell and heard a voice from the mother's heart saying, "Are you hurt, my child? Are you hurt?"

This literary work was describing the love of a mother. How much greater than that is the love of God in Heaven for each of us? When we look at ourselves, we realize how unworthy of that love we really are.

My wife will occasionally buy me a book of crossword puzzles to keep me from getting bored when I travel on airplanes as often as I do. Of course, in the back of each book you will find several pages with the answers to the puzzles. Sometimes I find myself turning back to the answer pages, and when I do that I don't want anyone sitting nearby to see me doing it.

One day I was doing this while the man next to me was sound asleep. At least I thought he was asleep. A few moments later I heard him say, "Aha! You're cheating."

Sometimes we feel nervous about God, knowing that He sees everything we do and hears everything we say. But God loves you and see you through Christ. As the hymn writer put it:

Man of sorrows, what a name;
For the son of God who came
Ruined sinners to proclaim:
Hallelujah, what a Savior!

Look at I Pet. 2:9. *"But ye are a chosen generation, a royal priesthood, an holy nation, a peculiar people; that ye should shew forth the praises of him who hath called you out of darkness into his marvellous light."*

If we believe that these blessings we have just read about are true, we should do everything we can to go out and be a blessing to other people. Our greatest joy comes not from what we get in life, but how we take what is given to us and use it to help others.

Chapter 11

SALVATION FOR A LIFETIME

"Wherefore, as by one man sin entered into the world, and death by sin; and so death passed upon all men, for that all have sinned: (For until the law sin was in the world: but sin is not imputed when there is no law. Nevertheless death reigned from Adam to Moses, even over them that had not sinned after the similitude of Adam's transgression, who is the figure of him that was to come. But not as the offence, so also is the free gift. For if through the offence of one many be dead, much more the grace of God, and the gift by grace, which is by one man, Jesus Christ, hath abounded unto many. And not as it was by one that sinned, so is the gift: for the judgment was by one to condemnation, but the free gift is of many offences unto justification. For if by one man's offence death reigned by one; much more they which receive abundance of grace and of the gift of righteousness shall reign in life by one, Jesus Christ.) Therefore as by the offence of one judgment came upon all men to condemnation; even so by the righteousness of one the free gift came upon all men unto justification of life. For as by one man's disobedience many were made sinners, so by the obedience of one shall many be made righteous. Moreover the law entered, that the offence might abound. But where sin abounded, grace did much more abound: That as sin hath reigned unto death, even so

115

might grace reign through righteousness unto eternal life by Jesus Christ our Lord." **(Rom. 5:12-21)**

Years ago, when my wife and I were newly married, I wanted to be the dutiful husband. Our little house on Ohio Avenue in a small Pennsylvania community had about four rooms, but there was a nice, big yard along with it. She liked yard work, so I got this brilliant idea that I would help her.

I got the feeling that she didn't have a great attitude about my presence in the yard helping her. One day as I was washing up at the sink after working, I looked out the kitchen window and noticed that she was redoing everything I did. I walked outside and asked, "What are you doing?"

"I'm redoing what you did."

"Why?"

"Because you don't know what you're doing."

To be honest, she was absolutely right. I didn't really want to do yard work anyway, so it was actually a good thing that she said that.

In this portion of Scripture we are looking at the same thing – God redoing what we did. Adam did something that was wrong, and a second Adam came and was placed on a cross to fix the wrong that had been done.

Some writers have called the fifth chapter of Romans the greatest chapter in the entire Bible regarding salvation. You may agree as we consider these wonderful verses.

There are several key words in this passage. One of those is the word *"one,"* which is found 11 times. Also important is the term *"much more,"* as well as the word *"reign."*

Think for a moment about Adam. God brought him into the world and gave him a beautiful garden, along with the responsibility of being the leader over that garden.

"You must not touch the Tree of the Knowledge of Good and Evil," God told him. "I have given you all of these beautiful things, but this one thing you must not do." God did not make Adam to be a robot, but a man with freedom to make moral choices.

You know the story. Eve came along, and she was the most beautiful woman Adam had ever seen. Men like to say that Eve was at fault in the fall, but Adam neglected his responsibility to protect Eve. Sin came into the world, and death came by that sin.

Because of this God sent the second Adam, who is none other than our Lord and Saviour Jesus Christ. There is a great contrast in this passage between the two Adams. The second Adam came to undo what the first Adam did.

The original Adam had dominion over the old creation. Christ came to have greater dominion over the new creation. His obedience brought righteousness and justification. Christ not only undid all of the damage done by Adam under the old covenant, but He did so much more in that He made a way for us to become children of God.

We have considered many questions during our study of Romans. One question that has not been asked is this: Was it fair for God to condemn the whole world because of one man's disobedience? Why blame us for what he did?

The fact of the matter is that it was not only fair, but it was wise and gracious because one's disobedience was brought to One's obedience to buy us back. If you and I had been in the Garden of Eden instead of Adam and Eve, it is very possible that we would have done far worse than they did. It is always easy to blame someone else for our sin.

In Romans 5 we learn that we are united, even racially, to Christ. We see that all of us die, that we went from a time of no law to a time of law, and that we continue to die. As I Cor. 15:22 says, *"For as in Adam all die, even so in Christ shall all be made alive."*

This passage in Romans deals with the very foundation and the basis for our salvation. In Adam all are sinners; in Christ all are saints. In Adam death reigns; in Christ there is deliverance. In Adam there is offense; in Christ the emphasis is on obedience.

With that in mind, notice in verses 12-14 the entrance of sin into the world. *"Wherefore, as by one man sin entered into the world, and death by sin; and so death passed upon all men, for that all have sinned. For until the law sin was in the world: but sin is not imputed when there is no law. Nevertheless death reigned from Adam to*

Moses, even over them that had not sinned after the similitude of Adam's transgression, who is the figure of him that was to come."

We all have the tendency to categorize sin, labeling some sins as terrible and others as not so bad. It's easy for us to talk about how horrible it is to kill someone, but in Romans we have seen that it is also horrible to gossip or show envy.

The book of Romans not only unveils the presence of sin in the world, but also the penalty for sin, which is death. This goes all the way back to Genesis, when God told Adam and Eve that if they ate from the forbidden tree they would die. Or course, the serpent came along shortly thereafter and assured them that they would not die.

Death is not annihilation; it is separation. In other words, when Adam sinned in the garden he did not die physically, but he died spiritually. His sin caused separation from God. When someone dies physically, the body goes back to the ground but the spirit goes on. For the unsaved person the soul goes on to spend eternity in Hell, totally separated from God. That is eternal death. The most tragic thing in the world is to be separated from God.

We have no problem pointing out everyone else's sin, but the bottom line is that we are all sinners. My sin might not seem as serious to me as it does to you, but your sin might seem very offensive to me. One of the greatest sins in the church today is the attitude that says, "I think I'm better than you are."

These passages also speak to us about the power of sin. Addiction is a word that we all use with regularity in today's society. If someone abuses alcohol to the point that he is drinking and it is affecting his body in a negative way, we call that alcohol addiction. People become addicted to everything from painkillers to pornography.

It is tempting for us to look at someone else's addiction and be critical, comparing ourselves to them and feeling good about how we are. But God wants us to look at Him and use Him as the standard for comparison. When we do that we see how great our own shortcomings are.

All of us have something that hangs us up. What is your hangup? The Bible calls it *"the sin which doth so easily beset us"* (Heb. 12:1). Sin affects all of us.

Now that we have seen the entrance of sin into the world, the next portion of this passage deals with the entrance of salvation, beginning with verse 15. *"But not as the offence, so also is the free gift. For if through the offence of one many be dead, much more the grace of God, and the gift by grace, which is by one man, Jesus Christ, hath abounded unto many."*

The word *"offence"* here is similar to a trespass, as if God had placed a literal "No Trespassing" sign in the Garden of Eden and Adam had gone past it. But this verse also talks about a free gift. It isn't often in life that something is truly free, without any obligation.

That is one of the things so difficult to understand about God. We are a performance-based people. Everything in our lives is based upon performance, and if you hold the people in your life to a performance-based standard you will often be disappointed. So often what we expect from people is what only God can do.

Salvation is free and it releases us from blame. Look at verse 16. *"And not as it was by one that sinned, so is the gift: for the judgment was by one to condemnation, but the free gift is of many offences unto justification."*

Adam's sin brought judgment. Christ's work on the cross brings justification. Salvation means that, in God's eyes, the blame and guilt that were once laid on you have been removed.

Verse 17 shows that salvation releases us from bondage. *"For if by one man's offence death reigned by one; much more they which receive abundance of grace and of the gift of righteousness shall reign in life by one, Jesus Christ."*

When Adam died, he did so without having lived under the law. The Israelites who lived under the law also died, as sin and its wages (death) reign in accordance with this verse. But while Adam represents a kinship lost, in Christ there is a kinship realigned.

This brings us to the thought that salvation is greater than our sin, as expressed in verses 18-19. *"Therefore as by the offence of one judgment came upon all men to condemnation; even so by the righteousness of one the free gift came upon all men unto justification of life. For as by one man's disobedience many were made sinners, so by the obedience of one shall many be made righteous."*

God's grace and salvation are greater than any sin we have ever committed.

Read Gen. 2:16-17. *"And the LORD God commanded the man, saying, Of every tree of the garden thou mayest freely eat: But of the tree of the knowledge of good and evil, thou shalt not eat of it: for in the day that thou eatest thereof thou shalt surely die."*

If you have children, you certainly have told them at various times, "Don't touch that." And what do they do? Usually they will go straight for the thing you don't want them to touch.

Once when I was a boy my mother was taking my temperature. When she put the thermometer in my mouth, she said, "Don't drop it." As it rested there, I started to wonder what would happen if I dropped it.

Guess what I did? I dropped it. It broke! When my mother came back in the room, she asked, "What happened?"

"It fell," I replied.

There is something in all of us that makes us want to behave as Adam did. In the garden Adam and Eve had everything they could possibly want, but they went after the one thing God told them not to touch, and the result was a world plunged into sin.

The closer you and I get to Christ, the better our relationships are with other people. If you are carrying heavy guilt, shame or a broken heart, the grace of God can help us overcome it if we strive to be closer to Him.

Verses 20-21 summarize the great theme of this entire passage, which is the entrance of God's grace into the world. *"Moreover the law entered, that the offence might abound. But where sin abounded, grace did much more abound: That as sin hath reigned unto death, even so might grace reign through righteousness unto eternal life by Jesus Christ our Lord."*

As sin continues to get worse, grace will always abound even more.

If you bring in front of your church a young child who was just saved and ask him what had just happened in his life, he might simply say, "I accepted Christ." Years later, if he has been living for God, the answer will likely be the same, perhaps with a bit of emotion, perhaps not.

But if you find someone who has had a rough childhood followed by a number of adult years in sin before coming to Christ, and ask that person to give a testimony, you are likely to see some tears. You almost feel the heartache yourself. Because of what that person has gone through, there is a unique understanding of the incredible grace of God.

If you and I were dangled for a few moments over a giant hole that led straight into Hell, where we could see the pain and suffering taking place there, and suddenly we had the chance to accept God's grace, we would shout from the heavens. We wouldn't be able to accept it quickly enough.

As Christians, that is how we are supposed to live out our lives – in grace. But too often we put people on certain levels and fail to give them the grace that God has given us.

Adam was a type of Christ, as stated in verse 14 (*"the figure of him that was to come"*). But how exactly is he a type of Christ?

Adam was made in the earth. Jesus came from Heaven to the earth. Adam was told to take care of the garden as he was surrounded by its beauty. Jesus came from beauty and was tempted in the wilderness.

Adam died spiritually in the garden. Jesus died physically and spiritually on the cross. Adam was a thief in that he took from God. Jesus turned to a thief on the cross next to His and promised to meet him that same day in paradise.

The Bible says in Gen. 5:1, *"This is the book of the generations of Adam."* But the book of Matthew begins with the words, *"The book of the generation of Jesus Christ."*

Now go to the last chapter of the last book in the Bible, Revelation 22. This is a picture of Heaven. If you think Heaven is here on earth, you are wrong. Verse 3 begins, *"And there shall be no more curse."*

That is the whole problem today. We are all living under a curse – the curse of sin. The devil does not want you to be with Christ. He wants your soul, but if he can't have that he wants your testimony.

The next part of that verse states, *"But the throne of God and of the Lamb shall be in it; and his servants shall serve him."* One thing we can have in this life is the pleasure of Christ living in us.

Adam brought sin and destitution into our lives, but Jesus brings something far greater.

Sin tells you something is OK when Jesus is telling you the opposite. Sometimes we hear people say, "The Lord led me to do such-and-such," when we know that is not the case because their actions go against the Bible.

Sin says it is OK to be an addict, or to lie, or to gossip and complain. But God says, "No, there is a better way."

Sin says, "Life is short, so do what you want. Besides, everyone is doing it."

God says, "No, there is a better way."

Sin says, "As long as no one else finds out, everything's fine."

God says, "No, there is a better way."

The sixth chapter of Romans, as we will see in the next portion of this book, shows how God takes this idea all the way. It begins with verses 1-2: "*What shall we say then? Shall we continue in sin, that grace may abound? God forbid. How shall we, that are dead to sin, live any longer therein?*"

Near the end of that chapter, verses 20-22 say, "*For when ye were the servants of sin, ye were free from righteousness. What fruit had ye then in those things whereof ye are now ashamed? for the end of those things is death. But now being made free from sin, and become servants to God, ye have your fruit unto holiness, and the end everlasting life.*"

Here is the key. It is what I like to call the redemptive quality of God. In the days of the Roman Empire it was very common to own slaves. These slaves would be brought into the town square and put on a block for prospective owners to inspect. The "shoppers" would carefully consider the physical qualities, whether male or female, to see what kind of work they could do. A brief conversation might reveal the slave's level of intelligence. The idea was usually for the purchaser to take the slave home for work inside or outside the house.

Sometimes, however, a person would walk up, pay the asking price, then tell the slave, "You are free to go and do what you want." Roman law allowed that practice, but historians say that in many of those cases the slave would respond, "If you are willing to purchase my freedom, I want to stay and work for you. I believe in you."

The English word to describe that process is redemption.

We are on the block in sin's slave market. But a Redeemer came along one day and said, "I will buy you back and give you freedom." That is what the second Adam did for the sins of the first Adam and every person who has lived since then.

God says, "I release you from those sins which have been held to your account." It is redemption that is bought by the precious blood of Jesus Christ.

You may have heard someone jokingly say, "I believe in the Golden Rule: He who has the gold rules." I want to tell you that the One who has the gold is Jesus Christ, and He rules. He has bought us all back, and it is by His grace that we are free today.

Christianity is not a performance. It is not what you do. There are no legalistic requirements to it. It is not driven by deeds or by deals with God. Its anointing in your life can be removed by disobedience to God and His Word. But His salvation is yours to keep. Christianity is all about the grace of an almighty God who has bought us back from the slave market of sin.

When our church observes the Lord's Table, I will often take the wafer and break it to symbolize how Christ took everything upon Himself. That is so true. Whatever you are carrying with you today or have ever gone through, He took that upon Himself.

John Newton, the great preacher and songwriter, penned these words:

I saw one hanging on a tree in agony and blood;
He fixed His languid eyes on me as near His cross I stood.
Never till my latest breath can I forget that look;
He seemed to charge me with His death, though not a word
    He spoke.
My conscience felt and owned the guilt, and plunged me in
    despair;
I saw my sins His blood had spilt and helped to nail Him
    there.
A second look He gave which said, "I freely all forgive:

This blood has for thy ransom paid – I died that you might
live."

Clench your fists together tightly as if in anger. Now release
them. That's forgiveness. That is what God has done for you.

You may need to do that for God because you are mad at Him.
Perhaps there is someone you know whom you need to forgive. That
is the essence of the grace of God and the basis for our salvation.

My father was a wonderful man. He was a full-blooded Italian
and, although he was kind and gracious, that temper could show
through at times.

One day he came home with a brand-new car, the first new car
he had ever bought. I was heading out to pitch in a baseball game
and I asked if I could take the car. "Sure," he said.

I remember the exact spot, on Howard Avenue going toward
Robinson Street in Binghamton, New York. The car in front of me
crossed, and I was talking to someone as I moved forward, thinking
the coast was clear. I looked up and saw another car coming right at
us. I didn't know what to do, and neither did the other driver.

He smashed into the front of that brand-new car, then it spun
around and was hit in the back as well. As I got out and inspected
the damage, I thought that this would be a good time for the Rapture,
because I didn't want to be around for what would happen later when
my father saw his car.

"Are you OK?" asked a bystander who saw blood on my face.

"No, I'm not," I replied. "I have to go home and face Dad."

As the police arrived, I walked over to my friend Gary's house
and called my father. "Dad," I said, "I've had a little accident."

"Are you OK?"

"I am if you are," I thought to myself.

He came over and saw this car, the first new one he ever owned.
Then he said to me, "I can always replace a car [although it was not
easy back then]. But I can never replace a son."

Of course, he lectured me later about looking both ways and the
rules of the road, but it was not nearly as bad as I thought it would
be. He showed a lot of grace. But that is not even a speck compared
to the grace God has shown to us.

John Newton was, by his own testimony, one of the most wicked men of his generation. But he was saved and became a firebrand for God. His most famous song is the classic "Amazing Grace." Think about those words you've sung for years and what they really mean.

If we are going to accept this grace that God gives to us so freely, we need to give it to others as well. You need to live out this grace in your life.

Redemption, forgiveness and grace go together, and this is expressed so well in Eph. 4:30-32. "*And grieve not the holy Spirit of God, whereby ye are sealed unto the day of redemption. Let all bitterness, and wrath, and anger, and clamour, and evil speaking, be put away from you, with all malice: And be ye kind one to another, tenderhearted, forgiving one another, even as God for Christ's sake hath forgiven you.*"

Doug Seamands wrote a great book called "Healing for Damaged Emotions." He talked about how much he hated his father as he went through his life. When he was an adult and a successful businessman, he could not get along with anyone who looked or sounded like his father. "You'd be surprised how many people look and sound like my father," he wrote.

One day he decided to say, "I forgive." It was not because of anything in him, but by the grace of God. When he did that, his life took on a whole new meaning.

Years ago I asked an elderly man named David Snider, who was a member of my church, what was the greatest lesson he had learned in life. "Every drop of legalism is out of my body," he said. I didn't know what he meant by that, but the older I get the more thankful I am for God's wonderful grace.

The more grace you get, the more you give. And God has shown us that it is all available to us.

Chapter 12

IT'S TIME TO DIE

"What shall we say then? Shall we continue in sin, that grace may abound? God forbid. How shall we, that are dead to sin, live any longer therein? Know ye not, that so many of us as were baptized into Jesus Christ were baptized into his death? Therefore we are buried with him by baptism into death: that like as Christ was raised up from the dead by the glory of the Father, even so we also should walk in newness of life. For if we have been planted together in the likeness of his death, we shall be also in the likeness of his resurrection: Knowing this, that our old man is crucified with him, that the body of sin might be destroyed, that henceforth we should not serve sin. For he that is dead is freed from sin. Now if we be dead with Christ, we believe that we shall also live with him: Knowing that Christ being raised from the dead dieth no more; death hath no more dominion over him. For in that he died, he died unto sin once: but in that he liveth, he liveth unto God. Likewise reckon ye also yourselves to be dead indeed unto sin, but alive unto God through Jesus Christ our Lord. Let not sin therefore reign in your mortal body, that ye should obey it in the lusts thereof. Neither yield ye your members as instruments of unrighteousness unto sin: but yield yourselves unto God, as those that are alive from

the dead, and your members as instruments of righteousness unto God. For sin shall not have dominion over you: for ye are not under the law, but under grace." **(Rom. 6:1-14)**

Right now you are probably thinking, "Couldn't he come up with a better chapter title than that?" But that is precisely what this passage in Romans is talking about. I am not speaking about a physical death, but the book of Romans tells us that it is time to die.

Death is a very interesting subject. If you look it up in the dictionary, you might come across something like this:

"A permanent cessation of all functions."

"The loss of life."

"Extinction."

You have often heard of someone being on his death bed. Obviously, that person is probably not going to live much longer.

But in the Bible, the word "death" does not denote extinction or even loss of life in some cases. Rather, it is about a separation. When you die physically, your soul is separated from your body. Spiritual death is a separation from God.

If you are living today without Christ, you are in spiritual death. If you die without Him, you will experience eternal death – being separated from God forever.

Suppose we were in a room with a dead person lying on the floor. I walk over to the dead man, lean down and ask, "How are you doing today?" You would probably think I was crazy, and you might say, "Why are you talking to him? He can't respond."

That lack of response is due to the soul – who the person really is – being separated from the body in death.

There are some key phrases in this passage from Romans that we should notice. The phrase *"know ye not"* in the form of a question appears in verses 3 and 16 of chapter 6 as well as Rom. 7:1. It is as if the Apostle Paul is stressing the importance of what he wants us to see by saying, "Don't you know…?" Also mentioned three times in these two chapters is the phrase *"through Jesus Christ our Lord."*

We have already discussed at length the idea of justification, which is our standing before God in righteousness as if we had never sinned. But there are objections to that, one of which is expressed in verse 1 of chapter 6: *"What shall we say then? Shall we continue in sin, that grace may abound?"*

The answer to that question is immediately provided in verse 2. *"God forbid. How shall we, that are dead to sin, live any longer therein?"*

I heard a story about a young boy who was being watched by his mother's friend one afternoon. The lady brought the boy a piece of chocolate cake and said, "I made this just for you."

"Thank you, ma'am," the boy replied.

The lady was so impressed. As he ate his snack and drank his milk, she commented, "It is so nice to see a young boy being so polite as to say 'thank you' and 'ma'am.'"

"Do you want to hear me say it again?" the boy asked.

"Why, yes, I would."

"Then give me another piece of cake."

That is the way we behave sometimes regarding God's grace. We thank Him for His grace but then think that we can just go on and live in our sin.

There were other objections raised over God's law and our ability to live as we please. All of these are covered in detail in the middle portion of Romans, with emphasis on victory (chapter 6), liberty (chapter 7) and security (chapter 8). In these chapters we find instruction on how to have victory over our sin life.

There are three key words for us here: *"know,"* which we have already seen; *"reckon,"* found in verse 11; and *"yield,"* mentioned twice in verse 13.

I want to give you four thoughts about this subject of death. First, death with Christ is a **revolutionary** idea.

Christian living depends on Christian learning. We identify with Adam in his sin, but we identify with Christ in His death. When Jesus was dying on the cross, He had you in mind above all else. He was identifying with us in our sin.

The first few chapters of Romans dealt with our sins (plural), but we see a shift in focus to our sin (singular) beginning with Rom. 5:12. "Wherefore, as by one man sin entered into the world, and death by sin; and so death passed upon all men, for that all have sinned."

Jesus died for our sins, but He also died unto sin. He paid sin's penalty and broke sin's power, which means we can be justified and live sanctified lives.

If you are a parent, you know all too well the feelings that can get hold of you concerning your children. The phone call comes from the principal, who says, "I need to talk to you about your child." You know that he is not calling just to tell you how wonderful your child is. There are so many ways your children tug at your emotions.

When Jesus went to the cross, through all of the agony and pain He suffered, He had you in mind the entire time. There is not one thing you and I will go through in life that He isn't already aware of and experiencing right along with you. You may think that no one understands your burden, but He does.

Look at verses 3-4. *"Know ye not, that so many of us as were baptized into Jesus Christ were baptized into his death? Therefore we are buried with him by baptism into death: that like as Christ was raised up from the dead by the glory of the Father, even so we also should walk in newness of life."*

This baptism into death is a spiritual baptism where, upon our salvation, we are placed into the body of Christ. Bible teacher John Phillips put it this way: "Baptism is the introduction or placement or a person or thing into a new environment."

Now we move on to verse 5. *"For if we have been planted together in the likeness of his death, we shall be also in the likeness of his resurrection."*

The word *"planted"* means to be united or joined together. It carries the idea of being grafted into the body of Christ. We are united to God and we share His very life.

Our church spent a Saturday during Thanksgiving week last year preparing and furnishing a meal for many of the homeless in our area. As you visit with a homeless person, often you will find a person who grew up in a family with parents who never imagined their child would be homeless. You will find someone who had a productive life a few years earlier, until something happened. It could have been a poor decision or just tough circumstances. But it is wonderful to see the family of God rising up to help them, as hundreds of churches do all across the country, because who knows where any of us would be except for the grace of God.

God is showing us in this passage that His desire for us to be in His family extends to everyone, regardless of our social or economic status. He had every one of us in mind.

My wife and I have four grown children, and sometimes when I am talking about them I get their names mixed up. I might have to go through the list and get them in order in my head while I'm talking. God makes no such mistakes.

When God made you, He knew all about you. He knows your beginning and your end. When Jesus died, if you had been the only person who ever lived, He would have died just for you.

That leads us to the second thought, found in verses 6-7, that death through Christ gives us a **reason** for living. *"Knowing this, that our old man is crucified with him, that the body of sin might be destroyed, that henceforth we should not serve sin. For he that is dead is freed from sin."*

These verses talk about God breaking the stronghold that sin had over our lives. The phrase *"old man"* refers to our old sin nature that brought Christ to the cross. When we accept Christ that old nature stays with us, and we have to put it to death on the cross with Him.

Verses 8-11 give us the third thought, which is the **results** of death in Christ. *"Now if we be dead with Christ, we believe that we shall also live with him: Knowing that Christ being raised from the dead dieth no more; death hath no more dominion over him. For in that he died, he died unto sin once: but in that he liveth, he liveth unto God. Likewise reckon ye also yourselves to be dead indeed unto sin, but alive unto God through Jesus Christ our Lord."*

When Jesus died on the cross, you and I died with Him. But He did not stay dead for long; as the Bible recounts, on the first day of the week He rose again. His resurrection is a fact of history as well as a fact of theology. As He lives again, so do we.

The word *"reckon"* in verse 11 is an accounting term, as if God is saying, "I put this on your account." When Jesus Christ died, He died for you and me. When He rose again, He rose for you and me. In doing this, He put on our account His righteousness.

The final thought I want to emphasize in this passage is the **reward** that death in Christ brings. Look at verses 12-14.

"Let not sin therefore reign in your mortal body, that ye should obey it in the lusts thereof. Neither yield ye your members as instruments of unrighteousness unto sin: but yield yourselves unto God, as those that are alive from the dead, and your members as instruments of righteousness unto God. For sin shall not have dominion over you: for ye are not under the law, but under grace."

Verse 12 plainly says we are not to continue in our sinful lives. It is not acceptable to God to have the attitude that says, "Well, this is just the way I am." When Jesus took your sins on the cross, He gave you the position for change and the power to have your life changed.

Our church has three Christian schools. We want to teach children academically, but we also want everyone to know that they are first and foremost Christian institutions, where Jesus Christ is the top priority. If He is Lord of all, that we should reflect that truth in everything we say and do.

Perhaps the most important words in this entire passage are those that make up the phrase *"the glory of the Father"* in verse 4. Our main purpose in life should be to bring glory to God.

Go back to Rom. 1:9. *"For God is my witness, whom I serve with my spirit in the gospel of his Son, that without ceasing I make mention of you always in my prayers."* There is no way that we can get to God the Father except through Jesus Christ. That is the only access.

Everyone in life needs a father. My physical father, who was my best friend, died a number of years ago. But I still have Heavenly Father. Through His death, burial and resurrection, Christ connects us to the Father.

Frederick Buechner, a noted theologian, tells a tragic story of a rebellious 13-year-old boy who took a gun and killed his father. When asked why he did it, he said, "Because I couldn't stand my father."

Later, a guard in the detention center reported that he heard this same boy sobbing in a corner, crying out, "I want my father. I want my father."

You may not have had a good relationship with your earthly father, but there is a Father in Heaven who wants your love and who loves you more than you can imagine.

Philip Yancey, in his great book "Disappointment with God," wrote about a visit he had with his mother after not seeing her for several years. As many mothers might do, she pulled out a scrapbook.

Yancey saw an old crumpled picture of himself as a baby, about 10 months of age. Noting the poor condition of the portrait, he suggested that his mother get rid of it.

"I would never get rid of this," his mother replied, and she told him the following story:

His father had suffered from polio, which at that time was as feared as cancer or AIDS might be today. He died in about three months. When he lay in a large metal cylinder during his treatment, he put up pictures of his wife and children to look at.

"Your father had only one thing in mind," Yancey's mother told him. "He wanted to think of you and pray for you."

There is a Father in Heaven today who feels the same way about you. He wants your love in return.

The greatest thing you can do for a child is to love God. There is nothing better than letting your children know that you have a loving relationship with your Heavenly Father, and that you care about them because of the way He cares for you.

The late R.G. Lee was a great preacher for many years, best known as pastor of Bellevue Baptist Church in Memphis, Tennessee. One day he took his first trip to the Holy Land and visited the site known as the Garden Tomb.

When the guide instructed the group to follow him, the elderly Lee ran ahead of everyone else. He reached a small landing from which one can look out on a hill known as Golgotha, which is the place where Jesus was crucified. Interestingly, that site now includes a Muslim cemetery as well as a Muslim-operated bus station.

As Lee gazed at that hill, the guide walked up beside him and said, "Dr. Lee, you act as though you have seen this place before. I thought you said you have never been to Israel."

With tears in his eyes, that prince of preachers replied, "I was here 2,000 years ago when my Jesus died there."

He turned around quickly and walked to the empty tomb, saying, "I was here also. This is where my Jesus rose again."

There are scores of people in every church in this country who sit in the pew on Sunday morning with hurting hearts and heavy burdens, and many more who really are trying to get a handle on just what God is all about. For all of those people, there is a connection through Christ to a Heavenly Father who can be reached at any time. We can talk to Him about any problem, large or small. He loves you just as you are.

Verses 12-14 reminds us that we do not have to be slaves to sin, but we have choices about how we can live for God. We are living under grace, and that grace comes to us from a loving, omnipotent Heavenly Father.

God is always thinking about you, and the way to love Him is by loving His Son. When the Father sees you through the Son, He sees righteousness.

When Jesus died and rose again, you were on His mind. If you were the only person who ever lived, He would have died and risen just for you.

Chapter 13

GOODBYE SIN, HELLO LIBERTY!

"What then? shall we sin, because we are not under the law, but under grace? God forbid. Know ye not, that to whom ye yield yourselves servants to obey, his servants ye are to whom ye obey; whether of sin unto death, or of obedience unto righteousness? But God be thanked, that ye were the servants of sin, but ye have obeyed from the heart that form of doctrine which was delivered you. Being then made free from sin, ye became the servants of righteousness. I speak after the manner of men because of the infirmity of your flesh: for as ye have yielded your members servants to uncleanness and to iniquity unto iniquity; even so now yield your members servants to righteousness unto holiness. For when ye were the servants of sin, ye were free from righteousness. What fruit had ye then in those things whereof ye are now ashamed? for the end of those things is death. But now being made free from sin, and become servants to God, ye have your fruit unto holiness, and the end everlasting life. For the wages of sin is death; but the gift of God is eternal life through Jesus Christ our Lord." (**Rom. 6:15-23**)

Have you ever had a guest stay in your home and wished he or she would leave? When that person finally did walk out the door, you said (at least to yourself) a cheerful "Goodbye." That is the attitude toward sin as expressed in this passage.

There is a belief in the world today that if you are saved by the grace of God you can go on and do whatever you want. That is not a Biblical teaching. We are saved and kept by God's grace, but Romans 6 gives us some excellent insight concerning the liberty that the Lord has given us. Where we once were slaves to sin, we now are slaves to God.

Ray Steadman was pastor of the Peninsula Bible Church in Palo Alto, California, for many years and he was also a gifted writer. He once told a story about walking down a street in his city and encountering a man who walked toward him. This man had a large sign hung over his shoulder, and on one side it read, "I am a slave for Christ."

As expected, that sign was very noticeable on this busy street. As people turned to look at this man, they could see another message on the back of the sign: "Whose slave are you?"

While that may sound like an odd thing to write on a sign, it is precisely what this chapter of Romans is talking about. There is no such thing as absolute freedom for anyone to do whatever they want to do just because God's grace has come into their lives. This chapter teaches us about the victory we have through Christ over sin and death, and when we realize this we begin to understand that God has given us something very important.

Notice in verses 15-16 that we have a **new liberty**. *"What then? shall we sin, because we are not under the law, but under grace? God forbid. Know ye not, that to whom ye yield yourselves servants to obey, his servants ye are to whom ye obey; whether of sin unto death, or of obedience unto righteousness?"*

The question in verse 15 is similar to the question posed at the beginning of Romans 6. The obvious answer in both cases is no, as sin is slavery and no one should desire to return to that type of slavery which leads to death, as verses 16, 21 and 23 point out.

We should not trust our own judgment about such things, but instead we need to trust the Word of God, which says that if we allow sin to reign in our bodies it will lead us to slavery. Christians are saved from all of their sins through Jesus' death on the cross, and those sins are taken away forever.

Look at what Jesus taught the Jews who followed Him, as portrayed in John 8:31-36. *"Then said Jesus to those Jews which believed on him, If ye continue in my word, then are ye my disciples indeed; And ye shall know the truth, and the truth shall make you free. They answered him, We be Abraham's seed, and were never in bondage to any man: how sayest thou, Ye shall be made free? Jesus answered them, Verily, verily, I say unto you, Whosoever committeth sin is the servant of sin. And the servant abideth not in the house for ever: but the Son abideth ever. If the Son therefore shall make you free, ye shall be free indeed."*

The only freedom that we have is in living for Christ. True Christianity can never lead us to a license to do whatever we want. That practice is known as antinomianism, and Jesus said over and over again that such behavior is the opposite of real freedom.

One thing we must realize as Christians is that we are living for an audience of one. Football aficionados are familiar with the term "twelfth man" which refers to a team's fans in the stands cheering their favorite players on to victory. That enthusiasm and support motivates the players on the field to play better.

When you become a child of God, the audience that matters to you as you live out your Christian life consists solely of Him. There is Someone who watches over you, cares for you and knows all about you, and that is your audience – the God of Heaven. We are instructed three times in verse 16 that He is one we are supposed to obey.

I read recently about a soldier in 19th-century England named Gen. Charles Gordon, who truly believed in the principle of the audience of one. He was sent out to battle one fateful day and he died. One of his men who loved him so much wrote these words about Gordon: "What struck me most was the way his oneness with God ruled over all of his actions and his mode of seeing things. I never saw a man who lived with so much understanding of the invisible One who was watching over him."

For those of us who know Christ, God not only watches over us but also lives in us. This new liberty proves the historical point that the shift from Christ to Christianity is in itself a mark of corruption. We often talk about being Christians, but if that is addressed as only a theological concept then it is merely religion. Christianity is not religion; it is a relationship with Jesus Christ. It is a walk with God that is like nothing else in the entire world.

Ralph Waldo Emerson once put it this way: "Every stoic was and is a stoic, but in Christendom where, then, is the Christian?"

Think about it. One in three people in the United States claim to be Christian. If that were so and everyone lived that way, there would be a revival sweeping across our country. There is a struggle taking place in your life and mine. God lives in me, and He rules and reigns, but I still have a problem with sin.

Go back and take a look at Rom. 6:13. *"Neither yield ye your members as instruments of unrighteousness unto sin: but yield yourselves unto God, as those that are alive from the dead, and your members as instruments of righteousness unto God."*

The word *"yield"* is also used in verses 16 and 19. We all know what it means to yield, especially when driving, although we may seldom do it. When you see a yield sign, you slow down and give up your position to the other motorist who has the right of way. The Greek word in these verses means literally to place oneself at another's disposal or to offer oneself as a sacrifice.

What God is saying here is this: You have a choice as a believer. There is the sin principle, and the principle of the One living within you. Where will you yield?

We often struggle with that choice, and Paul even writes in Romans about his own struggle in that regard. He writes in Rom. 12:1, *"I beseech you therefore brethren, by the mercies of God, that ye present your bodies a living sacrifice, holy, acceptable unto God, which is your reasonable service."* That word *"present"* has the same origin as the word *"yield"* in the previous passage.

You can yield to righteousness, or you can yield to sin. It's one or the other. That is the decision that every child of God faces.

In verses 17-18 we see an **attitude of liberty**. *"But God be thanked, that ye were the servants of sin, but ye have obeyed from the heart that form of doctrine which was delivered you. Being then made free from sin, ye became the servants of righteousness."*

The word *"form"* in verse 17 is an interesting word. It suggests a mold into which melted metal is poured so it can take its destined shape. The Gospel shapes our character and helps us to be free from sin. Gal. 2:20 says, *"I am crucified with Christ: nevertheless I live; yet not I, but Christ liveth in me: and the life which I now live in the flesh I live by the faith of the Son of God, who loved me, and gave himself for me."*

The first four chapters of Romans talk about our specific sins. Chapter 5 takes a different direction and addresses the sin in our lives in general, while chapter 6 covers the principle of sin. There are two key words we need to understand so that we can grasp this idea of saying goodbye to sin and living in freedom. The first word is "blood" and the second word is "cross."

One of the most familiar verses in the Bible is Rom. 3:23, which says, "For all have sinned, and come short of the glory of God." You may also know Rom. 5:8-9, which says, *"But God commendeth his love toward us, in that, while we were yet sinners, Christ died for us. Much more then, being now justified by his blood, we shall be saved from wrath through him."*

The blood was necessary for God. He looks at our standing based upon the blood.

In the Old Testament there was the day of atonement, when the blood was to be taken for the sin offering and brought into the holy place to be sprinkled seven times. The high priest was a type of Christ.

Remember the Lord's words regarding the Passover: *"When I see the blood, I will pass over you"* (Ex. 12:13). God's holiness demanded a penalty to be paid, and that is by the blood. When He sees us in our sins, He cannot allow us into His presence. But when He looks at us and sees the blood of Jesus Christ, His only Son, not one sin is ever held to our account again.

Some people look at that principle and say, "That's great. I can do whatever I want." But there is another word to be considered here. We are to be crucified with Christ on the cross.

Imaging that I am hanging on a cross and you walk up and say, "Come and go with me." Obviously I cannot go with you, because I am on the cross. If you instruct me to reach out and gather certain worldly possessions for myself, I can't do that because my hands are fastened to the cross.

When Jesus went to His cross so many years ago, He actually had your name and my name in mind. Your parents, either at birth or adoption, chose your name for you. You have a definite date of birth. In God's salvation economy, you were saved when you came to Christ on this earth at some point in your life, but He had you on His mind while on the cross some 2,000 years ago.

You start the day off thinking, "Boy, things are going good. I read my Bible and prayed today, and I'm feeling really great about my walk with God." Then, sometime in the afternoon or early evening, you do or say something to make you think you've blown it. So you promise yourself that you'll do better the next day, but the same thing happens. After a few days you are thinking, "What in the world is wrong with me?"

At the beginning of the Christian life, often we are more consumed by doing than by being. We become distressed because of what we have done (or not done) rather than who we are. We think that if we could only make things right and change actions, we would be OK. But it is more than just a case of trouble on the outside; it is a more serious matter on the inside.

We try to please God, but there is something inside of us that simply does not want to please Him. We want to be loving or humble or gracious, but we don't really feel that way. The more we try to rectify the trouble on the outside, the more we see the more deep-seated issues on the inside.

We have to realize that rather than saying, "Lord, I have done wrong," it would be correct to state, "Lord, I am wrong." We don't just sin; we are sinners. As Rom. 5:19 says, *"For as by one man's disobedience many were made sinners, so by the obedience of one shall many be made righteous."* We are all sinners, and we must live a crucified life.

In the Old Testament the Lord dwelled with His people in a variety of ways. He was in the tabernacle as a cloud, in what was known as the Shekinah glory. People followed the cloud and knew which way God wanted them to go.

In Solomon's day He was in the temple, a structure that today is underneath the rubble from past generations in Jerusalem. Needless to say, that is not the place where God dwells today.

Many people refer to their respective church buildings as "God's house." But when you leave your place of worship after a service on Sunday or any other day, it is only a building. If you are a child of God, your body is God's house. He dwells in you in the form of the Holy Spirit. When you accepted Christ as your Saviour, God came to live inside you.

Your hands do not belong to you. Neither do your feet, or your eyes, or your mind. All of that belongs to Him. When we live the crucified life, we are yielding or submitting ourselves to Him so that He can rule and reign in our lives as He should. That is the primary struggle of the Christian life.

Notice in verses 19-20 the **new longevity.** *"I speak after the manner of men because of the infirmity of your flesh: for as ye have yielded your members servants to uncleanness and to iniquity unto iniquity; even so now yield your members servants to righteousness unto holiness. For when ye were the servants of sin, ye were free from righteousness."*

These verses are talking about obedience. Paul is saying through his writing that he wants to be as good a saint as he was a sinner. The word that perhaps best expresses this thought is "sanctify," which means to set apart.

There are three tenses to consider regarding sanctification. When you were saved God set you apart. As you grow in your Christian life, He continues to set you apart – a process we call progressive sanctification. One day when you arrive in Heaven, you will be finally and permanently sanctified in His presence. Your sanctification gives you a very special position.

There are those who talk about bestowing sainthood upon certain people after they have been dead for many years. But Rom. 1:6-7 says, *"Among whom are ye also the called of Jesus Christ: To all that be in Rome, beloved of God, called to be saints: Grace to you and peace from God our Father, and the Lord Jesus Christ."* As a child of God you are already a saint.

The Vines Dictionary puts it this way: "The Lord enables you more and more to spend your lives in the interest of others in order that He may establish you in Christian character even now."

Verses 21-23 are very familiar to us. *"What fruit had ye then in those things whereof ye are now ashamed? for the end of those things is death. But now being made free from sin, and become servants to God, ye have your fruit unto holiness, and the end everlasting life. For the wages of sin is death; but the gift of God is eternal life through Jesus Christ our Lord."*

These verses tell us that we are emancipated from sin, we have security through Christ and will live forevermore. It is important for Christians to truly capture the message of Romans 6 in their hearts.

Look at Rom. 9:21. *"Hath not the potter power over the clay, of the same lump to make one vessel unto honour, and another unto dishonour?"* That verse was written specifically to the people of the nation of Israel, but it applies to us today as well.

If you were to take that verse along with the idea of what it means to yield, you would understand exactly what it means to live what I call the basic Christian life. You would be saying goodbye to sin and hello to freedom forever – still having to face the struggle with sin, but in submission to God.

When shopping in the old city of Jerusalem, you learn to negotiate with the merchants for good bargains. If you are told right up front that an item costs $20 and you hand over that amount of money, you've overspent – you can probably get the item for half that amount.

The first time I ever bought something there, I was so proud as I showed my wife the beautiful ring I had just paid $10 for. She looked at me and said, "Where is the stone?" I looked down and discovered that the stone had already fallen out. Once I bought it, I couldn't return it.

Many years ago, on my second trip to the Holy Land, one of the tour guides took me aside and told me a story I have never heard anywhere else.

In that part of town there was an expert known as the potter who would go down into the valley of Hinnom, or Gehenna. It was a garbage dump, with an overwhelming stench from where people had literally been burned to death. But there was a clay in that valley that was very precious.

The potter would find the right amount of clay to fit whatever idea he had, put it in his pack and bring it back home. A small place behind the potter's house contained a wheel and enough room for him to work. That was where he would mold and fashion that clay.

Sometimes he would grow tired of that clay, so he would put it on a shelf and leave it there for a day or a month. But he always came back to it and worked on it some more. Finally the day came when that lump of clay had become a beautiful vessel, and when he took the finished product to the streets of Jerusalem to sell it, he got whatever asking price he wanted for it. People knew the value of what the potter made.

The idea behind this story, the guide told me, was that God would fulfill what he had in mind for Israel just as He would for each of us in our lives. The finished vessel is presented to the Father and He says, *"Well done, thou good and faithful servant"* (Matt. 25:21).

The moment you came to Christ, God began to do a work in your life. There are times when you feel great about what He is doing, and there are other times when you don't like it as much.

Sometimes you think you've been placed on the shelf like that clay and you wonder, "God, where did You go? Why are You hiding?" Then He takes you down and works on you so fast it makes your head spin. But whether you realize it or not, God is at work in your life at every moment.

In that story about the potter, the guide mentioned that the potter always looked for clay that was "yielding." That meant it had to be moldable for whatever the potter had in mind. That is the same idea God has for us in Romans 6, where we are told to be yielded to Him. We will have problems and struggles in our daily lives, and we will often wonder what God is doing, but He is constantly working on us like clay to make us what He wants us to be.

Have you ever prayed about something, so certain in your own mind how it should come to pass, only to have God do something so much better that you can't believe you didn't pray that way to begin with? You see God do a work in your life and think how easy it seemed, then at other times you wonder why He seemed to make it so hard. It's all part of the process of presenting the vessel, just like the potter always did, only this time the potter is God.

Sometimes a person enters your life and you soon find that you would prefer that person not be there. But that might be someone God has sent to play a part in molding your life. On the other hand, people often leave our lives and we wish they would stay. That is also a part of the molding process, as God moves you into a new phase of your life.

The bottom line is this: God does not make junk. You are one of His saints. The issue is whether you will yield to Him and live the crucified life.

Chapter 14

GOODBYE LEGALISM, HELLO RESPONSIBILITY!

"Know ye not, brethren, (for I speak to them that know the law,) how that the law hath dominion over a man as long as he liveth? For the woman which hath an husband is bound by the law to her husband so long as he liveth; but if the husband be dead, she is loosed from the law of her husband. So then if, while her husband liveth, she be married to another man, she shall be called an adulteress: but if her husband be dead, she is free from that law; so that she is no adulteress, though she be married to another man. Wherefore, my brethren, ye also are become dead to the law by the body of Christ; that ye should be married to another, even to him who is raised from the dead, that we should bring forth fruit unto God. For when we were in the flesh, the motions of sins, which were by the law, did work in our members to bring forth fruit unto death. But now we are delivered from the law, that being dead wherein we were held; that we should serve in newness of spirit, and not in the oldness of the letter. What shall we say then? Is the law sin? God forbid. Nay, I had not known sin, but by the law: for I had not known lust, except the law had said, Thou shalt not covet. But sin, taking occasion by the commandment, wrought in me all manner of concupiscence. For without the law sin was dead. For I

was alive without the law once: but when the commandment came, sin revived, and I died. And the commandment, which was ordained to life, I found to be unto death. For sin, taking occasion by the commandment, deceived me, and by it slew me. Wherefore the law is holy, and the commandment holy, and just, and good." (**Rom. 7:1-12**)

The law does not reward us for keeping its commands. It only punishes us for breaking them.

Assume that a police officer stops me in my car on a typical Sunday morning and asks for my driver's license and proof of insurance. After examining those documents, he says, "Follow me." I drive to the police station wondering what I've done wrong. But once inside the station, I see other drivers with plaques of commendation for their excellent driving, and I am told that I will be getting one as well.

Has that ever happened to you? I didn't think so. That doesn't happen because the laws of the road were not created for that reason.

Now suppose that you are in the military. You get into a fight with another soldier in your barracks, and as a result you are put in detention for a few days. Maybe you criticize a superior officer when you are given an order, which would bring about a more severe result. If you are standing nearby when the president of the United States walks by and you assault him, you might lose your life.

Why would those three incidents produce three different outcomes? Because the weight of the offense varies based upon the status of the person you are offending.

When we think about sin and the law, we learn something about where our sin is really directed. We often think that our sin is OK if it doesn't affect anyone else, but we must remember that our sin is, first and foremost, against a holy God. After he sinned with Bathsheba, David addressed this statement to God: *"Against thee, thee only, have I sinned, and done this evil in thy sight"* (Ps. 51:4).

So the purpose of the law is not to show us what a good job we are doing, but to show us where our problems are. The seventh chapter of Romans helps us see the importance of the law in our lives. The word *"law"* appears 14 times in the first 12 verses of that chapter.

Up to now, the book of Romans has consisted of a series of questions. Time after time the Apostle Paul poses a question and immediately follows it with an answer. One of the best ways to learn is to ask questions.

A perfect example of this is found in Rom. 7:7. *"What shall we say then? Is the law sin? God forbid. Nay, I had not known sin, but by the law: for I had not known lust, except the law had said, Thou shalt not covet."*

God has a purpose and a reason for the law. But legalism is a killer.

Bible scholar and writer Warren Wiersbe gives this definition of legalism: "Legalism is the belief that I can be holy and please God by obeying laws. It is measuring spirituality by a list of DOs and DON'Ts. The weakness of legalism is that it sees sins and not sin, or the root of the trouble. It judges by the outward and not by the inward." If you are around legalistic people, you find that they tend to be critical, unloving and unforgiving.

I read an article recently by Mike Yaconelli, editor of a Christian satire publication called the Wittenburg Door. He wrote about how legalism leads to pettiness:

"Petty people are ugly people. They are people who have lost their vision," he wrote. "They are people who have turned their eyes away from what matters and focused instead on what doesn't matter. The result is that the rest of us are immobilized by their obsession with the insignificant. It is time to rid the church of pettiness. It is time the church refused to be victimized by petty people. It is time the church stopped ignoring pettiness. It is time the church stopped pretending pettiness doesn't matter. Pettiness has become a serious disease in the church of Jesus Christ, a disease which continues to result in terminal cases of discord, disruption and destruction. Petty people are dangerous people because they appear to be only a nuisance instead of what they really are – a health hazard."

Interesting words, aren't they? Yaconelli is not the only person to address this issue in print. Chuck Swindoll wrote a great book called "The Grace Awakening" in which he talks at length about legalism.

There is a purpose to the law. We are not to simply throw the law away. But the law cannot save you and will not keep you.

Paul begins his discussion of this important topic with an illustration regarding marriage in verses 1-5.

"Know ye not, brethren, (for I speak to them that know the law,) how that the law hath dominion over a man as long as he liveth? For the woman which hath an husband is bound by the law to her husband so long as he liveth; but if the husband be dead, she is loosed from the law of her husband. So then if, while her husband liveth, she be married to another man, she shall be called an adulteress: but if her husband be dead, she is free from that law; so that she is no adulteress, though she be married to another man. Wherefore, my brethren, ye also are become dead to the law by the body of Christ; that ye should be married to another, even to him who is raised from the dead, that we should bring forth fruit unto God. For when we were in the flesh, the motions of sins, which were by the law, did work in our members to bring forth fruit unto death."

These verses are not talking about divorce and remarriage, but rather the dissolution of a marriage due to a spouse's death. There is a unique and powerful application to be made here.

The husband's death represents the old life, while the wife's remarriage represents the new life. Now she and her new husband are walking in newness of life.

When you accept Jesus Christ as your Saviour, you still have the old sin nature. Sin is still in your life. But at the time of salvation a new person comes to live within you – the Holy Spirit.

Look at Rom. 8:4. *"That the righteousness of the law might be fulfilled in us, who walk not after the flesh, but after the Spirit."* Our motivation for our life is not the law; it is the Spirit of God.

I can look at you and tell you that I see sin in your life. I can even point it out to you. You could do the same thing to me. We are all sinners.

Many years ago I was invited to speak at a conference, and I received in the mail a form listing the requirements and standards for workers in that particular church, all of which also applied to guest speakers. It was a very long list.

The items on the list included abstinence from alcohol and tobacco, no theater attendance, short hair on men and long dresses on women, etc. But the last item on the list was this: "No wire-rimmed glasses." I wore such glasses at that time. I called to inquire about it, and they told me, "Just don't wear them in the pulpit."

Let me be clear. I respect the rules that any church may adopt. That is the right of each individual church. The problem that often arises, however, is that people tend to think those kinds of rules are what make them righteous.

You might remember the long list of sins mentioned in Rom. 1:29-31. *"Being filled with all unrighteousness, fornication, wickedness, covetousness, maliciousness; full of envy, murder, debate, deceit, malignity; whisperers, Backbiters, haters of God, despiteful, proud, boasters, inventors of evil things, disobedient to parents, Without understanding, covenantbreakers, without natural affection, implacable, unmerciful."*

That detailed list is used to stress the point that we are all sinners, and the law points this out. The law doesn't tell us how good we are. It tells us how good God is and how bad we are.

Back in chapter 7, verse 6 begins the lesson that results from the marriage illustration. *"But now we are delivered from the law, that being dead wherein we were held; that we should serve in newness of spirit, and not in the oldness of the letter."*

The Christian life is not one of rebellion. We are united with Christ. God's commandments were originally written in stone, but under grace they are also written in our hearts.

The law cannot exercise authority over a dead person. We died to the law that we might be married to Christ. Our authority comes to us under grace. So why do we have the law?

We are all familiar with the Ten Commandments, but did you know that more than 600 laws were given in the Old Testament? In most churches today the majority of members could not quote the Ten Commandments in order, let alone those other laws. How can you keep the law when you don't know the law?

We are told in Rom. 3:20 why the law exists. *"Therefore by the deeds of the law there shall no flesh be justified in his sight: for by the law is the knowledge of sin."* The law reminds us that we are sinners.

This is also emphasized in Rom. 4:15. "Because the law worketh wrath: for where no law is, there is no transgression."

Now look at James 1:22-25 for a different perspective on following the law. *"But be ye doers of the word, and not hearers only, deceiving your own selves. For if any be a hearer of the word, and not a doer, he is like unto a man beholding his natural face in a glass: For he beholdeth himself, and goeth his way, and straightway forgetteth what manner of man he was. But whoso looketh into the perfect law of liberty, and continueth therein, he being not a forgetful hearer, but a doer of the work, this man shall be blessed in his deed."*

Our church in south Florida has two campuses, and I have an office at each location. In each office I have a mirror. I love to watch people come into my office. They look in the mirror and instinctively fix themselves up. I do it a dozen times a day as I go in and out, and I don't really know why. I think we all do it because we can't help it.

Have you ever participated in a group picture? If you are asked to choose from several poses in a group picture, you will base your choice upon how you look in the picture. Everyone else may be looking straight at the ceiling or have their eyes closed, but if you like the way you look, it's OK. We all want to look good.

God says that if you look at yourself in the mirror of His Word, you cannot come away looking good. His law shows us how bad we really are.

Verses 8-9 demonstrate how the law can lead us into rebellion. *"But sin, taking occasion by the commandment, wrought in me all manner of concupiscence. For without the law sin was dead. For I was alive without the law once: but when the commandment came, sin revived, and I died."*

According to I Cor. 15:56, *"The sting of death is sin; and the strength of sin is the law."* People consumed by legalism unknowingly are moving toward rebellion because they are living by commandments that continually accuse them of more sin.

Bible scholar John Phillips illustrated this point with a story about a wealthy landowner who received a visitor one day. They enjoyed a wonderful meal together, but there was one place at the table with a plate and a note that said, "Do not touch."

The landowner left the room and the visitor couldn't stop looking at that plate. When he could no longer resist, he leaned over and tipped the plate ever so slightly. Feathers began to fly everywhere, and the man was caught.

I was walking through a town square one day and saw a bench with a sign that warned passersby not to touch because of wet paint. I suppose a half-dozen people or more walked by and touched that bench in just a few minutes. (I know because I was one of those people.) What is there about us that makes us do that?

The law ultimately destroys, as indicated in verses 10-11. *"And the commandment, which was ordained to life, I found to be unto death. For sin, taking occasion by the commandment, deceived me, and by it slew me."* The law cannot give life; it can only show that the sinner is guilty.

What is worse, an alcoholic or a gossip? Both of them lead to ruined lives. How about murder vs. jealousy? We talk about "white lies" as if they are different from other types of lies.

We make those comparisons based upon our presuppositions about life. But in God's eyes, sin is sin.

In the Old Testament there are 15 Hebrew words to describe sin. There are many in the New Testament as well. Words like wickedness, evil, ungodliness, disobedience, transgressions, trespasses, iniquity, error, fault are all used in the Word of God to portray sin.

When you and I try to promote our own goodness rather than the grace of God, we become miserable people. The law is a good thing, but it is not the main thing. The law cannot save, because that is the prerogative of grace.

Sin is not mistakes or weakness. It is sin, and we have a sin nature. The law says that we are sinners.

Consider Paul's words in Rom. 7:24-25. *"O wretched man that I am! who shall deliver me from the body of this death? I thank God through Jesus Christ our Lord. So then with the mind I myself serve the law of God; but with the flesh the law of sin."*

He continues this thought in Rom. 8:1. *"There is therefore now no condemnation to them which are in Christ Jesus, who walk not after the flesh, but after the Spirit."* This verse leads into a discussion of the Spirit-filled life.

We must understand that the law reveals what we are really like. But who wrote the law? It was our Lord. Jesus said, *"Think not that I am come to destroy the law, or the prophets: I am not come to destroy, but to fulfil"* (Matt. 5:17).

If we are to understand what the law is all about and how it relates to us, then we must understand how Jesus relates to us.

We often think about what Jesus might have looked like. Many pictures we have seen depict Him as a handsome, European-looking fellow. But the Bible only speaks once about His appearance, in the book of Isaiah, and that is a description of how He looked on the cross: *"His visage was so marred more than any man, and his form more than the sons of men"* (Is. 52:14).

Think about Christ's attitude toward people. The Bible says that He would often praise people. He would say to many of them, as He did in Matt. 9:22, *"Thy faith hath made thee whole."* He called Peter the rock upon which He would build His church.

Consider what Jesus did. He often went to feasts, and twice He arrived late to find that people had died. He was ridiculed, but in both instances He spoke and the dead people came to life – Jarius' daughter and Lazarus. Remember how He said, *"Lazarus, come forth."* Someone rightfully said that it's a good thing He called Lazarus by name, or else every dead body in every tomb would have risen.

Jesus took a small group of men that no one seemed to want, and they changed the world. He faced all types of questions from religious leaders and His own disciples. Think about the stories He told and the messages He preached during His earthly ministry.

When the religious leaders brought the adulterous woman before Him, it was a prime example of men putting their emphasis on the law. What did He say to them? *"He that is without sin among you, let him first cast a stone at her"* (John 8:7). Jesus was known as a friend of sinners.

Author Salman Rushdie said, "The true battle of history will not be between the socialists and capitalists or the rich and poor, but it will be between the epicurean and the puritan." He is referring to those who believe that anything goes and those who do not. But the important question is this: What does God think?

When you see the law, you start to understand what God is really like. He is absolutely pure and holy, righteous and loving.

George Buttrick, who was chaplain at Harvard, used to have students come to him and say, "I don't believe in God." He would then disarm them by saying, "Tell me what kind of god you don't believe in, because I probably don't believe in him, either." That would give him the opportunity to tell students what God is really like.

Sometimes we like to make up in our own minds what we want God to be. But think about what Jesus said about Him. We can call Him "Abba Father," or Papa Father. When Christ said, *"For the Son of man is come to seek and to save that which was lost"* (Luke 19:10), He was saying that while we search for Him, in reality He is looking for us.

Think of the Father who loved the world so much that He gave His only Son. Think of the Holy Spirit who has come as a comforter and encourager. Our God, who is a God of the law, loves us unconditionally. There is not a single reference in the Koran that attaches love to God, but the Bible is full of examples that show us a loving God.

What does the law mean to you? We have already seen that Christ came to fulfill the law.

If you were sitting on an airplane reading a book that you wrote and noticed the person sitting next to you looking over to see what you were reading, you would feel pretty good about it. If that person verbally expressed that he liked your book, you would be impressed at his wisdom and feel even better.

153

But if that person did not understand your book at all, and your efforts to explain it only made things more confusing, you would think, "Either something is wrong with him, or something is wrong with the book."

There is nothing wrong with God's law. It is a teacher. It is a schoolmaster. God's law tells you where to go and what to do.

Look at Rom. 8:11-14. *"But if the Spirit of him that raised up Jesus from the dead dwell in you, he that raised up Christ from the dead shall also quicken your mortal bodies by his Spirit that dwelleth in you. Therefore, brethren, we are debtors, not to the flesh, to live after the flesh. For if ye live after the flesh, ye shall die: but if ye through the Spirit do mortify the deeds of the body, ye shall live. For as many as are led by the Spirit of God, they are the sons of God."*

When you accept Jesus Christ into your life, you begin to understand that there is something different and unique about you, and you sense the leading of the Holy Spirit within you. God wrote the law, the Spirit leads and guides you according to the law, and Christ fulfilled everything there is relating to the law. The law drives us to Christ, and if it doesn't do that it will absolutely condemn us.

Take a moment and think back to when you were saved. Do you remember who led you to Christ? That person is important to you, as is the event that led to your salvation. You sensed at that moment that something was different in your life, and there was something that drove you to that point.

As we get ready to explore the eighth chapter of Romans and discover what it is to live the Spirit-filled life, we must remember that the law does not drive us there, but Christ does – and it is the law that drives us to Christ.

Rom. 8:1 says, *"There is therefore now no condemnation to them which are in Christ Jesus, who walk not after the flesh, but after the Spirit."* We are not condemned because of what Christ has done for us.

The law has a great message for all of us. But the law by and of itself is empty. When we use the law as our teacher to drive us to Christ, it is fulfilled in Him.

God came to this earth in embryonic form and took on the flesh of a man. He went to a cross and died for our sins so that we might have eternal life with Him.

Without Jesus, what would the law mean to any of us? As you read the Bible and consider the law, remember that its purpose is to drive you to Jesus Christ.

Chapter 15

LAW & ORDER

"Was then that which is good made death unto me? God forbid. But sin, that it might appear sin, working death in me by that which is good; that sin by the commandment might become exceeding sinful. For we know that the law is spiritual: but I am carnal, sold under sin. For that which I do I allow not: for what I would, that do I not; but what I hate, that do I. If then I do that which I would not, I consent unto the law that it is good. Now then it is no more I that do it, but sin that dwelleth in me. For I know that in me (that is, in my flesh,) dwelleth no good thing: for to will is present with me; but how to perform that which is good I find not. For the good that I would I do not: but the evil which I would not, that I do. Now if I do that I would not, it is no more I that do it, but sin that dwelleth in me. I find then a law, that, when I would do good, evil is present with me. For I delight in the law of God after the inward man: But I see another law in my members, warring against the law of my mind, and bringing me into captivity to the law of sin which is in my members. O wretched man that I am! who shall deliver me from the body of this death? I thank God through Jesus Christ our Lord. So then with the mind I myself serve the law of God; but with the flesh the law of sin." **(Rom. 7:13-25)**

fter seeing in the previous two chapters the transformation
from sin to liberty and from legalism to responsibility, we now
are faced with a massive tug-of-war against our flesh that we will
have to struggle with until Jesus Christ returns. It is, quite literally,
a war of wills.

Can you have law and order in your life, plus victory over the
burden of sin now as well as down the road? To find the answer to
that question, we will examine one of the most paradoxical and diffi-
cult-to-understand passages in the New Testament, as Paul's conversation with himself makes him sound as though he is not even a
Christian.

Paul wanted to know two basic things:

"Can I live a victorious Christian life?"

"Can I have order over my flesh and my sinful nature before I
die?"

He was trying to reconcile the law of God with the desire for
order in his life. He wanted to know if he could do away with greed,
envy, lust and all of the other things humans have struggled with for
thousands of years. He was a divided man in three different ways.

First is the **conflict**. This is laid out in verses 14-16, beginning
with Paul's admission that he is "carnal, sold under sin." As a Jew
and a former Pharisee, he thought at one time that he could live as he
should by following the law. He later learned that the law could not
save him, but it could kill him by tempting him to sin and keeping
him separated from God. He discovered that the law is actually a
mirror, a reflection of God's holiness and justice that showed him
how incapable he was of earning God's favor and grace.

You may have seen on television how evangelists Ray Comfort
and Kirk Cameron would go out on the street and talk to people
about the Ten Commandments. The interesting thing about that exercise is that when you find someone who thinks he has everything
figured out regarding God, the Ten Commandments will cut him
down to size in an instant. Those who stand with pride because they
have never committed adultery during their marriages or murdered
anyone are reminded of Christ's admonition that harboring hatred in
the heart toward another can be akin to murder, not to mention the

connection between lust and adultery. There is simply no way you can keep the law in its entirety.

The first three chapters of Romans tell us that conscience and the law condemn us all. Chapters 4-6 show that we are justified by faith in Christ which redeems us and gives us victory over the bondage of sin. Everything looks pretty clear until we get into chapter 7, and especially verse 14, which includes the phrase, *"But I am carnal, sold under sin."* That bothers me, and it should bother you as well.

The word "carnal" literally means "of flesh." It refers to the lusts and passions that are tied to our sinful bodies. In Romans 5 Paul wrote of the fact that he was sold into the slavery of sin because of Adam's curse, but it was in the past tense. In this passage he is speaking as if he is still carnal and bound by sin. Does that sound like a contradiction to you? It does to me. There is a conflict here that is expressed in more detail in verses 15-16.

This war between the will and the flesh is ever-present. Paul wrote in Galatians 5 about the lust of the flesh against the Spirit. So who is this man in Romans 7? Is he a believer? There are three primary arguments that have been advanced for many years regarding this subject.

Some people believe that this passage is about a man who is unsaved. They think Paul is referring to the unregenerate Saul of Tarsus. The early writings of Augustine show that many in the early church would seem to agree.

Paul's statement in Romans 7:14 appears to contradict his words in the previous chapter. Rom. 6:17-18 says, *"But God be thanked, that ye were the servants of sin, but ye have obeyed from the heart that form of doctrine which was delivered you. Being then made free from sin, ye became the servants of righteousness."*

The problem here is the context. Look at Rom. 7:18 and it becomes a bit clearer. *"For I know that in me (that is, in my flesh,) dwelleth no good thing: for to will is present with me; but how to perform that which is good I find not."* We see here that Paul has a desire to do good. That does not sound like an unbeliever. He even expresses a delight in the law, as we see in verse 22.

The grammatical differences in Romans 7 cannot be overlooked. Whereas Paul spoke in the past tense in verses 7-13, he uses the present tense in verses 14-25 and frequently uses the personal pronoun "I." He is saying, "This is how I am today." This is an obvious contrast when compared to Paul's other letters that speak of his pre-conversion life.

Look at Phil. 3:4-6. *"If any other man thinketh that he hath whereof he might trust in the flesh, I more: Circumcised the eighth day, of the stock of Israel, of the tribe of Benjamin, an Hebrew of the Hebrews; as touching the law, a Pharisee; Concerning zeal, persecuting the church; touching the righteousness which is in the law, blameless."* The legalistic Pharisee in this passage is quite different from the man struggling with sin in Romans 7.

Another view of this passage, one that is popular as well as plausible, is that Paul is a backslidden Christian. The problem with that is the idea of Christ as fire insurance – wanting Him as Saviour but not as Lord.

Paul clears this up in Rom. 8:5-8. *"For they that are after the flesh do mind the things of the flesh; but they that are after the Spirit the things of the Spirit. For to be carnally minded is death; but to be spiritually minded is life and peace. Because the carnal mind is enmity against God: for it is not subject to the law of God, neither indeed can be. So then they that are in the flesh cannot please God."*

If you are so wrapped up in your flesh that your carnality is your whole life, you don't have the Spirit. You cannot be 100 percent carnal and still have the Lord. There must be some change, some life transformation and regeneration at some point in your life. This idea is echoed many times in the Bible.

So that leaves us with the third (and most likely) possibility, which is that Paul is a born-again Christian like the rest of us, struggling every day with the battle between the will and the flesh, longing for law and order in our lives. This is the consensus of many great theologians and Bible teachers of history.

You see this struggle in some of the great heroes of the faith. David, known as "a man after God's own heart," committed adultery with Bathsheba and conspired to have her husband killed. He later wrote Psalm 51 as his prayer of confession, which includes these words in verse 3: *"For I acknowledge my transgressions: and my sin is ever before me.*" He acknowledged that his sin was against God and he was a sinner from the moment he came into the world.

In the New Testament, we read about how Peter claimed he would never deny Christ but ultimately did so three times. We can relate to his words in I Pet. 2:11, which says, *"Dearly beloved, I beseech you as strangers and pilgrims, abstain from fleshly lusts, which war against the soul."* He was telling believers in this verse that they could expect to fight this tug-of-war against sin for their entire lives.

Following the conflict is the **capacity**, in Rom. 7:17-20. This is the constant war that is fought in sanctification, and it cannot be won without the Holy Spirit.

A lot of us would be happy to just skip chapter 7 completely and go straight into chapter 8, which means victory. We'd love to bypass this subject. But just as the law cannot justify you, it also cannot sanctify you. God wants us to be sanctified – unique, holy, set apart for Him.

Here is the clash between the old Adamic nature and the new man. We can all relate to Paul in the two main ideas of this passage: We do not do good as we should and we often do bad as we shouldn't.

All of us need to be digesting the Word daily, praying without ceasing, fellowshipping with the saints whenever possible, and spending as much quality and quantity time with our families as we can. But we struggle against the lure of big bucks that may require 60-hour work weeks, along with the temptation of worldly entertainment that is either filthy or just wastes too much of our time. That is the struggle, and Paul wrestled with the same problems as us because he had the same big capacity to sin.

He recognized in verses 17-18 the sinful nature that lives within him, sounding almost as if he has excused himself or just given up because he knows he can't win the battle. It sounds a lot like the way Eve responded to God after she was caught eating the forbidden fruit, or the "victim attitude" that is so prevalent in our society today.

Our sinful nature is depraved. Even after we are saved we struggle with sin. We might not be as bad as we could be, but in God's eyes we're a mess. Because we still live in a sin-drenched, sin-cursed world, we have no capacity on our own to win the tug-of-war.

There is a way to win, but it is difficult and takes some effort on our part. There is no easy way through spiritual warfare, although in America today that is exactly the way we want it. We want a simple method we can read in a book or learn in a multi-step program. It doesn't happen that way.

Now let's look at the **conclusion** of this battle in verses 21-25. The first part of that deals with Paul's captivity that he specifically mentions in verse 23. Paul cannot do what he wants to do because he is still held captive to some extent by sin.

This sounds strange when viewed next to two verses from the previous chapter:

> *"Knowing this, that our old man is crucified with him, that the body of sin might be destroyed, that henceforth we should not serve sin"* (Rom. 6:6).
> *"For sin shall not have dominion over you: for ye are not under the law, but under grace"* (Rom. 6:14)

If these matters appear to be settled in chapter 6, why is Paul wrestling with them in chapter 7? It's because now he is not talking about possession, but about submission. A believer in Christ who is walking in the Spirit can crucify the desires of the flesh. You can say no to sin. It won't always happen, but it can be done.

Unbelievers have no ability to overcome sin. They are acting the way they are supposed to act, because their father is the devil, as Jesus stated in the New Testament. You and I can remember when we were in the same spot, so we are not too harsh on them regarding their struggle. They do not have the power of Holy Spirit, so they are utterly powerless against sin.

But if you are a child of God, you can say no to sin and you must do so. Sin no longer has absolute controlling power over you.

Paul's use of the word *"wretched"* in verse 24 denotes his constant trials and continuing burden. Many of us can relate to this. Actually, the Greek root word here refers to a scale with weights on it, implying that we are constantly burdened with a weight that we just can't hold up. It's as if Paul is saying, "Who is going to get this weight off my back?"

The phrase *"the body of this death"* in verse 24 is a fascinating one. Scholars believe that Paul is making an analogy to a particularly gruesome ancient form of execution that was practiced near his homeland of Tarsus. A convicted killer would be bound in a way that he lay face-to-face against the corpse of his victim, and when the two were set out in the hot Mediterranean sun the forces that consumed the dead body would begin to eat away at the live one. Paul used that symbol to describe our life in Christ, where we have a new nature but still fight against the old one.

So can we achieve law and order in our lives and obtain victory more often than not? Paul's final thoughts in this chapter are in verse 25: *"I thank God through Jesus Christ our Lord. So then with the mind I myself serve the law of God; but with the flesh the law of sin."* He acknowledges that it will be a struggle throughout his earthly life, but he will have the final victory through Christ. That is the case with us as well. Not only that, but you can win more battles than you lose when you just let the Lord take control of your life and guide you by His Spirit.

What is sanctification? It is best defined in three stages.

In the past, you were sanctified when you were saved. God set you apart to be holy, and that happened at the moment of salvation and justification.

In the present, you are in the process of being sanctified. You are being more holy and set apart every day as you strive to be conformed to His image. It's not about your perfection, but your direction.

In the future, you will be sanctified ultimately when Jesus comes again and you receive a resurrected body. It's no longer a body of death, but a body of permanent life. This stage of sanctification is what we call glorification.

No matter how bad the struggle is right now, we will have ultimate victory. With this in mind, let's encourage one another for a moment with the words of I Cor. 15:52-57. *"In a moment, in the twinkling of an eye, at the last trump: for the trumpet shall sound, and the dead shall be raised incorruptible, and we shall be changed. For this corruptible must put on incorruption, and this mortal must put on immortality. So when this corruptible shall have put on incor-*

ruption, and this mortal shall have put on immortality, then shall be brought to pass the saying that is written, Death is swallowed up in victory. O death, where is thy sting? O grave, where is thy victory? The sting of death is sin; and the strength of sin is the law. But thanks be to God, which giveth us the victory through our Lord Jesus Christ."

In the meantime, we need to let Christ feel at home within us. That is what walking in the Spirit is all about. Let's put on the whole armor of God, strip away whatever weighs us down, present ourselves as a living sacrifice and renew our minds. Only in the power of God and His Spirit can we have victory over sin.

Chapter 16

GO AND LIVE YOUR SPIRIT LIFE

"There is therefore now no condemnation to them which are in Christ Jesus, who walk not after the flesh, but after the Spirit. For the law of the Spirit of life in Christ Jesus hath made me free from the law of sin and death. For what the law could not do, in that it was weak through the flesh, God sending his own Son in the likeness of sinful flesh, and for sin, condemned sin in the flesh: That the righteousness of the law might be fulfilled in us, who walk not after the flesh, but after the Spirit. For they that are after the flesh do mind the things of the flesh; but they that are after the Spirit the things of the Spirit. For to be carnally minded is death; but to be spiritually minded is life and peace. Because the carnal mind is enmity against God: for it is not subject to the law of God, neither indeed can be. So then they that are in the flesh cannot please God. But ye are not in the flesh, but in the Spirit, if so be that the Spirit of God dwell in you. Now if any man have not the Spirit of Christ, he is none of his. And if Christ be in you, the body is dead because of sin; but the Spirit is life because of righteousness. But if the Spirit of him that raised up Jesus from the dead dwell in you, he that raised up Christ from the dead shall also quicken your mortal bodies by his Spirit that dwelleth in you." **(Rom. 8:1-11)**

James Montgomery Boice, who for many years was pastor of the Tenth Street Presbyterian Church in Philadelphia and went verse-by-verse through the Bible during much of his radio ministry, once said that the eighth chapter of Romans was the greatest chapter in all the Bible.

Warren Wiersbe has called this chapter "the one chapter that tells us about freedom and fulfillment."

Donald Trumble has written these words: "The book of Romans begins with no condemnation and ends with no separation, and in between there is no defeat."

An old German commentator named Spencer said, "If the Bible was a ring and the book of Romans its precious stone, chapter 8 would be the sparkling point of the jewel."

This chapter tells us something very important. It tells us to get our eyes off ourselves and all of the little things that bother us; to get our eyes off our families and our material possessions; and to get them on the Lord.

President Franklin Delano Roosevelt addressed Congress Jan. 6, 1941 on the state of the war in Europe. He said that to have a successful republic required four essential human freedoms: freedom of speech, freedom of worship, freedom from want and freedom from fear. These are the things our country must defend to survive something like a world war, he said.

In the eighth chapter of Romans are also four freedoms that we must defend, and I would call them "Four Greater Freedoms." They are freedom from judgment (verses 1-4), freedom from defeat (v. 5-17), freedom from discouragement (v. 18-30) and freedom from fear (v. 31-39).

A key word used throughout this chapter is the word "*in*." Verses 1-2 contain the phrase "*in Christ Jesus*," while verses 3 and 9 talk about living "*in the flesh*." Verse 4 addresses the fulfillment of the law "*in us*," and subsequent verses deal with living "*in the Spirit*" (v. 9) and Christ living "*in you*" (v. 10-11). This chapter talks about a glorious relationship that we have in Christ.

Four of the greatest words in the entire book of Romans are found here in verse 1: "*therefore now no condemnation*." Let me explain those words in a different order.

The word *"condemnation"* is very interesting. It is a forensic term which includes not only the sentence but also the execution of that sentence. If you are condemned in this context, you have absolutely no hope.

The word *"now"* points to the change that comes to us because we are justified. The condemnation is gone immediately with our justification.

The word *"no"* is simple yet permanent. It means that a Christian can never be in a state of condemnation. When you are a child of God, it is impossible to be condemned by God.

The final word in that phrase is *"therefore,"* which means "because of what has been said it is true." It connects the dots. As I have often said, when you find a *"therefore"* in the Bible, you must then find out what it is "there for." It also appears in this chapter in verse 12.

To help us understand this we will go back to John 8 and look at a very familiar story. We begin in verse 2: *"And early in the morning he came again into the temple, and all the people came unto him; and he sat down, and taught them."*

The religious leaders of that day did not want Jesus teaching the people, and they did everything they could to interrupt that teaching, which they did here in verses 3-4. *"And the scribes and Pharisees brought unto him a woman taken in adultery; and when they had set her in the midst, They say unto him, Master, this woman was taken in adultery, in the very act."*

It's one thing to accuse someone of adultery; it is quite another to catch that person in the act. I can't help but wonder where the man is in this situation. They did not hesitate to take the woman and charge her, but the man is nowhere to be found. It is obvious that this was motivated not by their concern for this woman's sin, but their desire to interrupt the teaching of Jesus.

Their words in verse 5 are an attempt to put Jesus on the spot. *"Now Moses in the law commanded us, that such should be stoned: but what sayest thou?"*

If you and I are answerable to the law, we will always be condemned. Remember, there are more than 600 laws given in the Old Testament. Many of us struggle to name all of the Ten

Commandments, let alone the all of the other laws. No one can keep the law successfully and without failing, no matter what he or she thinks.

Imagine the shame and embarrassment this woman feels as she stands before Christ as well as her accusers. She knows how sinful her actions are. Some of the men have no doubt reached down and gathered stones in their hands before Jesus even begins to respond. We see more of their evil intentions in verse 6: *"This they said, tempting him, that they might have to accuse him. But Jesus stooped down, and with his finger wrote on the ground, as though he heard them not."*

Has someone ever said something to you in an accusing manner, and you wished you had just the right thing to say or could easily ignore your accusers just to get under their skin? We know that Jesus always said and did exactly the right thing. No one knows what He wrote on the ground in this instance, although some scholars believe it was something pertaining to the law.

Just when they thought He wasn't going to give them the time of day, Christ uttered an immortal thought, as we see in verses 7-9. *"So when they continued asking him, he lifted up himself, and said unto them, He that is without sin among you, let him first cast a stone at her. And again he stooped down, and wrote on the ground. And they which heard it, being convicted by their own conscience, went out one by one, beginning at the eldest, even unto the last: and Jesus was left alone, and the woman standing in the midst."*

Imagine these proud religious men standing in silence, then dropping their stones one by one and walking away. You probably could have heard a pin drop.

Notice how the older accusers departed first, then the younger. The older members of any group will typically be wiser. Younger people tend to jump into something without thinking, then wonder how they will get out.

This wonderful story concludes in verses 10-11. *"When Jesus had lifted up himself, and saw none but the woman, he said unto her, Woman, where are those thine accusers? hath no man condemned thee? She said, No man, Lord. And Jesus said unto her, Neither do I condemn thee: go, and sin no more."*

There is that word *"condemned"* that we just saw in Romans. In keeping with the definition of the word here, the woman's accusers were ready to sentence her and then execute her immediately before Jesus intervened with forgiveness and the admonition that she leave her life of sin.

The first 11 verses of the eighth chapter of Romans take us to a new level in our Christian walk. Once we come to Christ, we are commanded to live a Spirit-filled life, and this passage shows us several reasons why.

As verses 1-4 point out, the first reason is that **we are not condemned**. Verse 1 says, *"There is therefore now no condemnation to them which are in Christ Jesus, who walk not after the flesh, but after the Spirit."*

When we are saved, the Holy Spirit comes to live within us. This does not mean that we no longer make mistakes or experience failure, and these verses do not suggest that.

Consider some of the heroes of the Bible. Abraham lied. David committed adultery. Moses killed a man, and Peter tried to kill someone. There are always consequences for sin, but when you are in Christ there is no condemnation.

Verses 2-4 show us a new law that goes into effect when we come to Christ. *"For the law of the Spirit of life in Christ Jesus hath made me free from the law of sin and death. For what the law could not do, in that it was weak through the flesh, God sending his own Son in the likeness of sinful flesh, and for sin, condemned sin in the flesh: That the righteousness of the law might be fulfilled in us, who walk not after the flesh, but after the Spirit."*

A new law has been given to us, and it is the law of the Spirit of God. The old law is contained in the many rules and regulations in the Old Testament. A writer put it in the following manner: "But that law cannot claim you, since the law of sin and death was the result of the old Mosaic law; it cannot condemn you, because the law is simply a tutor to bring you to Christ; and it cannot control you – legalism promotes obeying God in our own flesh, but God sent Jesus in the flesh, untainted by the fall, who never yielded to a wrong thought or action because His coming fulfilled the law."

Christ's life does not save me, but His death saves me. Living the Spirit-filled life is a way to show the world that I am not condemned. Jesus can forgive an adulterer, a murderer, or even a Pharisee who thinks his morality will get him to Heaven.

You and I would have a much different outlook on life if we could fully grasp this idea that we are not condemned. If you want to go on and live in your sin, that's one thing. But when you understand that no condemnation will come upon your life, it should give you all the motivation you need to make you want to follow Christ.

In verses 5-8 we learn that in the Spirit-filled life **we are not defeated**. There is a major difference between the seventh and eighth chapters of Romans. We read a lot of "*I*," "*me*" and "*my*" in Romans 7. In fact, Paul uses 28 personal pronouns referring to himself in verses 14-21 of that chapter. He understood that the problem lay with him, namely his own sinful condition. That's our problem as well.

Even after we come to Christ, many times we feel defeated because we are doing things in the flesh instead of allowing the Holy Spirit to direct us. In this passage from Romans 8 we see a series of contrasts that show us how to live a life that is not defeated.

Verse 5 shows the contrast between being in Christ and being in the flesh. "*For they that are after the flesh do mind the things of the flesh; but they that are after the Spirit the things of the Spirit.*"

An unsaved person can do good things, and a saved person can do bad things. The difference is that the saved person has the Holy Spirit of God working in his or her life. If you are a child of God, the Holy Spirit begins to convict you when you do wrong. One of the ways you can know that you are saved is that Someone is living within you – Someone who knows you, watches you, guards you, and reminds you that you are not condemned.

When I was a child I was blessed with good, Godly parents. My mother was an old-fashioned disciplinarian and I used to think that she knew everything I did without anyone telling her. I thought she had eyes in the back of her head. Whenever I thought I could get away with something, even if my mother were nowhere to be found, I had this sinking feeling that she was right around the corner watching me.

When you are saved, you know the Holy Spirit of God is in your life. Someone lives within you and will give you victory in your life. You know something is different. That is the contrast between being in Christ and being in the flesh.

Does that mean a Christian is perfect? Absolutely not. There are numerous examples in the Bible of great men and women of God who did things they should not have done. Abraham married Hagar. Lot chose Sodom. Moses killed an Egyptian. Solomon, considered the wisest man of his day, married 700 heathen wives (What was he thinking?). Jonah set out for Tarshish instead of Nineveh. Peter chopped off a man's ear.

We all do things in our lives we shouldn't do, just like these men did. It's all a matter of submitting to the Holy Spirit.

Do you ever have one of those days where you feel as though you're living in complete victory only to do something that just ruins everything? "What's the matter with me?" you wonder. I'll tell you what's the matter – you still have the flesh in you. But that doesn't mean you have to live your Christian life in defeat or thinking there's no future.

During the fall of 2007 the Miami Dolphins, our hometown team, came dangerously close to a winless season. As the weeks went by and the record fell to 0-6, 0-7 and 0-8, I would be greeted by five or six people each Sunday morning at church who said, "Today is the day. We're finally going to get a win today." Thankfully, that win came in the final month of the season.

That's the kind of attitude we need to have as Christians. We need to wake up every morning believing that we're going to be winners. You don't have to live a defeated Christian life.

Notice in verse 6 the contrast between death and life. *"For to be carnally minded is death; but to be spiritually minded is life and peace."*

In Israel the beautiful Sea of Galilee is fed from the waters to its north and feeds the Jordan River to the south. Because water comes in and out, there is life in that sea. But the Jordan River flows into the Dead Sea, also known as the Salt Sea, and there is nowhere for the water to go from there. Because of that, everything dies.

In your Christian life you must give as your receive. If you just take and take without giving, holding onto everything for yourself, it's like living in death. Some of the unhappiest people in the world are Christians who do not give of themselves. The most defeated people are Christians who do not want to live the victorious Christian life.

The contrast between war with God and peace with God is addressed in verse 7. "*Because the carnal mind is enmity against God: for it is not subject to the law of God, neither indeed can be.*"

Verse 8 speaks of the contrast between pleasing God and pleasing self. "*So then they that are in the flesh cannot please God.*"

I learned when our children were small how futile it is to try to please the flesh. On Christmas morning they would eagerly wade through the mountain of gifts that we had scrimped and saved to be able to buy. When that last gift is opened, however, there is that unmistakable look on each child's face: "Is this all there is?" On top of that, later in the day the kids end up playing with the boxes that the gifts came in.

We can never please ourselves. A short time after you buy a new house, you want a better one. The same goes for a new car. All of our stuff has to be bigger and better than before. But it's not just material possessions; many of us are constantly trying to "upgrade" our relationships.

As long as you live to please yourself, you will continue to live in defeat. The Spirit-filled life is not a life of defeat.

The great preacher Jonathan Edwards wrote an article entitled "The Treatise Concerning Religion and Affections." He said some interesting things about what people considered to be aspect of a victorious life.

"If you have fervency, that is not necessarily a sign of victory," he wrote. "If you have fluency and can speak the Gospel well, that is not necessarily a sign of victory." He went on to say the same for excitement, zeal, religious affections and even praising God.

"The sign of victory is when the Holy Spirit of God is at work in your life," wrote Edwards. "Everything else is a result of that."

That is why the Bible tells us so often to live the Spirit-filled life. You know the presence of the Holy Spirit in your life by the way you look at life in general. Things that used to seem so important to you now just aren't important. Certain things that would never have gotten a reaction from you in the past now bring a tear to your eye. Nothing is as important as glorifying and honoring God. There is a difference in your life.

Verses 9-11 show us that when we live the Spirit-filled life **God works through us**. Verse 9 addresses our past. *"But ye are not in the flesh, but in the Spirit, if so be that the Spirit of God dwell in you. Now if any man have not the Spirit of Christ, he is none of his."*

But there is a change brought about by salvation. Verse 10 speaks of our present. *"And if Christ be in you, the body is dead because of sin; but the Spirit is life because of righteousness."*

Notice how these verses refer simply to Christ and not the Lord Jesus Christ. Why is that? Lord means "master," Jesus is His human name, and Christ means "the anointed one." It is the word we speak to designate Him as Messiah, but that is not the connotation in these verses. It is a reference to the anointed One living within you.

We must have the anointing of God if we are to serve Him. What is that? It is the touch of God on your life for the task that He has in store for your life.

Someone can stand on the platform at your church and sing a great song like "Amazing Grace" with such eloquence and fluency, yet it doesn't make contact with the spirit. On the other hand, the same song that is sung with far less of what our human minds consider to be talent and ability will touch every heart in the building. The difference is the touch of God.

You and I cannot really begin to enjoy the Christian life until we live by faith. If you are living from Sunday to Sunday so you can say that you put in your time for God by coming to church, you are missing out. You need to live out your whole life with the anointing of God upon you.

When we do this, we are alive not only to God but also to the Bible. God's Word begins to speak to us forcefully and regularly, and God touches our lives through it. Also coming alive is our relationship with other believers as we see the significance of being part of the family of God.

173

Verse 11 refers to the Christian's future, the natural progression of the thoughts conveyed in verses 9-10. We must also note that in verse 11, in addition to another reference to Christ there is a separate citation of the name Jesus. *"But if the Spirit of him that raised up Jesus from the dead dwell in you, he that raised up Christ from the dead shall also quicken your mortal bodies by his Spirit that dwelleth in you."*

There is another example in Rom. 3:26 of the name Jesus being separated unto itself. This use of His human name is to emphasize the One who died physically and rose again physically. It drives home the point that we are alive spiritually because of what the man Jesus did for us on Earth through His death, burial and resurrection.

There are two main thoughts I want to emphasize from this passage. The first is that you can always know that you are a Christian. You don't have to doubt that you are saved and your sins are forgiven. Your past, present and future are all secured in the eyes of God.

H.A. Ironside, a pastor many years ago in Chicago, was traveling by train to a conference in California. A gypsy lady came up to him and, just trying to make a little money, asked him if he would like for her to tell his future.

"I already know my future," he replied, reaching for his Bible. "Let me tell you about it."

After he explained to her that his future in Heaven was secure because of his salvation in Christ, the lady walked away realizing that she had picked the wrong man from whom to make any money as a fortune teller.

You don't need a gypsy or a horoscope to tell you about your future. If you are in Christ it is settled. It is a done deal.

The other thought I want to emphasize here is that the Christian life can only be lived as a life of faith. Remember those important words from the first chapter of Romans: *"The just shall live by faith."*

The older I get, the quicker the years seem to go by. As each year passes, you and I need to assess how we are living out our faith and what that faith has taught us. I believe that God wants to move mightily in each of our churches and throughout America, but it cannot happen unless we live by faith and ask God for His anointing to do whatever task He has called us to do.

Chapter 17

DOES THE SPIRIT HAVE YOU?

"Therefore, brethren, we are debtors, not to the flesh, to live after the flesh. For if ye live after the flesh, ye shall die: but if ye through the Spirit do mortify the deeds of the body, ye shall live. For as many as are led by the Spirit of God, they are the sons of God. For ye have not received the spirit of bondage again to fear; but ye have received the Spirit of adoption, whereby we cry, Abba, Father. The Spirit itself beareth witness with our spirit, that we are the children of God: And if children, then heirs; heirs of God, and joint-heirs with Christ; if so be that we suffer with him, that we may be also glorified together." (**Rom. 8:12-17**)

Many Christians live defeated lives. Sometimes we look at our families, our finances, our future, and even the fun we have as part of the foundation of our lives. Everything has its place, but we will never attain true living in this realm, and this portion of Scripture takes us from the position of living in the flesh to that of living in the Spirit.

The book of Romans has told us over and over again about the law. The Bible has a lot to say about the law. While it brings us to Christ, the law cannot save us. If you think you can be saved by keeping the law, you are mistaken.

We are not under the Pentateuchal law or the moral code of the Old Testament. We are not even under the Decalogue, or the Ten Commandments. This does not take away our moral responsibility as Christians who should live to please God.

The basis for our morality is directly linked to the Person of Jesus Christ and the principles urged by His sacrifice. The new covenant God has given us impels us to live through His abiding Holy Spirit. We do not live out our Christian life by keeping the law, but by the work of the Holy Spirit.

As we look at these verses we need to examine just who we are talking about when we refer to the Holy Spirit. He is certainly an encourager and influencer, but He is also much more than that. The Holy Spirit is God.

Remember the story of Ananias and Sapphira? This couple held back some money while lying about it, claiming that they had given their all. The Bible says in Acts 5:3-4, *"But Peter said, Ananias, why hath Satan filled thine heart to lie to the Holy Ghost, and to keep back part of the price of the land? Whiles it remained, was it not thine own? and after it was sold, was it not in thine own power? why hast thou conceived this thing in thine heart? thou hast not lied unto men, but unto God."* Notice how the Bible says in verse 3 that they lied to the Holy Spirit and in verse 4 that they lied to God. This is because God and the Holy Spirit are one.

The opening verses of Genesis talk about the Spirit of God moving on the face of the waters. When we talk about the Holy Spirit, we are talking about God. We refer to Him often as the third Person of the Trinity (Father, Son and Holy Spirit), but that does not in any way suggest that He is inferior to the other two. All three are equal, and all three are God.

It must be emphasized that the Holy Spirit is a distinct Person. As verse 16 says, *"The Spirit itself beareth witness with our spirit, that we are the children of God."* That is the work of a definite Person.

He is our great influencer. When Jesus Christ was baptized, God the Father appeared and said in Matt. 3:17, *"This is my beloved Son, in whom I am well pleased."* In the previous verse we see that the Holy Spirit came *"descending like a dove."* That is an important symbol.

I remember many times during my youth in upstate New York going to the town square and seeing the courthouse. It always seemed as though a few hundred pigeons decided to have a convention there. They always swarm around looking for food. A dove does not act like that, but stays in the background until it is truly welcome. It was no accident that the Holy Spirit appeared as a dove at Christ's baptism.

The Bible says in Eph. 4:30, *"And grieve not the holy Spirit of God, whereby ye are sealed unto the day of redemption."* The next verse adds, *"Let all bitterness, and wrath, and anger, and clamour, and evil speaking, be put away from you, with all malice."* So if you have an attitude of bitterness in your life, the Holy Spirit is not working in your life but remains in the background. As powerful as He is, He will not work in someone who is living like that.

He is also our great encourager. John 6 talks about how He comes alongside us to help us, as does John 14. The great theologian Charles Ryrie wrote, "The Spirit will help break down the indifference of a person who has no conviction of sin, who has a low regard for righteousness and pays no heed to the warnings of a coming judgment." In other words, the Holy Spirit can work amid some difficult circumstances.

The word used in the book of John that portrays the Spirit as our helper is the same word from which we get the English word "paraclete" – an advisor, advocate or intercessor. This is the One who dwells in your life when you accept Christ as your Saviour. He convicts you and teaches you as you go through life.

When Jesus left this earth and ascended into Heaven, He told the people that He would be sending them Someone else. A few weeks later, on the day of Pentecost, the Holy Spirit came down to be with them, and He does the same thing for every person who is born again today.

Now let's look at this section of Romans and see what happens when the Spirit has control of your life. First, He puts to death the things of the flesh and reproduces the things of the Spirit. As verse 14 says, *"For as many as are led by the Spirit of God, they are the sons of God."*

Go back a couple of chapters and look at Rom. 6:12. *"Let not sin therefore reign in your mortal body, that ye should obey it in the lusts thereof. Neither yield ye your members as instruments of unrighteousness unto sin: but yield yourselves unto God, as those that are alive from the dead, and your members as instruments of righteousness unto God."*

Paul is writing to Christians here and he is asking to whom you are going to yield your life. He continues the thought in Rom. 6:16. *"Know ye not, that to whom ye yield yourselves servants to obey, his servants ye are to whom ye obey; whether of sin unto death, or of obedience unto righteousness?"*

These verses show us that we must give ourselves to the Lord and not just continue living in the flesh. But how do we do that?

We who accept Christ must understand that not only are we justified, which we have discussed previously, but we are also to be sanctified, or set apart to grow in the Lord. That growth is accomplished through God's Word and prayer.

I want to encourage every person reading this book to set aside some time each day for God and His Word. You can find helpful devotional materials on our church's Web site (www.thegathering-placefl.org) and in many other places in print and online. Get a separate book or journal with blank pages for writing down your prayer requests. Then, when God answers a prayer in your life, you can check it off and write down the date. This will give you quite a testimony.

Try to spend time with the Lord every day, and don't go on a guilt trip if you miss a day. Just pick it back up the next day. When you make this a part of your regular routine, God gives you a wisdom you didn't know you had. Sometimes a person will ask me a question and I will give an answer I didn't even know until that morning when I was having my own quiet time. That person will think I'm pretty smart when I'm really just trying to stay in the Word like everyone else should. When you are led by the Spirit, you can make a difference in other people's lives.

Also, when you are led by the Spirit you show that you are part of the family of God, as reflected by Rom. 8:14-17. *"For as many as are led by the Spirit of God, they are the sons of God. For ye have not received the spirit of bondage again to fear; but ye have received the Spirit of adoption, whereby we cry, Abba, Father. The Spirit itself beareth witness with our spirit, that we are the children of God: And if children, then heirs; heirs of God, and joint-heirs with Christ; if so be that we suffer with him, that we may be also glorified together."*

Every year during the holiday season, like most other pastors, I am contacted by people who are concerned about certain others they know who have no family and are approaching Christmas all alone. Our church family tries to help these people, as I'm sure your church does. Doctors tell us that loneliness is one of the greatest diseases known to mankind.

But when you become a child of God you join a mighty big family. The word "*adoption*" in this passage is not used in a way we might typically use that word. When you adopt a child, that child is yours but the bloodline is not there. In the family of God, however, everyone comes under the same bloodline – by the blood of Christ. In this case the word "*adoption*" means being placed as an adult.

This adoption is taken a step further in verse 23. "*And not only they, but ourselves also, which have the firstfruits of the Spirit, even we ourselves groan within ourselves, waiting for the adoption, to wit, the redemption of our body.*" This shows us that one day each of us will have a new body.

The nation of Israel is included in this adoption process, as we see in Rom. 9:4. "*Who are Israelites; to whom pertaineth the adoption, and the glory, and the covenants, and the giving of the law, and the service of God, and the promises.*"

Consider two other examples of this divine adoption:

"*To redeem them that were under the law, that we might receive the adoption of sons*" (Gal. 4:5).
"*Having predestinated us unto the adoption of children by Jesus Christ to himself, according to the good pleasure of his will*" (Eph. 1:5).

As soon as we come to Christ we need to begin growing in the things of God. When you see a baby spill some milk and start to cry, you want to comfort him. If a 20-year-old does that, you want to say, "Grow up." You expect to change a baby's diaper and you do so with loving attention, but soiled pants on an adult suggest a physical disability. A certain level of maturity is expected with advancing age, and the same applies to our spiritual lives.

It is important for each of us to look within ourselves and be certain that we are not the same Christians this year as we were last year. We have to maintain growth – to get past where we have been and move on to the next stage of life. If you struggle with that, you are not alone. Everyone faces that same struggle.

The next thought is also found in verse 14. If the Spirit has you, you are being led willingly by the Spirit. That is the idea conveyed by the verb in that verse.

There is a philosophy being taught in Christianity today that says, "When you receive Christ, everything is great. All of your troubles and heartaches are gone. Everything is just super." But you have likely found out through personal experience how untrue that line of thinking is. I spoke to a man recently who said he had more trouble in his life since he came to Christ than he did before.

Look at what verse 18 says. *"For I reckon that the sufferings of this present time are not worthy to be compared with the glory which shall be revealed in us."* If you want to live out your life for Christ, the devil will fight you because he doesn't want you to do that. You will encounter opposition that you never expected.

The Apostle Paul was stoned and left for dead in a city called Lystra. During that time he saw Heaven for a brief period of time, and this is partially chronicled in II Corinthians 12. Look at verses 2-4. *"I knew a man in Christ above fourteen years ago, (whether in the body, I cannot tell; or whether out of the body, I cannot tell: God knoweth;) such an one caught up to the third heaven. And I knew such a man, (whether in the body, or out of the body, I cannot tell: God knoweth;) How that he was caught up into paradise, and heard unspeakable words, which it is not lawful for a man to utter."*

God did a marvelous work in Paul's life with this episode, and he explains it to some degree in verse 7. *"And lest I should be exalted above measure through the abundance of the revelations, there was given to me a thorn in the flesh, the messenger of Satan to buffet me, lest I should be exalted above measure."*

There has been a great deal of discussion about who did what to Paul in this passage. Many people believe that the *"thorn in the flesh"* was a physical malady such as his poor eyesight. We don't know for certain, but we often wonder why it was allowed to happen.

When you are trying to live for God, Satan will put something in your life to preoccupy your mind. You will think about it when you wake up in the morning and when you go to bed at night, and all through the day whether you are thinking about nothing else or many other things.

"You can't live for the Lord," Satan tells you. "You can't do this great thing God wants you to do."

Paul pleaded with God three times for that infirmity to be removed, as II Cor. 12:8 indicates. I must say that I respect him for only asking three times; I would likely have kept begging God the rest of my life.

Verse 9 shows what Paul learned from this: "And he said unto me, My grace is sufficient for thee: for my strength is made perfect in weakness. Most gladly therefore will I rather glory in my infirmities, that the power of Christ may rest upon me."

If you live a life that is led by the Spirit, sooner or later you will encounter times of suffering. The devil is opposed to the kingdom of God and the work of Jesus Christ, and he does not want that work to go forward. He is more powerful than you and I, but he is no match for our Saviour.

The fourth thought I want to convey from this great passage in Romans 8 is that we have a new Father, as stated in verse 15. *"For ye have not received the spirit of bondage again to fear; but ye have received the Spirit of adoption, whereby we cry, Abba, Father."*

In this verse *"Abba"* is the Aramaic term for Papa or Daddy. You may have a wonderful relationship with your earthly father, or he may be someone you hardly know. But every child of God has a wonderful heavenly Father, and we are to live out our Christian lives under the auspices of this father-child relationship.

It is common for people to wonder just how this process of being led by the Spirit actually works. One day a man came to our house to sell a product, and he couldn't get it to work. Finally my wife asked him, "Shouldn't you plug it in?" That was the problem.

How do you get plugged in to this Spirit-led life? How do you work out what God is teaching us here?

To dig deeper into this relationship with our heavenly Father, let's look at what Jesus said in John 15, starting with the first four verses. "*I am the true vine, and my Father is the husbandman. Every branch in me that beareth not fruit he taketh away: and every branch that beareth fruit, he purgeth it, that it may bring forth more fruit. Now ye are clean through the word which I have spoken unto you. Abide in me, and I in you. As the branch cannot bear fruit of itself, except it abide in the vine; no more can ye, except ye abide in me.*"

Recently my wife and I spent nearly an entire day together at home with no one else around, just enjoying each other's company. We talked to each other and listened to each other – we were abiding in each other. Christ wants to abide in us, and He wants us to abide in Him.

Now look at verses 5-7. "*I am the vine, ye are the branches: He that abideth in me, and I in him, the same bringeth forth much fruit: for without me ye can do nothing. If a man abide not in me, he is cast forth as a branch, and is withered; and men gather them, and cast them into the fire, and they are burned. If ye abide in me, and my words abide in you, ye shall ask what ye will, and it shall be done unto you.*"

We have gone from "*fruit*" to "*much fruit*", and God's wonderful promise of how He will do what we ask of Him when we abide in Him.

That takes us to verses 8-10. "*Herein is my Father glorified, that ye bear much fruit; so shall ye be my disciples. As the Father hath loved me, so have I loved you: continue ye in my love. If ye keep my commandments, ye shall abide in my love; even as I have kept my Father's commandments, and abide in his love.*"

We have already mentioned how God does not expect us to be under the moral law of the Old Testament. We are not saved or kept by the law; that is not its purpose. The law brings us to Christ. So which commandments are we talking about?

Read on in verses 11-13. *"These things have I spoken unto you, that my joy might remain in you, and that your joy might be full. This is my commandment, That ye love one another, as I have loved you. Greater love hath no man than this, that a man lay down his life for his friends."*

Christ is saying here, "Do you want to know what love really is? Watch me. I am about to lay down my life for you."

His commandment is simplified even further in I John 3:23-24. *"And this is his commandment, That we should believe on the name of his Son Jesus Christ, and love one another, as he gave us commandment. And he that keepeth his commandments dwelleth in him, and he in him. And hereby we know that he abideth in us, by the Spirit which he hath given us."*

We are commanded to love one another. That doesn't mean we have to approve of or agree with each other all the time. This is agape love.

A pastor friend of mine once had another friend who did something he never should have done. This man ended up in jail, separated from his family and friends, and was ostracized by most people he knew. But my pastor friend did not do that.

Every other Saturday, whenever possible, he visited the man in jail. Through his actions he showed his friend that, while he did not approve of his actions, he loved him and was there for him. That is the kind of love Jesus is talking about.

The book "Tuesdays with Morrie" is about a man dying with Lou Gehrig's disease and his friend who gives of himself and comes to see him every week, helping him through this trial until his death. That is the kind of love Jesus is talking about.

I know of a family in my church that asks me every year for the names of people they can help financially during the holidays. They give a great deal of money to others without any recognition whatsoever, because they believe that is what Jesus wants them to do.

The commandment of our Lord is to be led by the Spirit, and if you do that you are not living just by the law. If you live by the law you will also die by the law, because it cannot save you and keep you. Only Jesus can do that.

If we are going to live out the Christian life as we should, we must do so with this unconditional love that Christ espouses here. You must love even those who reject you; you cannot do that alone, but with the Spirit's help you can. When we respond to others' bad attitudes with similar bad behavior, that dove that is the Holy Spirit will hesitate to get involved in your life and instead remain in the background.

People are sinners, and even saved people need to grow. God just wants us to believe in Him and love one another. It's a simple concept, even if the execution can be a bit difficult at times.

We see leaders in churches and denominations have problems with this. Holy wars are raged over insignificant differences in theology or practice. People who have been friends for many years turn on each other at the slightest provocation. You don't have to agree completely or go along with something you don't believe in, but you can show forgiveness and move on with your life.

Take one final look at Rom. 8:12-13. *"Therefore, brethren, we are debtors, not to the flesh, to live after the flesh. For if ye live after the flesh, ye shall die: but if ye through the Spirit do mortify the deeds of the body, ye shall live."*

We are indebted to Him, and in return we must live out our Christian lives with unconditional love, led by the Spirit of God.

Chapter 18

SOME THINGS TO CONSIDER

"For I reckon that the sufferings of this present time are not worthy to be compared with the glory which shall be revealed in us. For the earnest expectation of the creature waiteth for the manifestation of the sons of God. For the creature was made subject to vanity, not willingly, but by reason of him who hath subjected the same in hope, Because the creature itself also shall be delivered from the bondage of corruption into the glorious liberty of the children of God. For we know that the whole creation groaneth and travaileth in pain together until now. And not only they, but ourselves also, which have the firstfruits of the Spirit, even we ourselves groan within ourselves, waiting for the adoption, to wit, the redemption of our body. For we are saved by hope: but hope that is seen is not hope: for what a man seeth, why doth he yet hope for? But if we hope for that we see not, then do we with patience wait for it. Likewise the Spirit also helpeth our infirmities: for we know not what we should pray for as we ought: but the Spirit itself maketh intercession for us with groanings which cannot be uttered. And he that searcheth the hearts knoweth what is the mind of the Spirit, because he maketh intercession for the saints according to the will of God. And we know that all things work together for good to them that love God, to them who are the called according to

*his purpose. For whom he did foreknow, he also did predes-
tinate to be conformed to the image of his Son, that he might
be the firstborn among many brethren. Moreover whom he
did predestinate, them he also called: and whom he called,
them he also justified: and whom he justified, them he also
glorified."* **(Rom. 8:18-30)**

There are very few passages in the Word of God as potent and as powerful as this.

The first three words are *"for I reckon,"* which can also be translated as "for I consider." I want you to consider some of the things the Apostle Paul is writing about in these verses.

The word "consider" is a very interesting word. In our English Bible there are nine different Greek words that are translated as "consider" or similar word such as "reckon." In this particular instance the meaning is to think about or discover something. The idea is that you have been thinking over something you may have learned and you finally discover something new.

Perhaps the most-asked question in this section is the most difficult question to ask about God: Why does a loving God allow suffering and pain in the lives of His people?

Many years ago one of my mentors was the great pastor and evangelist B.R. Lakin. He had only one son, and one night he received a phone call informing him that his son had been killed in an auto accident. Often in his preaching he would say, "I know a little something about what it means to give your only son." One might wonder why the son of this servant of God was taken rather than the son of an atheist who mocked God.

Another well-known evangelist had a wife who loved God and served Him faithfully, yet their five children grew up questioning God. All of them had various problems throughout their lives.

George Truett was perhaps the best-known pastor in the United States at the beginning of the 20th century, leading the First Baptist Church of Dallas, Texas. One day while on a hunting trip he accidentally shot and killed his best friend.

Dr. Wendell Kempton led a great mission work based in Pennsylvania for many years. Upon his retirement, while traveling the world and preaching – having the time of his life – he discovered after a routine checkup that he had cancer all over his body, and he died only a few months later.

Dr. John McArthur, the teacher in southern California, had a young man come to his church for counseling. A short time later the man took his own life, and his family sued the church, saying it was to blame. Why would something like that happen when the church was only trying to help this troubled man?

It would not be unusual for a Christian to occasionally wonder, "Why does God allow these things to happen? Why doesn't He just inflict that pain on Muslims and leave His children alone?"

A few years ago Antony Flew, a leading British philosopher and atheist for decades who debated creationists and Christian leaders around the world, announced at the age of 81 that he had changed his view and now believed in God. It was an incredible confession by this man. He gave three reasons for his decision.

First, he cited the laws of nature. "Someone had to put all of these laws together," he said. His other reasons were the existence and organization of the universe, as he noted that there must be some reason behind its creation.

While many people applauded these statements, he was also quick to add while he believed there is a God, he still did not understand suffering.

Notice in our text that the word "*groan*" appears three times. The first two times it is from the same word that produced our English word "grieve," talking about a sigh or unexpressed sorrow in dealing with life's difficulties – a groaning of the Spirit. But you cannot read these verses without coming away with a feeling of great enthusiasm despite the numerous references to suffering in life.

If you live long enough, you will suffer. It's that simple. All of us will question these things at some point in life. But why must suffering happen to the Christian? We might understand if it happened to other people, to bring them to God – but not us.

Let's look in verses 18-22 at what I like to call **creation's groan**. Verse 18 says, "*For I reckon that the sufferings of this present time are not worthy to be compared with the glory which shall be revealed in us.*"

Look at I Pet. 5:10. *"But the God of all grace, who hath called us unto his eternal glory by Christ Jesus, after that ye have suffered a while, make you perfect, stablish, strengthen, settle you."*

We can surmise from these verses that there is a purpose, a meaning and a reason for suffering. We have peer counseling at our church, which means that people are counseled by others who have been through similar experiences. Paul emphasizes in verse 18 that our suffering now does not compare to the later glory, but our suffering is important because people notice how we handle it.

Verse 19 says, *"For the earnest expectation of the creature waiteth for the manifestation of the sons of God."* One translation puts it this way: "The whole creation is on tiptoe to see the wonderful sights of the sons of God coming into their own."

Here is our problem today. We are living in a world that is cursed. The Bible says in II Cor. 4:17, *"For our light affliction, which is but for a moment, worketh for us a far more exceeding and eternal weight of glory."* Our suffering teaches us that our bodies, like this planet we live on, is under a curse.

I remember well an episode when my wife and I were riding in our car down the interstate. "They don't make the lettering on the road signs as large as they used to," I told her. "I can hardly read them."

My wife didn't hesitate. "Honey, it's your eyes," she said.

"No, my eyes are fine," I insisted.

It was only a few months later that I was being introduced to the world of eyeglasses and contact lenses. Now I find myself checking those every year or so because things still seem to be getting smaller. I am part of the cursed creation.

I love to play tennis. When I was younger I could chase the ball down and keep hitting it back until my opponent was worn down. Now my mind tells me to go get the ball but my body says, "No, we're staying right here." Our bodies break down because of the curse of creation.

Verses 20-21 talk about a life of emptiness and bondage similar to that of a slave. We are enslaved to our bodies and to ourselves.

If I told you I was going to the top of a skyscraper in downtown Miami, a few miles from my home, watch some birds for a few moments to see how they fly and then do the same thing myself, you would tell me, "Pastor, that will never happen." You might even call some professionals in white coats and tell them to have a strait jacket standing by. In short, I am not a bird. I am what I am, and I will never fly under my own power.

We have a new dog at our house. He is small and full of life, although not too smart at this point. He will go in our back yard, where hundreds of birds seem to have decided to hold a convention, and chase those birds. He will even try to soar through the air like they do, but he only gets a few inches off the ground. He's not a bird; he's a dog.

We are in bondage to this world, and verse 21 even calls it "*the bondage of corruption*," or a state of decay. Verse 22 goes on to speak about pain. But in the midst of this there is a contrast that is present throughout this passage.

It starts in verse 18, when Paul points out that our present suffering cannot compare to our future glory. Verse 19 contrasts the present state of creation with the glorious fact that we will one day be changed. The word "*vanity*" in verse 20, which could also be translated as "futility," is contrasted with "*hope.*" Verse 21 differentiates between "*the bondage of corruption*" and "*the glorious liberty of the children of God.*"

The pain described in verse 22 brings to mind the travails of a woman giving birth. Some women have gone through that pain many times, but the goal is always the same – the delivery of that beautiful child. One day our sufferings will result in a delivery to glory. We must strive to see that our character survives our suffering, as people see how we react to what we are facing.

That brings me to the second thought, which is the **Christian's groan**. The word "*hope*" is used a number of times in this passage (four times in verse 24 alone), and as we have discussed previously, this refers to a confident expectation. The phrase "*earnest expectation*" appears in verse 19, and here it means "to watch with an outstretched head." We are stretching and even straining our necks to see what is going to happen, and until the fulfillment is realized we are constantly looking ahead. Phil. 1:20 also speaks of this "*earnest expectation.*"

When children get out of bed on Christmas morning, the first thing they want to do is run to the Christmas tree and unwrap their gifts, fulfilling the expectation of the past several weeks. I was at a meeting in Orlando a few years ago when a rocket was being launched at the Kennedy Space Center, and we all walked outdoors and strained to get a glimpse of the spacecraft soaring into the sky from some 40 miles away. That is the type of expectation Paul is referring to in these verses.

This is prophecy. The next event we are all looking forward to is when Jesus Christ will come again. It could happen at any time, even today. That is the rapture of the church, which is immediately followed by seven years of tribulation and then the Lord's kingdom on this earth for 1,000 glorious years, after which He rules and reigns in Heaven forever. Don't focus on your suffering today; focus instead on what God is doing for your future.

We can go back to II Cor. 4:15-18 and see more verses that speak to what we are studying in this portion of Romans. *"For all things are for your sakes, that the abundant grace might through the thanksgiving of many redound to the glory of God. For which cause we faint not; but though our outward man perish, yet the inward man is renewed day by day. For our light affliction, which is but for a moment, worketh for us a far more exceeding and eternal weight of glory; While we look not at the things which are seen, but at the things which are not seen: for the things which are seen are temporal; but the things which are not seen are eternal."*

An important story regarding the children of Israel is illustrated in Numbers 13. According to verses 23-25, *"And they came unto the brook of Eshcol, and cut down from thence a branch with one cluster of grapes, and they bare it between two upon a staff; and they brought of the pomegranates, and of the figs. The place was called the brook Eshcol, because of the cluster of grapes which the children of Israel cut down from thence. And they returned from searching of the land after forty days."*

When the spies returned from the land of Canaan, they began to understand what was happening and they brought back a taste of what was there. While you and I are living in this present world, we must understand that God will give us a taste of Heaven by the Holy

Spirit at various times in our lives and it will make us want to see the land that God has prepared for us. Your suffering here is temporary and it doesn't compare to the eternal things God has waiting for us over there.

We can also have a taste of Heaven when we realize how God is working in us and doing something great through us, and the way we deal with our suffering shows others how they can deal with theirs. While we are *"waiting for the adoption, to wit, the redemption of our body"* as Rom. 8:23 puts it, we realize that the best is yet to come.

I conducted a funeral service some months ago, and as I got out of the car at the cemetery and prepared to lead the casket to the grave site I noticed a man seated near where the hearse was parked. He appeared 75 or 80 years old, and he sat with his Bible open to Matthew 24-25, which speaks about the coming of the Lord. Next to him was a fresh grave that appeared to be the resting place of his wife.

I made a mental note to speak to this man after the service, and when I came back by I asked him if his wife's body lay there. "Yes," he said. "I'm waiting here for the Lord to come."

Jesus Christ is coming again, and some of you are probably wondering right now why He doesn't just show up. Have you ever noticed how you don't think about His coming as much when things are going well? But when things are going bad, you say, "Even so, come, Lord Jesus."

When I was preparing to get married, I didn't want the Lord to come because I wanted to spend many years with my wife. Once all four of our children arrived, there were a few days that I thought would be great opportunities for His return.

The reason we think that way so often is that for the child of God, the best is yet to come. Our best times are still ahead.

Verses 25-30 tell us about the Holy Spirit's groan. We see from these verses that the Holy Spirit is sensitive to our groaning and suffering.

Why does the Lord not simply come now and end our suffering? Look at II Pet. 3:9. *"The Lord is not slack concerning his promise, as some men count slackness; but is longsuffering to us-ward, not willing that any should perish, but that all should come to repentance."*

But one day the last soul will be brought into the family of God, and Jesus will come. Until that time, the Holy Spirit is praying for us.

Consider these amazing words in verse 26. *"Likewise the Spirit also helpeth our infirmities: for we know not what we should pray for as we ought: but the Spirit itself maketh intercession for us with groanings which cannot be uttered."* You probably have realized at times that you didn't really know just what to pray for. The Holy Spirit does, and He helps you.

Bible scholar John Phillips put it this way: "Most of us feel particularly helpless in the matter of prayer. We stand appalled at times before the deep antipathy of our hearts to pray. Perfunctorily we say our prayers, but seldom do we really pray. There is not merit in saying prayers; even an unsaved person can do that. But only a Spirit-taught believer can really pray, because the ministry of prayer is a purely spiritual ministry and we stand in need of the Holy Spirit to help our infirmities in like manner."

The word *"help"* that is referred to in verses 26-27 comes from a word that is found in only one other place in the New Testament. It is the familiar story in Luke 10, where Mary and Martha are with Christ, but Mary is worshipping while Martha is doing all of the work. When Martha got tired of Mary getting all of the good things from the Lord while she worked, she asked Jesus to tell Mary to come and help her. This word is used again in this portion of Romans to emphasize the fact that God wants to help us, even in our prayer lives. Also, the word *"groan"* is a different word here, talking about standing before someone who will come to your defense.

There are three reasons that He goes to our defense in prayer. First, He is searching our hearts. Second, He knows our hearts in all things. Third, He is helping us pray according to the will of God.

Many times we have prayed as if to say, "Lord, here is what we're going to do." Then, when God doesn't do it just as we instructed Him, we wonder if He is listening to us. God does not operate that way.

When you look back at things, you will find that God has done things in your life in a pretty good way. Even when you have gone through some of the most difficult suffering of your life. You have to admit that the Spirit of God was in it.

When you pray, the Holy Spirit is praying for you. That is an awesome thought.

If people come to you and say they have been praying for you, and you know they really mean it, that's a pretty good feeling. I am telling you today that the Holy Spirit is doing the same thing. He is saying to each of us, "I am praying for you." Prayer is worth more than we could ever imagine.

We quote Rom. 8:28 over and over again, especially when things are going wrong. *"And we know that all things work together for good to them that love God, to them who are the called according to his purpose."* But this is just one of many things God is saying in this passage. The Spirit of God is encouraging us not to faint, and for us to succeed there is a process that we must follow, which is outlined in verses 29-30.

"For whom he did foreknow, he also did predestinate to be conformed to the image of his Son, that he might be the firstborn among many brethren. Moreover whom he did predestinate, them he also called: and whom he called, them he also justified: and whom he justified, them he also glorified."

I remember when I tried out for the baseball team in high school as a pitcher and third baseman. As would-be players were dropped from the team, we would anxiously consult the sheet that was posted at the school announcing the members of the team. If you weren't on the list, you had been cut. God is telling us here that He already has our name down and He is not taking it off.

Predestination refers to the fact that we have been ordained to one day be like the Son of God. Our goal in life is to be more like Jesus. No one is predestined to be condemned; one is only condemned because of his refusal to trust Christ as Saviour. This is reinforced in John 3:18-21.

"He that believeth on him is not condemned: but he that believeth not is condemned already, because he hath not

believed in the name of the only begotten Son of God. And this is the condemnation, that light is come into the world, and men loved darkness rather than light, because their deeds were evil. For every one that doeth evil hateth the light, neither cometh to the light, lest his deeds should be reproved. But he that doeth truth cometh to the light, that his deeds may be made manifest, that they are wrought in God."

People die and go to Hell not because God sent them there. It is only because they did not accept Christ. That is the choice each of us has.

Verses 29-30 of Romans 8 point out that we are not only predestined, but we are called. As we see in II Thess. 2:13-14, *"But we are bound to give thanks alway to God for you, brethren beloved of the Lord, because God hath from the beginning chosen you to salvation through sanctification of the Spirit and belief of the truth: Whereunto he called you by our gospel, to the obtaining of the glory of our Lord Jesus Christ."*

We are also justified and glorified. Jesus said in John 17:22, *"And the glory which thou gavest me I have given them; that they may be one, even as we are one."*

All of this brings us to the ultimate purpose of what God is teaching us here. The first thing is the matter of His glory. We have to accept the fact that we are not here on this earth for God to make us happy. That is very hard for most of us to accept.

God did not intend for us to have a great deal of wealth or success just for our own benefit. We are here for no other reason except to bring glory back to Him. A lot of people just want to have fun, and I like to have fun. But that's not the only reason to live; it's only temporary. You can have a good time as a child of God, but mainly because you are glorifying Him.

God also has us here for our own good. Go back to our original question: Why does a loving God allow suffering? Anyone who claims to have all of the answers on this subject has not experienced very much suffering.

But when you get your eyes on Jesus at the cross, you will start to get a better idea of suffering. Nothing we can go through in this life can compare to His suffering, and He did it all just for you. We must also remember that suffering is temporary, while eternity is forever.

You will not have full satisfaction from anything in life – your spouse, family, career, whatever – because you expect a kind of satisfaction that only Jesus can give to you. I have learned that nothing you look forward to in this world is all that you expected it to be. That's just the way life is. But when you get to Heaven you will find that it is far better than you expected it to be.

I met a family whose son had been killed as a young man. Their pastor, Jerry Falwell, met with them and put his arms around them, telling them, "It's going to be OK."

Whatever you are going through in life, at the end of the day it's going to be OK. One day you will look back and agree that it was all for your good and God's glory, and our only responsibility is to obey what God has told us.

Chapter 19

NEVER TO BE
SEPARATED AGAIN

"What shall we then say to these things? If God be for us, who can be against us? He that spared not his own Son, but delivered him up for us all, how shall he not with him also freely give us all things? Who shall lay any thing to the charge of God's elect? It is God that justifieth. Who is he that condemneth? It is Christ that died, yea rather, that is risen again, who is even at the right hand of God, who also maketh intercession for us. Who shall separate us from the love of Christ? shall tribulation, or distress, or persecution, or famine, or nakedness, or peril, or sword? As it is written, For thy sake we are killed all the day long; we are accounted as sheep for the slaughter. Nay, in all these things we are more than conquerors through him that loved us. For I am persuaded, that neither death, nor life, nor angels, nor principalities, nor powers, nor things present, nor things to come, Nor height, nor depth, nor any other creature, shall be able to separate us from the love of God, which is in Christ Jesus our Lord." **(Rom. 8:31-39)**

The first time in my life that I experienced real separation from someone I dearly loved was at the death of my father. He was a wonderful man whom I respected greatly, but he was also a great friend. We had some wonderful times together.

He was recovering from a massive heart attack when he suffered a second heart attack that took his life. I remember the phone call from my mom as if it were today. I rushed to their house and saw him lying there, knowing he was gone even though the paramedics were working feverishly to revive him.

A number of things go through your mind at a time like this. My first thought was that I would never see my father on this earth ever again. I recalled his great sense of humor that we often shared, and I quickly realized that all future visits to that house would not be to see Mom and Dad – it would be to see Mom.

We talked about sports a lot, as you might imagine, but we also talked a great deal about theology. I would tell him my theology and he would tell me his; we were probably both wrong, but we had a great time of discussion. We took fishing trips together and made many fantastic memories.

As he lay dead I recognized that there was now a separation. He was gone. At the funeral I put my hand upon his hand in the casket and said to myself, "This isn't my father. He's gone, and I will see him again."

No matter the circumstances, earthly separations are difficult. But this passage in Romans tells us that there is no separation between you and your God. That relationship will last throughout your entire life and continue for eternity.

The word "separate" means to depart or put asunder. Leaving is a constant part of life. Any special occasion spent with family or friends must come to an end, and we go our separate ways until the next gathering. There are always going to be times of separation.

But that's not the case regarding the Christian's relationship with God. Just as verse 1 of Romans 8 tells us there is *"no condemnation"* for those who are in Christ, the final verse of that great chapter points out that there is no separation from His love. This portion of Scripture addresses a wonderful truth of the Bible known as the security of the believer.

Christ loved us in the past, He loves us now and will continue to love us in the future, no matter what. It is hard to imagine this kind of love, but it is there. We are secure in Him because of what He has done and our acceptance of Him.

The first eight chapters of Romans make up an important section of the Bible. It begins by telling us how bad we were, then what God did for us, and now this elevated position we have in Jesus Christ. These nine verses that conclude Romans 8 give us at least five arguments that show why we are secure in Christ.

The first argument is the fact that **God is for us**. What an amazing thought. During the Civil War someone asked Abraham Lincoln, "Whose side is God on? Is it the North or the South?" Lincoln wisely replied, "That is the wrong question. We should instead be asking, 'Are we on God's side?'"

After outlining in Romans 8 so many great things God has done for us, Paul writes these telling words in verse 31: *"What shall we then say to these things? If God be for us, who can be against us?"* You need to realize today that God is for you. He loves you regardless of what you have done, and His love is something you could never earn anyway. Simply put, He has chosen to love you.

Verse 33 shows us that God the Father loves us. *"Who shall lay any thing to the charge of God's elect? It is God that justifieth."*

Verse 34 shows us that God the Son loves us. *"Who is he that condemneth? It is Christ that died, yea rather, that is risen again, who is even at the right hand of God, who also maketh intercession for us."*

Back in verse 26 we see that God the Holy Spirit loves us. *"Likewise the Spirit also helpeth our infirmities: for we know not what we should pray for as we ought: but the Spirit itself maketh intercession for us with groanings which cannot be uttered."*

God is for us – Father, Son and Holy Spirit. At times it seems that everything is working against us, even though we are His children, but we have to remember that He is always working things out for our best.

You are probably familiar with the story of Joseph, who endured many things in his life we would not want to endure. When he finally revealed himself in Genesis 45 to his brothers, who thought for years that he was dead, he did so with tears in his eyes. In verse 5 of that chapter he said to them, *"Now therefore be not grieved, nor angry with yourselves, that ye sold me hither: for God did send me before you to preserve life.*" He showed them that, while they did a terrible thing to him, he was being used of God all along.

Joseph's brothers had a plan for getting rid of him, but God had other plans. Gen. 50:20 says, "*But as for you, ye thought evil against me; but God meant it unto good, to bring to pass, as it is this day, to save much people alive.*"

This story is a prime example of the principle in Rom. 8:28. "*And we know that all things work together for good to them that love God, to them who are the called according to his purpose.*"

Every day, if you are a child of God, He is working in your life. There is no need to fear because He is in control. We may often think that He isn't doing such a great job because of things that are happening to us, but if God is for us, then He knows what is best for us. Remember the words of Jer. 29:11. "*For I know the thoughts that I think toward you, saith the LORD, thoughts of peace, and not of evil, to give you an expected end.*"

I spoke recently to a group of physicians as part of a new ministry one of our church members started called Doctors for Christ. I asked them what their dreams in life were, then I told them, "If you have a dream and God is in it, when you get to the end of that dream it will look a lot different than you thought it would look when you started." I believe that with all my heart.

God loves you because He has chosen to love you. He is for you because that is His desire. "Jesus loves me, this I know, for the Bible tells me so."

Many years ago I went to visit one of my professors in college; he was a man who had been a mentor in my early life. I had heard that his wife suffered from Lou Gehrig's disease.

He welcomed me into his home and took me back to the bedroom where she lay as an invalid. Actually it was somewhat amusing because they were watching "I Love Lucy" on television.

"We're glad you came to see us," he said, "but we want to watch the end of the show. Please join us."

We watched it together, although I don't remember what the episode was about. Then as we visited for a few moments, I noticed how he carefully fed his wife from a bowl of soup and even scratched an itch on her nose without her telling him. It was incredible to see the love this man had for his wife.

The two of us walked back to the living room and he asked me to pray for him, which I was honored to do. After I finished praying he said to me, "You know, I love that woman in there. I will do anything I can for her."

That is a lot of love. However, your God loves you far greater than that.

The second argument is that **Christ died for us**, as expressed in verse 32. *"He that spared not his own Son, but delivered him up for us all, how shall he not with him also freely give us all things?"*

This is what is referred to in the debating arena as "the lesser to the greater." The point here is that when we were sinners God gave us His best, and now that we are His children He will give us exactly what we need. God cared for people before the law; He cared for them under the law; and He continues to care for them in the age of grace. If God cares for the sheep, the birds and the lilies of the field, don't you think He also cares for us?

God gave us His best, and there is nothing better. When Adam sinned he was declared unrighteous, but Jesus died and rose again so that we could be declared righteous. Christ's work on the cross brings about justification, and as He died on the cross and rose again, so have we died and risen in Him. We need to understand as Christians that we can live in victory because of what He has given to us.

Many Christians try to put one foot in the world and the other in the Kingdom, but it doesn't work that way. I have to remember that because my union in Christ is secure, I must live out my life for Him.

Look at Col. 3:1. *"If ye then be risen with Christ, seek those things which are above, where Christ sitteth on the right hand of God."* A child of God will not live in deliberate sin because of his new identification in Christ. We have the Spirit of God upon our lives.

So many Christians act like they are going to live in depression for the rest of their days; they never smile or show any joy. My friend, Jesus loves you and cares about you. That is reason enough to smile all day long. But if God thought enough of you to send His

Son to die for you, don't you think He might have something special in mind for your life?

The reason most of us don't smile is that we just look at our circumstances, which always have a tendency to weigh us down. Satan used our circumstances to discourage us.

Go back to the Old Testament and look at Zech. 3:1. *"And he shewed me Joshua the high priest standing before the angel of the LORD, and Satan standing at his right hand to resist him."* This is a picture of your life and mine, as Satan is constantly on guard and ready to accuse us. If Satan cannot have your soul, he wants to take away your testimony or your influence.

But look at the next four verses of that chapter. *"And the LORD said unto Satan, The LORD rebuke thee, O Satan; even the LORD that hath chosen Jerusalem rebuke thee: is not this a brand plucked out of the fire? Now Joshua was clothed with filthy garments, and stood before the angel. And he answered and spake unto those that stood before him, saying, Take away the filthy garments from him. And unto him he said, Behold, I have caused thine iniquity to pass from thee, and I will clothe thee with change of raiment. And I said, Let them set a fair mitre upon his head. So they set a fair mitre upon his head, and clothed him with garments. And the angel of the LORD stood by."*

When you and I stand before God, it is in these same *"filthy garments."* Isaiah even calls them *"filthy rags,"* which actually is a reference to leprous rags. We have nothing whatsoever to offer to God.

Satan says, "Look at your condition. You don't amount to anything." But along comes grace in the form of Jesus Christ, and now you stand before God clothed in the righteousness of Christ, and God considers you one of His children now and forever.

The third argument, illustrated in verse 33, is **justification**. This has been in important topic throughout the book of Romans.

Notice how we are referred to in that verse as *"God's elect."* Satan tries to tell us that we don't belong in the family of God, but we are in there – not because of what we have done, but because of what Christ has done. That will never change; we may accuse ourselves, but God will never accuse us because He has justified us.

Go back to the beginning of Romans and you can see, from Rom. 1:8 to 3:23, the description of our awful condition as sinners. A good example is found in Rom. 1:32. *"Who knowing the judgment of God, that they which commit such things are worthy of death, not only do the same, but have pleasure in them that do them."*

That thought is continued in the very next verse, which is Rom. 2:1. *"Therefore thou art inexcusable, O man, whosoever thou art that judgest: for wherein thou judgest another, thou condemnest thyself; for thou that judgest doest the same things."* It is easy for us to judge other people, but too many are caught up in their own morality and religion, neither of which ever saved anyone.

Look at Rom. 3:20. *"Therefore by the deeds of the law there shall no flesh be justified in his sight: for by the law is the knowledge of sin."* Some people think one is saved by the law, but the law only exists to show us how wicked we are.

But right after declaring in Rom. 3:23 that all of us are sinners, these are the wonderful words of verse 24: *"Being justified freely by his grace through the redemption that is in Christ Jesus."* Grace is the only instrument that can save anyone. We are not saved by anything we have done in the church or anywhere else; it is only by the grace of God.

Chapter 4 of Romans talks about being justified by faith, and chapter 5 shows us how faith triumphs in so many areas of life. The transformation from being slaves of sin to slaves of God is covered in chapter 6, while chapter 7 highlights our freedom from the law. That takes us into this chapter, which concludes so wonderfully with our security as children of God.

If everything in these chapters is true, then we should all be living like it. Each of us should live as a child of God in attitude and action, and all of us should be living in victory.

The fourth argument, in verse 34, is that **Christ intercedes on our behalf**. *"Who is he that condemneth? It is Christ that died, yea rather, that is risen again, who is even at the right hand of God, who also maketh intercession for us."*

Jesus is praying for you. That is an amazing thought. As we saw earlier in verses 26-27, the Holy Spirit also prays for us. Christ died for us, intercedes for us and gives us all of the grace we need.

The book of Hebrews reminds us that when we are tempted and tested, God has already been there with you. That means we are victors. Our society is obsessed with winning and losing; just ask the coaches of your favorite college and professional teams if there is not pressure on them to win. There is something in all of us that wants to win, and this section of Scripture shows us that we are winners. We should be rejoicing in that.

Look at how this victory is expressed beginning in Rom. 8:35. *"Who shall separate us from the love of Christ? shall tribulation, or distress, or persecution, or famine, or nakedness, or peril, or sword?"*

Those first two examples are the trials and circumstances of life. The reference to persecution is particularly timely, as there is more persecution for the cause of Christ in our world today than at any point in human history (and more martyrs). Paul also cites economic hardship and the absence of peace in a society as other possible situations. But none of these dark moments of life can separate us from God's love.

We all struggle with the concept of unconditional love. As fickle people, we are easily offended and prone to turn our backs on people who hurt us. But that is nothing like the character of God.

Look at verses 36-37. *"As it is written, For thy sake we are killed all the day long; we are accounted as sheep for the slaughter. Nay, in all these things we are more than conquerors through him that loved us."*

We are conquerors, and we should act like it. This position, as plainly stated in verse 37, is because of Christ.

That leads us to the fifth argument, which is that **Christ loves us**. Read verses 38-39. *"For I am persuaded, that neither death, nor life, nor angels, nor principalities, nor powers, nor things present, nor things to come, Nor height, nor depth, nor any other creature, shall be able to separate us from the love of God, which is in Christ Jesus our Lord."*

These verses say something very powerful and profound. I want you to consider three particular thoughts regarding this passage.

First, the fact that Christ loves us does not mean that God will always shelter us from difficulties of life, because we need those difficulties for spiritual growth. Rom. 5:3-5 says, *"And not only so, but we glory in tribulations also: knowing that tribulation worketh patience; And patience, experience; and experience, hope: And hope maketh not ashamed; because the love of God is shed abroad in our hearts by the Holy Ghost which is given unto us."*

As we saw in a previous chapter, the patience we gather through our trials is what builds character, and then the hope of what God will do in our lives.

Second, the difficulties of life are always working for us and not against us. That is hard to understand when you are going through a tough time, but that's exactly what God is teaching us.

An evangelist was conducting a crusade back in the days of the great tent meetings and he said there was nothing happening at this meeting; it was dead. He preached to a handful of people each night and no one seemed to respond. Finally an old man came forward and asked to pray with this preacher, and he agreed.

"Lord, I don't like sugar all by itself," the old man began praying. "I don't like vanilla or flour by itself."

Just as the evangelist began to wonder if the old man had lost his mind, he said, "But Lord, when all of it is mixed together, I sure love the taste of that chocolate cake."

The evangelist realized the truth of that prayer. Life is made up of many things, some of which may seem unpleasant on their own. But God knows how the cake will taste when it is finished, even though we don't. He is working for us, and everything is happening for our good.

Third, God gives us the power to conquer. The promises in the final verses of Romans 8 do not have conditions attached to them. This security in Christ is an established fact, not based on anything we may or may not do for Him now and in the future.

There is no faith like the Christian faith. All other faiths involve works on our part, but Christianity is not based upon what we accomplish.

William Barclay was asked late in life, after many years teaching and lecturing around the world, about what he considered the greatest truth he knew. He replied, "Jesus loves me, this I know; for the Bible tells me so."

We all know what we are really like, and we don't want other people to know it because we're afraid they won't like us. God knows all about us, and He loves us in spite of that. Love is a choice, and we should choose to love others in our lives just as He has chosen to love us.

Can anything separate us from Him? As this passage has shown us, the answer to that question is no. He will continue to love you no matter what.

Chapter 20

DOES GOD MAKE MISTAKES?

"I say the truth in Christ, I lie not, my conscience also bearing me witness in the Holy Ghost, That I have great heaviness and continual sorrow in my heart. For I could wish that myself were accursed from Christ for my brethren, my kinsmen according to the flesh: Who are Israelites; to whom pertaineth the adoption, and the glory, and the covenants, and the giving of the law, and the service of God, and the promises; Whose are the fathers, and of whom as concerning the flesh Christ came, who is over all, God blessed for ever. Amen. Not as though the word of God hath taken none effect. For they are not all Israel, which are of Israel: Neither, because they are the seed of Abraham, are they all children: but, In Isaac shall thy seed be called. That is, They which are the children of the flesh, these are not the children of God: but the children of the promise are counted for the seed. For this is the word of promise, At this time will I come, and Sarah shall have a son. And not only this; but when Rebecca also had conceived by one, even by our father Isaac; (For the children being not yet born, neither having done any good or evil, that the purpose of God according to election might stand, not of works, but of him that calleth;) It was said unto

her, The elder shall serve the younger. As it is written, Jacob have I loved, but Esau have I hated." (**Rom. 9:1-13**)

Does God make mistakes? The quick and easy answer would be no, but we all must admit that there are times when we wonder if He knows what He is doing.

Anyone who reads the Bible even casually can recognize from hundreds of references in the Old and New Testament that God has a chosen nation. Israel is the apple of His eye. But did God make a mistake with Israel now that everyone has the opportunity to become part of the family of God?

Do you ever wonder why some people are saved and others are not? Certainly you have wondered at various times why some people seem to have it easier in life than others. A constant question for thousands of people is why they have been able to live in the United States of America, a land of plenty, while billions of people have so little in other parts of the world.

Perhaps the greatest question is why it often seems that some people suffer a great deal and others hardly suffer at all, if ever. That motivates many observers to ask if God has made a mistake or two.

In Romans 9-11 the Apostle Paul begins to talk about what God has done and how He deals with certain issues, and part of that discussion centers on the nation of Israel, which was the chosen of God throughout the Old Testament. These passages in Romans address whether God abandoned the Israelites or what kind of future they might have.

It is awesome to be a child of God. I consider it awesome to be a part of my church, and you probably feel the same way. But the most awesome thing about life is to understand who God is. The word "awesome" is often misused in our society today, but it cannot be overstated when that word is used to refer to God.

The ninth chapter of Romans is directed at the nation of Israel, the only nation on this earth with a history as complete as it is. We can trace its origin back to Abraham, who lived thousands of years ago. It still exists today and we know its future because the Bible lays it out for us. Our country, the United States, began in 1776 and we often do not know what its future holds. But we know the future of Israel.

As we have seen, the book of Romans paints a picture of what God has done for us. In the opening verses of chapter 9 Paul tells of the burden of his heart, that his countrymen would know these great truths about God.

As parents and grandparents we all have a burden for our children. But what is that burden? First and foremost, it should be a burden that they know the Lord and want to follow Him. We can be burdened for their education and their choices regarding marriage and career, but that shouldn't be all we worry about regarding our children.

Saul of Tarsus was a Jew of the Jews. He had been a man who sought to have Christians put in jail and even to death. On the Damascus Road he saw that this Jesus whom he had been persecuting was more than he expected Him to be, and Saul of Tarsus became the great missionary we know as the Apostle Paul. But he also was known as a traitor to the Jewish nation.

He ministered to the Gentiles and taught about freedom from the law. He preached in the synagogues and was seen as a troublemaker. He had a questionable reputation with the Jewish leaders.

During a presidential campaign the media bombards us with information. Recently Oprah Winfrey was asked if she would ever run for public office and she replied that she would not because she could not stand the public scrutiny. Our candidates today are living in glass houses, with every move they make being examined under a microscope.

Paul was seen in a similar light because of his former notoriety as a Jewish leader. Now he has spoken out about his burden that his fellow Jews, whom he loves, come to know the Lord. This leads to questions concerning the future of Israel.

Paul taught that Israel's election as a chosen nation of God would stand firm, and God would not break His promise. Did God make a mistake concerning Israel? No, and He has made no mistakes in your life, either.

Here is what we have in Romans 9-11: Israel's past election in chapter 9, its present rejection in chapter 10, and its future restoration in chapter 11. Paul is defending the character of God in chapter 9 by showing that Israel's past history magnified the characteristics and attributes of God. Four attributes are shown in this chapter: His faithfulness (verses 1-13), His righteousness (14-18), His justice (19-29) and His grace (30-33).

When we ask if God makes any mistakes, we are actually looking at whether He is faithful to do what He says He will do. I try to be a faithful husband because my wife deserves it. She has been good to me through our years of marriage before and after our children arrived. It's easy for me to want to be a faithful husband because she has been good to me. She deserves that.

But we need to understand that God is faithful to us when we don't deserve His faithfulness. God is faithful because He has chosen to be faithful. If He promises to bless and honor Israel, then you can rest assured that He will follow through on that promise.

Look at Israel's election in verses 4-5. *"Who are Israelites; to whom pertaineth the adoption, and the glory, and the covenants, and the giving of the law, and the service of God, and the promises; Whose are the fathers, and of whom as concerning the flesh Christ came, who is over all, God blessed for ever."*

Paul expressed in verse 3 the great burden he had for his people, the Jews, even suggesting that he be separated from God if it meant that they could come to Him.

Sometimes a child has a burden for a father who has forsaken him, or a widow is burdened about a husband who has passed away. The burden of a parent might be a child who is not living right. Paul's burden was for his people to be brought into the family of God.

The *"covenants"* mentioned in verse 4 refer to the Abrahamic covenant, in which God promised to *"bless them that bless thee, and curse him that curseth thee"* (Gen. 12:3). By the way, we should remember as a country and as individual Christians that it is our responsibility to bless the nation of Israel. That is God's plan, and He has not broken His promise. Other covenants shared with Israel include the law given to Moses and the promise to David that the Messiah would one day sit on his throne.

When you read the Old Testament you will not often find God mentioned as a father. It was when Jesus came on the scene that this aspect of God came to light, as Christ referred to Him as "Abba Father" or Papa Father. How wonderful to have that kind of relationship with God.

Verse 6 says, "*Not as though the word of God hath taken none effect.*" That is a straightforward declaration that God's promises will be fulfilled and come to pass. This phrase is actually translated as to refer to a ship veering off-course.

You book a cruise and there is a pre-planned itinerary. But it can change. You might be scheduled to stop in Cancun but a storm comes along and sends you to Cozumel instead. You might start wondering where else you'll end up. But God will follow through on what he says and there will be no deviation from that course. If you love God and follow Him, He will come through for you time after time. He always comes through exactly as He wishes, because He is God and can do whatever He wants.

Have you ever rooted for a team in a big game that came down to the final play? It was pretty nerve-wracking up to that point, but your team came through. That is how God works sometimes. You may have issues in your life and you're wondering if God is going to come through for you. I can assure you that He will – but it will be at the time of His choosing.

Look at the basis of God's election in verses 7-10. "*For they are not all Israel, which are of Israel: Neither, because they are the seed of Abraham, are they all children: but, In Isaac shall thy seed be called. That is, They which are the children of the flesh, these are not the children of God: but the children of the promise are counted for the seed. For this is the word of promise, At this time will I come, and Sarah shall have a son. And not only this; but when Rebecca also had conceived by one, even by our father Isaac...*"

The basis of the election of Israel was not of natural descent. Stop and think about it for a moment. Ishmael was born, then Isaac. When Isaac's twins were born, Esau came out before Jacob. In Jewish families the oldest is considered the patriarch or the son of promise, but God chose Isaac and then Jacob. Those were His choices to make.

I have had people tell me, "I was born a Catholic, I am still a Catholic today, and I will die a Catholic." Others have said the same thing about being a Baptist, Methodist, Democrat, Republican, New York Yankees fan, or whatever. But your status or religious affiliation is unimportant compared to the crucial question of whether you have accepted Christ as your Saviour. That is the only thing that matters.

God chose the Jewish nation through which to send us the Messiah, even though it was not of traditional descent. But as we see in verses 11-13, it was not of human merit, either.

"(For the children being not yet born, neither having done any good or evil, that the purpose of God according to election might stand, not of works, but of him that calleth;) It was said unto her, The elder shall serve the younger. As it is written, Jacob have I loved, but Esau have I hated."

God chose Jacob over Esau before either of them were born. They had done nothing good or evil to merit this choice. I believe that this is a reference to the nations. God chose Israel in a very special way.

God's election of Israel was not based on human merit, and Israel's disobedience does not negate the promises of God. He will do what He says every time. If God is after you, stop running because He will get you one way or another.

In 2007 I had the opportunity to meet with the chief rabbi of Israel when he visited south Florida. I sat right next to him at lunch and he asked me, "When did you evangelicals begin?"

I wondered for a moment if I could come up with the right answer, but I believe God put it in my mouth just in time. "We began with Abraham," I said, "and we have been grafted into the family of God."

God has only one Saviour and one way to Heaven. There is not a Jewish way and a Gentile way, or a Catholic way and a Baptist way. The only way is through Jesus Christ.

Go back for a few moments in your mind's eye and picture Jesus dying on the cross. We like to categorize sin, but God does not do that. A lady in my church gave a great definition of a redemptive church when she said, "It is a church that is not prejudiced against certain sins, but treats them all equally. Sin is sin."

Whatever sin you have in your life, the Son of God took that upon the cross just for you as if you were the only person who had ever lived. The message of the Gospel is that anyone can come and be a part of the family of God. No matter how wicked you think you are, Jesus died for you, and if He is calling you today there is no reason for you to hesitate another moment before coming to Him. Why would you refuse Him?

I was in India several years ago preaching in a series of meetings. We went to a place called Mud Island, and that is literally what it was – an island surrounded by filth and debris. Each day we would take a boat ride to the site of the services and I was extra careful not to fall into the water.

There were multitudes of people at these meetings, and they represented various faiths such as Islam and Hinduism. Many of them wanted to have Jesus in addition to their other gods. We stressed to them continually that if they had Jesus, they would not need any of the others.

God, in His sovereign election, chose the nation of Israel. He used that nation to send us the Messiah – our one and only Saviour. We don't need anything else.

Chapter 21

WHO IS IN CHARGE AROUND HERE?

"What shall we say then? Is there unrighteousness with God? God forbid. For he saith to Moses, I will have mercy on whom I will have mercy, and I will have compassion on whom I will have compassion. So then it is not of him that willeth, nor of him that runneth, but of God that sheweth mercy. For the scripture saith unto Pharaoh, Even for this same purpose have I raised thee up, that I might shew my power in thee, and that my name might be declared throughout all the earth. Therefore hath he mercy on whom he will have mercy, and whom he will he hardeneth. Thou wilt say then unto me, Why doth he yet find fault? For who hath resisted his will? Nay but, O man, who art thou that repliest against God? Shall the thing formed say to him that formed it, Why hast thou made me thus? Hath not the potter power over the clay, of the same lump to make one vessel unto honour, and another unto dishonour? What if God, willing to shew his wrath, and to make his power known, endured with much longsuffering the vessels of wrath fitted to destruction: And that he might make known the riches of his glory on the vessels of mercy, which he had afore prepared unto glory, Even us, whom he hath called, not of the Jews only, but also of the Gentiles? As he saith also in Osee, I will call them my people, which were

not my people; and her beloved, which was not beloved. And it shall come to pass, that in the place where it was said unto them, Ye are not my people; there shall they be called the children of the living God. Esaias also crieth concerning Israel, Though the number of the children of Israel be as the sand of the sea, a remnant shall be saved: For he will finish the work, and cut it short in righteousness: because a short work will the Lord make upon the earth. And as Esaias said before, Except the Lord of Sabaoth had left us a seed, we had been as Sodoma, and been made like unto Gomorrha. What shall we say then? That the Gentiles, which followed not after righteousness, have attained to righteousness, even the righteousness which is of faith. But Israel, which followed after the law of righteousness, hath not attained to the law of righteousness. Wherefore? Because they sought it not by faith, but as it were by the works of the law. For they stumbled at that stumblingstone; As it is written, Behold, I lay in Sion a stumblingstone and rock of offence: and whosoever believeth on him shall not be ashamed." **(Rom. 9:14-33)**

Recently I visited some of the elementary classes in our Christian school. In each case the teacher introduced me as the pastor, and I enjoyed spending a few moments with those precious children.

It was interesting to me that in nearly every class, a certain child would step forward and act as if he were the leader of that class, telling the other children what to do and perhaps even making an impression on the teacher regarding his leadership. It happens in so many instances, regardless of the type of group that is assembled – someone will invariably make his or her presence known as the leader of the pack. Leadership is a special gift from God.

At this writing, in the fall of 2008, two men – John McCain and Barack Obama – are vying to be the next president of the United States. That position is traditionally considered the top leadership position in this country, but there are many others in close proximity. Some might even consider the nine members of the U.S. Supreme Court to be the ultimate leaders.

But who is really in charge of this world? Who is in charge of your life?

We have seen in the first eight chapters of Romans the great salvation given to us by God. Now we must ask ourselves if we can trust Him with this great salvation, and we will once again look at Israel at the many promises from God concerning it.

A number of questions have been asked throughout the book for Romans, and now we have a new question: Is God just? Is He righteous? Since Israel has been elected by God, what will He do with all of the other nations of the world?

In the last chapter we presented four attributes of God – His **faithfulness, righteousness, justice** and **grace**. God's faithfulness was addressed in greater detail in that chapter, and the other three will be covered here.

The absolute righteousness of God is seen in verses 14-18. Indeed, it is addressed point-blank in verse 14: *"shall we say then? Is there unrighteousness with God? God forbid."* God is the only one who is truly righteous.

God chose Israel and made that nation certain promises. He will not ever go back on His promises. We must remember this, because the Bible clearly states that those who curse Israel will be under the curse of God, but those who bless Israel will be under the blessing of God.

But now the book of Romans shows us that everyone, Jew and Gentile, can be welcomed into the family of God by trusting in Christ. So where does that leave Israel?

Go back to the Old Testament for a moment. God raised up a man named Joseph who led his people through a great famine, saving the Israelites via his position in Egypt. As the book of Genesis comes to a close and Exodus begins, we find that Israel has a new leader named Moses.

Moses makes the first of several visits to Pharoah in Ex. 5:1-3. *"And afterward Moses and Aaron went in, and told Pharaoh, Thus saith the LORD God of Israel, Let my people go, that they may hold a feast unto me in the wilderness. And Pharaoh said, Who is the LORD, that I should obey his voice to let Israel go? I know not the LORD, neither will I let Israel go. And they said, The God of the Hebrews hath met with us: let us go, we pray thee, three days' journey into the desert, and sacrifice unto the LORD our God; lest he fall upon us with pestilence, or with the sword."*

The people only wanted to take three days for a feast and to worship, but notice Pharoah's response in verse 2 to that request. He said that he did not know their God.

We know that this is part of the process that God is using to lead His people to the promised land. To put this in proper context, look at Ex. 1:6-8.

"And Joseph died, and all his brethren, and all that genera-tion. And the children of Israel were fruitful, and increased abundantly, and multiplied, and waxed exceeding mighty; and the land was filled with them. Now there arose up a new king over Egypt, which knew not Joseph."

Those last four words – *"which knew not Joseph"* – are very important.

God stands in the way of those who are against His will. He will not allow anyone or anything to stop His plan. Even though Pharoah did not know God or recognize Him in any way, God's plan would not be delayed by him. We find 15 references in the book of Exodus to the hardening of Pharoah's heart.

In the opening verses of Exodus 7, God says that He will harden Pharoah's heart. In other instances, Pharoah hardens his own heart. Did Pharoah do it, or did God? They are one in the same, but ulti-mately God's plan came to pass.

Look at the conversation between God and Moses in Ex. 3:3-4. *"And Moses said, I will now turn aside, and see this great sight, why the bush is not burnt. And when the LORD saw that he turned aside to see, God called unto him out of the midst of the bush, and said, Moses, Moses. And he said, Here am I."* We see here how God called Moses.

Whatever God says to you or lays on your heart during your time with Him can never be taken away from you. Don't let anyone talk you out of what God has said to you, especially concerning your salvation. Trust in what He has promised in His Word and what

Christ did for you on the cross. If there is anything else God gives you that is confirmed by Scripture, don't let anyone take it away.

Moses used every excuse he could think of to avoid doing what God was calling him to do. But God was raising up this man to do His will in that hour, and nothing would stand in the way.

When I was in college I received a great deal of training in Calvinism and hyper-Calvinism. I must stress that hyper-Calvinism is a very dangerous thing, and we need to remember that "whosoever will" can be saved. If it is your desire to be saved, I guarantee that God is ready to save you today. As II Pet. 3:9 says, God is *"not willing that any should perish, but that all should come to repentance."*

But God is not going to be hindered in His sovereign work. I believe that what took place with Pharoah in these passages is very similar to the unpardonable sin that we read about in the New Testament – taking the works of God and attributing them to another. Pharoah said that he wanted nothing to do with the God of Israel, but God's righteousness was extended because Israel is the apple of God's eye.

Back in Romans 9, we see a wonderful description of the justice of God in verses 19-29. There are three important questions found in this section.

First, who are we to argue with God? All of us have done this, but we know it doesn't get us anywhere. Verse 21 uses the illustration of the potter and his clay to show us God's power, and it is also expressed using the example of Pharoah in verse 17; although he refused to even acknowledge God, Pharoah was used by God to accomplish His purpose. God is working on all of us, like that clay, to make us who He wants us to be, and we must be very careful not to harden our hearts toward Him.

Do you ever notice how someone can get mad at church, leave that church to go to another church, only to have the same thing happen again? Eventually you hear how "the church is full of hypocrites" and these people are not happy anywhere. A Christian cannot harden his heart in the same way as Pharoah did, but you can quench or grieve the Holy Spirit and eventually become miserable and totally ineffective because you are not letting God work in your life.

Second, what will God do with tyrants? That is a question that comes up from time to time throughout history, from the Old Testament examples such as Haman to the 20th-century standouts like Hitler.

On a trip to Israel I heard a story by the chief rabbi (which he also told during a speech he gave at the United Nations) about how Hitler had come into what is now Israel and damaged a number of synagogues, proclaiming all the while that he would obliterate the Jewish people. Today those synagogues have been rebuilt and much of Israel is thriving, and that rabbi made this comment at the U.N.: "Hitler, Hitler, where are you?"

The answer is simple. God deals with the Hitlers and Pharoahs of life. He always has and He always will.

Verses 22-23 talk about God's desire to obtain glory and show mercy, which is something he wants to do in every Christian's life. We must always remember the importance of God's mercy. No one can claim that he or she deserves to be saved. Our salvation is possible because of the mercy, love and holiness of an almighty God. If you think about the events that led to your salvation, God's mercy becomes even more evident.

Third, what will happen to the nation of Israel? The name "Osee" in verse 24 is what we know to be Hosea, and the words in Romans 9 are taken from that book of the Bible, especially Hos. 1:10. *"Yet the number of the children of Israel shall be as the sand of the sea, which cannot be measured nor numbered; and it shall come to pass, that in the place where it was said unto them, Ye are not my people, there it shall be said unto them, Ye are the sons of the living God."*

Isaiah is also quoted in Romans 9, beginning in verses 27-28. *"Esaias also crieth concerning Israel, Though the number of the children of Israel be as the sand of the sea, a remnant shall be saved: For he will finish the work, and cut it short in righteousness: because a short work will the Lord make upon the earth."*

Whatever God has promised, you can rest assured that He will make it happen. When He says that His chosen people will be given their land, we know it will come to pass. When He says that Jesus Christ will come again one day, we know that will happen as well.

God is not unjust in saving and judging others. In these passages we see that He is fulfilling Old Testament prophecies given centuries earlier. He keeps His word. God's election reveals grace by providing salvation to the Gentiles, and we have the opportunity to become members of the family of God.

Look at verse 29. *"Except the Lord of Sabaoth had left us a seed, we had been as Sodoma, and been made like unto Gomorrha."*

The word *"Sabaoth"* is from a Hebrew word which is translated as "the Lord of hosts" or "the Lord of the armies." It is a designation of Him who is supreme over all spiritual agencies, and it means in essence that the Lord is sovereign. You and I can trust God because we know He is sovereign.

During each election cycle, from the presidential elections down to the local level, it is easy to notice how the candidates attempt to connect with so many different groups and be everything to everyone. On the other hand, God does not do anything to try to please any group of people. Everything on His radar screen is intended for His glory.

As I said before, no one deserved to be saved. Some believe that God arbitrarily thrusts certain people into Hell, but the Bible tells us that it is our own choices regarding the acceptance or rejection of Christ that determine where we spend eternity. God's offer of grace is expressed throughout His Word, even to one of the last six verses of the Bible: *"And whosoever will, let him take the water of life freely"* (Rev. 22:17).

But God is sovereign above all, and nothing will stand in the way of what He wants to see accomplished. One can debate or discuss whether He worked Pharoah or Judas Iscariot into His plan out of necessity or if He had their roles determined before they were even born. There comes a point where we need to stop trying to get into the mind of God (we have enough trouble managing our own minds) and just concentrate on obeying God.

Look at verses 30-31. *"What shall we say then? That the Gentiles, which followed not after righteousness, have attained to righteousness, even the righteousness which is of faith. But Israel, which followed after the law of righteousness, hath not attained to the law of righteousness. Wherefore? Because they sought it not by faith, but as it were by the works of the law. For they stumbled at that stumblingstone."*

This begins the progression to personal responsibility that will be addressed in later chapters of Romans. We see here that the Gentiles progressed to righteousness by grace through faith, while those in Israel who clung solely to the law did not. Remember the words of Rom. 3:22-23. *"Even the righteousness of God which is by faith of Jesus Christ unto all and upon all them that believe: for there is no difference: For all have sinned, and come short of the glory of God."*

God has given to us what we need in Christ. Man's free will and God's sovereignty do not compete; they cooperate.

The conclusion of this thought comes in verse 33: *"As it is written, Behold, I lay in Sion a stumblingstone and rock of offence: and whosoever believeth on him shall not be ashamed."*

Don't harden your heart against God. If you are struggling with salvation, stop struggling and come to Christ. If you are a Christian but you are mad at God because of things in your life right now, be careful not to let others determine what your relationship with God will be. Recognize that if you harden your heart, in the long run you will be the loser and have many regrets.

Chapter 22

WHY DO PEOPLE REJECT CHRIST?

"Brethren, my heart's desire and prayer to God for Israel is, that they might be saved. For I bear them record that they have a zeal of God, but not according to knowledge. For they being ignorant of God's righteousness, and going about to establish their own righteousness, have not submitted themselves unto the righteousness of God. For Christ is the end of the law for righteousness to every one that believeth. For Moses describeth the righteousness which is of the law, That the man which doeth those things shall live by them. But the righteousness which is of faith speaketh on this wise, Say not in thine heart, Who shall ascend into heaven? (that is, to bring Christ down from above:) Or, Who shall descend into the deep? (that is, to bring up Christ again from the dead.) But what saith it? The word is nigh thee, even in thy mouth, and in thy heart: that is, the word of faith, which we preach; That if thou shalt confess with thy mouth the Lord Jesus, and shalt believe in thine heart that God hath raised him from the dead, thou shalt be saved. For with the heart man believeth unto righteousness; and with the mouth confession is made unto salvation. For the scripture saith, Whosoever believeth on him shall not be ashamed. For there is no difference between the Jew and the Greek: for the same Lord over

all is rich unto all that call upon him. For whosoever shall call upon the name of the Lord shall be saved. How then shall they call on him in whom they have not believed? and how shall they believe in him of whom they have not heard? and how shall they hear without a preacher? And how shall they preach, except they be sent? as it is written, How beautiful are the feet of them that preach the gospel of peace, and bring glad tidings of good things! But they have not all obeyed the gospel. For Esaias saith, Lord, who hath believed our report? So then faith cometh by hearing, and hearing by the word of God. But I say, Have they not heard? Yes verily, their sound went into all the earth, and their words unto the ends of the world. But I say, Did not Israel know? First Moses saith, I will provoke you to jealousy by them that are no people, and by a foolish nation I will anger you. But Esaias is very bold, and saith, I was found of them that sought me not; I was made manifest unto them that asked not after me. But to Israel he saith, All day long I have stretched forth my hands unto a disobedient and gainsaying people." **(Rom. 10:1-21)**

Rejection is a very difficult thing to go through in life. All of us have experienced this, whether being turned down for a job or forsaken by a would-be friend.

Now imagine how God felt after coming down to the world He had created and feeling that same rejection. Have you ever wondered why people would reject Christ – or, more specifically, why the chosen nation of Israel rejected its Messiah?

The Bible is full of passages that speak about this rejection. Consider I Pet. 2:4 and 7. *"To whom coming, as unto a living stone, disallowed indeed of men, but chosen of God, and precious...Unto you therefore which believe he is precious: but unto them which be disobedient, the stone which the builders disallowed, the same is made the head of the corner."*

When my wife and I were newlyweds we both attended college and had jobs. Her job paid for our tuition, while mine covered the rent and kept food on the table. At that time I sold fire alarms, which were a relatively new amenity and not yet in many homes.

I learned my presentation very well and went into many homes extolling the advantages of a fire alarm. I stressed to each family how it could save their house and even their lives. But my passion in every presentation was motivated by the simple fact that if I did not sell those fire alarms, I would not eat well that week. Of course, whenever a prospective client chose not to make purchase I felt rejection.

The word "rejection" as used in the Bible means "to examine something and be disproved." It's one thing to be rejected, but it's another thing when someone has examined something about you and disproved it.

Christ spoke many times about how He was rejected by those He came to save. Matt. 21:42 says, *"Jesus saith unto them, Did ye never read in the scriptures, The stone which the builders rejected, the same is become the head of the corner: this is the Lord's doing, and it is marvellous in our eyes?"* This is almost identical to what Jesus said in Mark 12:10-11.

Look at Luke 9:22. *"Saying, The Son of man must suffer many things, and be rejected of the elders and chief priests and scribes, and be slain, and be raised the third day."*

Perhaps this constant rejection is best summed up in John 1:11. *"He came unto his own, and his own received him not."* Why would anyone reject the Son of God?

We know for a fact that if you die with Jesus you go to Heaven, and if you die without Him you go to Hell. Why would anyone reject Jesus?

When you are saved you have a purpose for living. Your life begins to make sense. Life for the unsaved will never make sense. So why would you reject Jesus?

These questions can be answered in the 10th chapter of Romans as we look at how Christ came to His chosen people and they chose to reject Him. The reasons for their rejection are laid out in verses 1-13.

The first reason, in verse 1, is that they did not see a need for salvation. Paul's first word was *"Brethren,"* speaking as one Jewish man to another, when conveying his heart's desire that they be saved. But the Jews as a whole believed that, while the Gentiles needed salvation, they did not need it themselves.

Have you ever felt that way? You sit in the pew and hear a message, thinking, "This is good. I hope So-and-so is listening; he really needs this." If that's what you are thinking, you are probably the one who needs that sermon the most. The Jews always felt that way about the Gentiles, saying, "Those people really need God."

This is illustrated dramatically in the story of the prodigal son. When the younger son returns home to his father, the older son asks, "Why is he making such a fuss over him?" The older son had not gone astray, but now he was filled with pride. One of our biggest problems today is pride, and the Jewish people had a big problem during the time of the book of Romans. They did not want to accept the fact that their Messiah had come.

So many people today like to say that they are on a spiritual quest. But if that quest does not end up in Jesus, it is a false quest.

All of us remember vividly where we were the morning of Sept. 11, 2001. I was in Washington, D.C., with some other Christian leaders getting ready to enter a special briefing at the White House with the vice president. Suddenly a guard came out and told us that a plane was bearing down on the White House. I thought he said to run to J Street, but I later realized there was no such street.

We left there in a hurry although we didn't know yet what all was going on. Then we heard about the planes crashing into the World Trade Center and saw the smoke in the distance from the attack on the Pentagon. Everything changed on that day.

For the next six weeks people flocked to churches all over this country. You could hardly find a seat in our church during that time. People were afraid of what might happen next. But thousands of those people who turned to the house of God at that time have since fled the house of God because they feel safe once again.

We need Christ not because of a fear of terrorism or a need to feel safe, but because we are all lost without a Saviour. That is why you come to the house of God in the first place.

Paul was burdened about the Jews because they didn't see the need for salvation. Also, as indicated in verse 2 of Romans 10, they had a false knowledge of salvation.

When Israel returned from Babylonian captivity there was a sense that they had been cured of their idolatry. They went to the synagogues and studied the law with zeal, but it was a zeal without knowledge. Rom. 3:20 says, *"Therefore by the deeds of the law there shall no flesh be justified in his sight: for by the law is the knowledge of sin."* We have seen over and over in Romans that the law's purpose is to remind us how we need the grace of God. Aren't you glad you're under grace and not under the law?

Verse 3 shows the extent of their problem with pride in that they sought *"their own righteousness"* rather than God's. Israel had been told so many times about the Lord and for many it was simply a matter of refusing to submit to Him. Pride is perhaps the toughest problem we face in our Christian lives.

Robert Murray McCheyne, the great Scottish preacher of the 1800s, once gave a tract to an eminent lady he met on the street. She looked at him and said, "Sir, you must not know who I am."

"Madam," he replied, "there is coming a day of judgment, and on that day it will not matter who you are."

Spencer Williamson, who was the founding pastor of a great church in south Florida, was on the golf course one day with football legend Joe Namath. After their round was over, Namath commented to Williamson's son Jerry, "I guess he doesn't know who I am."

"No, he doesn't know," the younger Williamson replied. "And he doesn't care. All he knows is that people are going out into eternity, and that's all he cares about."

In the end, that's all that really matters. We may feel pretty good about ourselves but that will get us nowhere on the day of judgment.

Notice in verses 4-13 that the Jewish people misunderstood the meaning of the law. This is emphasized in verse 4, which says, *"Christ is the end of the law."* These verses are in many instances repeated phrases from the Old Testament.

The law is referred to in Gal. 3:24 as *"our schoolmaster to bring us unto Christ."* As individual Christians and as a church family we should be passionate about seeing lost people brought to Christ. People need the Lord, and we need to tell people about Him.

Verse 5 essentially tells us, as Moses did in Leviticus, that if we are going to depend upon the law, we had better keep all of it. But our own righteousness cannot stand in God's eyes because we all will break the law at some point.

Verses 6-8 quote various passages from Deuteronomy and the emphasis is on accepting the Word of God from the heart, not through outward acts of obedience. Paul is repeating them here to encourage us to allow the law to point us to Christ.

God's way of salvation is not difficult or complicated. Christ experienced sin and death for us, and we do not need to perform difficult works to be saved. We must trust Christ and Him alone.

That brings us to verse 9, one of the most familiar passages in the entire Bible. *"That if thou shalt confess with thy mouth the Lord Jesus, and shalt believe in thine heart that God hath raised him from the dead, thou shalt be saved."* Verse 11 adds that those who accept Christ will not be ashamed of Him.

Verse 13 is another famous verse: *"For whosoever shall call upon the name of the Lord shall be saved."* It is similar to Joel 2:32, which says, *"Whosoever shall call on the name of the LORD shall be delivered."* Salvation is open to everyone, and only Christ can do what the law could never do.

If righteousness is by the law, then it is only for the Jew. If righteousness is by grace through faith, then "whosoever will may come."

The law's righteousness focuses on works. When you are truly born again, you want to serve the Lord; you are *"created in Christ Jesus unto good works"* (Eph. 2:10). But the law's righteousness is self-righteousness, while faith's righteousness is the righteousness of God, as He looks at you and sees the righteousness of Jesus Christ, not your own.

The law says, "Obey the Lord." Faith says, "Come to the Lord." A wrong emphasis on the law always leads to pride, but faith brings glory to God. If you are a child of God there is a desire in your heart to bring glory and honor back to Him.

If someone offered you a dollar you might turn it down. You might turn down $100. If you were offered a million dollars and rejected it people would wonder what is wrong with you. God is offering you eternal life. Why would anyone reject that?

As we said before, the bottom line is pride. Before the creation of the world there was only God and His angels. An angel named Lucifer decided that he wanted to be just like God. In the passage from Isaiah 14 that recounts this story, we see Lucifer saying "I will" five times. He said, "This is what I am going to do." But God dealt with him as He always deals with pride. He cast him out of Heaven, and Satan has been mad every day since.

Remember when he came to the Garden of Eden as a serpent and wound his way to Eve? He told her that if she and Adam ate of the forbidden tree *"ye shall be as gods, knowing good and evil"* (Gen. 3:5). It was an attack intended to capitalize on their pride.

Verses 14-17 talk about the method God intends to be used to take the message of the Gospel to people. We are living in a world today in which the Gospel is going out like never before. Every day about 74,000 people around the world come to faith in Jesus Christ. There are more than 1,000 agencies broadcasting Christian programming on radio and television. The "Jesus" film has been seen by some 3 BILLION people in more than 200 countries, with nearly 200 million of them indicating a commitment to Christ.

In the 1990s the number of born-again believers in the world reportedly doubled. In Africa today about 20,000 people are added to the body of Christ every day. That continent was believed to be 3 percent Christian in 1900; today 50 percent claim to be born again.

In places like Indonesia hundreds of thousands of Muslims are turning to Christ. Even the best efforts of the government cannot stop the Gospel in China. There were an estimated one million believers there in 1950 when the government closed the country to missionaries; now there are more than 80 million, many of whom meet in underground churches, and an average of 20,000 new converts every day.

God is doing a great work in the world today, and we all need to be a part of it. This is a wonderful age. Is Jesus Christ coming soon?

He probably is; He could come today. In these last days we need to be doing all that we can for our Lord.

E. Myers Harrison put it this way: There is a command from above that says, "Go ye into all the world." There is a cry from beneath like that of the rich man who said, "Go and tell my brothers." There is a cry from without as in Acts 16 that says, "What must I do to be saved?" And there is a command from within which is the love of God that constrains us.

In the conclusion of Romans 10 we see how Israel is guilty, having heard the message as shown in verse 18. The next two verses show that the Gentiles are guilty as well. Paul closes the chapter with these words: *But to Israel he saith, All day long I have stretched forth my hands unto a disobedient and gainsaying people."* But God is not finished with the nation of Israel yet.

When I first moved to south Florida in the mid-1990s I met a young Jewish man, barely 20 years of age, and began witnessing to him. At first he wasn't sure what to do, but when I pointed out that Jesus was a Jew, he decided that he would accept Christ right then.

We need to be passionate about taking the Gospel to people. At the end of the day that is all that really matters.

Chapter 23

BACK TO THE WITNESS STAND: ISRAEL ON TRIAL

"I say then, Hath God cast away his people? God forbid. For I also am an Israelite, of the seed of Abraham, of the tribe of Benjamin. God hath not cast away his people which he foreknew. Wot ye not what the scripture saith of Elias? how he maketh intercession to God against Israel saying, Lord, they have killed thy prophets, and digged down thine altars; and I am left alone, and they seek my life. But what saith the answer of God unto him? I have reserved to myself seven thousand men, who have not bowed the knee to the image of Baal. Even so then at this present time also there is a remnant according to the election of grace. And if by grace, then is it no more of works: otherwise grace is no more grace. But if it be of works, then it is no more grace: otherwise work is no more work. What then? Israel hath not obtained that which he seeketh for; but the election hath obtained it, and the rest were blinded. (According as it is written, God hath given them the spirit of slumber, eyes that they should not see, and ears that they should not hear;) unto this day. And David saith, Let their table be made a snare, and a trap, and a stumblingblock, and a recompence unto them: Let their eyes be darkened, that they may not see, and bow down their back alway. I say then, Have they stumbled that they should

fall? God forbid: but rather through their fall salvation is come unto the Gentiles, for to provoke them to jealousy. Now if the fall of them be the riches of the world, and the diminishing of them the riches of the Gentiles; how much more their fulness? For I speak to you Gentiles, inasmuch as I am the apostle of the Gentiles, I magnify mine office: If by any means I may provoke to emulation them which are my flesh, and might save some of them. For if the casting away of them be the reconciling of the world, what shall the receiving of them be, but life from the dead? For if the first-fruit be holy, the lump is also holy: and if the root be holy, so are the branches. And if some of the branches be broken off, and thou, being a wild olive tree, wert grafted in among them, and with them partakest of the root and fatness of the olive tree; Boast not against the branches. But if thou boast, thou bearest not the root, but the root thee. Thou wilt say then, The branches were broken off, that I might be grafted in. Well; because of unbelief they were broken off, and thou standest by faith. Be not highminded, but fear: For if God spared not the natural branches, take heed lest he also spare not thee. Behold therefore the goodness and severity of God: on them which fell, severity; but toward thee, goodness, if thou continue in his goodness: otherwise thou also shalt be cut off. And they also, if they abide not still in unbelief, shall be grafted in: for God is able to graft them in again. For if thou wert cut out of the olive tree which is wild by nature, and wert grafted contrary to nature into a good olive tree: how much more shall these, which be the natural branches, be grafted into their own olive tree? For I would not, brethren, that ye should be ignorant of this mystery, lest ye should be wise in your own conceits; that blindness in part is happened to Israel, until the fulness of the Gentiles be come in. And so all Israel shall be saved: as it is written, There shall come out of Sion the Deliverer, and shall turn away ungodliness from Jacob: For this is my covenant unto them, when I shall take away their sins. As concerning the gospel, they are enemies for your sakes: but as touching the election, they are beloved for the father's sakes. For the gifts and calling of God are without repentance. For as ye in times past have not believed God, yet have now obtained mercy through their unbelief: Even so have these also now not believed, that through your mercy they also may obtain mercy. For God hath concluded them all in unbelief, that he might have mercy upon all. O the depth of the riches both of the wisdom and knowledge of God! how unsearchable are his judgments, and his ways past finding out! For who hath known the mind of the Lord? or who hath been his counsellor? Or who hath first given to him, and it shall be recompensed unto him again? For of him, and through him, and to him, are all things: to whom be glory for ever. Amen." **(Rom. 11:1-36)**

I took my first trip to Israel in 1974. I went with a friend of mine, and there were 40 or 50 in our group. At the time I had no idea how that land would captivate me and my understanding of the Scriptures. I led another group a few years later, and for a long time I have been going there every two years with various groups from my church and others.

When you become a child of God and begin to grow in the Lord and get into the depths of His Word, you will find the tremendous background for our faith that is in the Judeo-Christian teachings of the Old Testament. The 11th chapter of Romans is key to helping us understand how the nation of Israel relates to what God has in store for us.

If you look back through history you cannot deny that the nation of Israel has been persecuted more than any other people who ever lived. As far back as the story of Esther and up to the time of Hitler's Nazi Germany, we have seen examples of those who would annihilate the Jewish people if they could. In Jesus' day the Romans called the Jews the "nefarious sect," meaning that there was no need for them to be around, and one great historian even called them the "fossil generation."

Romans 11 proves that God is not through with the nation of Israel. Yes, He has raised up the church of Jesus Christ and we are now living in the church age, when Jews and Gentiles alike can come to God through Christ. But God is not done with Israel, and He is not done with us.

We learn in the very first verse of this chapter that the Apostle Paul is not writing to the church, but to Israel. *"I say then, Hath God cast away his people? God forbid. For I also am an Israelite, of the seed of Abraham, of the tribe of Benjamin."*

There is a theology known as replacement theology, not really found in the Bible, that suggests the church has replaced Israel. But Romans 11 tells us clearly about the future of Israel, which is directly referenced by name in verses 2, 7, 25 and 26. God has a great plan for Israel.

One thing that Christians can take great delight in is the fact that God has charge over everything. He knows exactly what He is doing and has a plan for all of it. Many times we have plans that don't turn out just like we thought they would.

Maybe you're a control freak, like I am. If anyone is truly in control, it is God, not us. Many people over the course of history have tried to do away with His special nation, but God has a plan.

Imagine for a moment a courtroom in which we put Israel on the witness stand. There are five witnesses in all for this case.

The first witness is the Apostle Paul. We have seen again in verse 1 his burden for his people, as he states without hesitation his lineage and race. Many people try to suggest that a Jew who comes to Christ somehow turns into a Gentile, but a Jew is a Jew and a Gentile is a Gentile. Both can have the same Messiah and the same Saviour.

Paul was formerly known as Saul, who was struck to the ground on the road to Damascus and asked, *"Who art thou, Lord?"* in Acts 9:5. When he saw that great light he knew he was dealing with the very one he had been persecuting. While his pockets held letters from the governor authorizing him to imprison any Christians he came across, he actually became a Christian. The story is repeated in Acts 22 and 26, as Paul tells it in Rome.

His conversion is a picture of how Israel will be saved when Jesus establishes His kingdom on the earth. There is coming a day when the nation of Israel will see the return of our Lord. Zech. 14:4 says, *"And his feet shall stand in that day upon the mount of Olives, which is before Jerusalem on the east, and the mount of Olives shall cleave in the midst thereof toward the east and toward the west, and there shall be a very great valley; and half of the mountain shall remove toward the north, and half of it toward the south."* He will establish a kingdom of righteousness.

Remember when Jesus ascended into Heaven and the angels came down to tell the disciples, *"Ye men of Galilee, why stand ye gazing up into heaven? this same Jesus, which is taken up from you into heaven, shall so come in like manner as ye have seen him go into heaven"* (Acts 1:11).

Rev. 1:7 puts it this way: *"Behold, he cometh with clouds; and every eye shall see him, and they also which pierced him: and all kindreds of the earth shall wail because of him. Even so, Amen."*

The Messiah who came the first time is coming a second time. He came first as the Lamb of God, and He will come next as the Lion of Judah. Many of our Jewish friends say that when the Messiah comes, they will ask Him, "Were you here before?" The answer to that question will be yes. He came the first time to die, and He is coming the second time to rule and reign in righteousness.

The second witness, found in verses 2-10, is the prophet Elijah. Israel is the elect nation of God, chosen in the Old Testament to get His Word out to the world. Although Israel rejected God as a nation, He was not finished with them, and when Elijah thought the country had completely abandoned God he discovered a remnant of 7,000 prophets that had remained.

Look at Rom. 9:27. *"Esaias also crieth concerning Israel, Though the number of the children of Israel be as the sand of the sea, a remnant shall be saved."* This is a repeat of a quotation from Is. 10:22-23 indicating that Israel still has a future, although being a member of that nation does not automatically make one a follower of Yeshua. The word *"remnant"* here means something that is left or saved by the Gospel of our Lord. Verses 5-6 of Romans 11 show that the remnant is saved by grace, not works.

Look at Rom. 9:30-33. *"What shall we say then? That the Gentiles, which followed not after righteousness, have attained to righteousness, even the righteousness which is of faith. But Israel, which followed after the law of righteousness, hath not attained to the law of righteousness. Wherefore? Because they sought it not by faith, but as it were by the works of the law. For they stumbled at that stumblingstone; As it is written, Behold, I lay in Sion a stumblingstone and rock of offence: and whosoever believeth on him shall not be ashamed."*

Israel has been blinded as a nation, but many Hebrew people are coming to Christ. Even today, many are returning to Israel. It is interesting to note that while wars rage all over the world, whenever there is a single skirmish in Jerusalem it is reported by every major media outlet. You see stories from Jerusalem like "6 killed in seminary" or "2 killed on street." Murders happen often in south Florida, where I live, but you often don't see it reported on the national and international news.

Go back through spiritual history to the origin of Lucifer, the archangel who wanted to be like God and was cast out of Heaven. Lucifer's sin was pride. He came to earth in the form of a serpent to tempt Eve, and judgment came once again because of pride. Whatever God is for, Satan is against.

The nation of Israel, God's chosen nation, has given us a great gift in the form of the Old Testament Scriptures. Satan hates Israel and would do anything in his power to wipe it off the map, which is why its people have been so persecuted for so long. But if God has made a special place for Israel and we are the people of God, we should stand firm alongside Israel.

The people of Israel turned their blessing into a burden by rejecting Christ when He came. According to Ps. 69:22-23, *"Let their table become a snare before them: and that which should have been for their welfare, let it become a trap. Let their eyes be darkened, that they see not; and make their loins continually to shake."*

This passage from one of what is known as the Messianic Psalms is repeated in Rom. 11:8-10, as the blessing became a burden and the rituals of their religion became a substitute for the blessing of salvation. All of our rituals and practices, no matter how sincere, do not bring us to God. Only Christ can do that.

Verse 25 of Romans 11 reminds us that the hardening of Israel is neither fatal nor final. *"For I would not, brethren, that ye should be ignorant of this mystery, lest ye should be wise in your own conceits;*

that blindness in part is happened to Israel, until the fulness of the Gentiles be come in." Those are powerful words.

The existence of the Jewish remnant today, as it was in Elijah's day, is the promise to us that God always has a plan.

Our faith is not based upon traditions. It has nothing to do with the color of the carpet or curtains, or the type of pulpit that is being used on the platform. Some people can take a potentially good thing, like a picture of Jesus, and turn it into an object of worship. It's fine to have a cross as a symbol or reminder of Christ, but it's not essential for your faith.

Simply put, we should worship the Lord our God and Him alone – not symbols, traditions or rituals. This was a big problem with Israel, particularly the fact that it was consumed by the law.

This brings us to verses 11-15 and the third witness, the Gentiles. How unusual this arrangement might be. If you had a situation where you were involved in a court case and your worst enemy came to testify for you, it is likely that you would be nervous about whether that person said the right thing in your favor. Well, the Jews and Gentiles could hardly be categorized as good buddies during this time, so it might seem like a similar situation.

Notice this phrase in Rom. 11:11. *"Have they stumbled that they should fall? God forbid."* This is one of many passages where a question is asked and the answer is a resounding no. We have already covered several of these in Romans (3:9, 6:1, 6:15 and 7:13, to name a few). In verse 11 it indicates one more time that God is not finished with Israel.

Through the fall of Israel salvation has come to the Gentile world. That doesn't mean that Gentiles couldn't be saved in the Old Testament. The message of salvation was given to the Jewish people first. Today, however, both Jew and Gentile alike become one in the body of Christ when they accept Him.

Rom. 9:24-26 says, *"Even us, whom he hath called, not of the Jews only, but also of the Gentiles? As he saith also in Osee, I will call them my people, which were not my people; and her beloved, which was not beloved. And it shall come to pass, that in the place where it was said unto them, Ye are not my people; there shall they be called the children of the living God."* The *"Osee"* in verse 25 is a reference to Hosea, as Paul once again quotes the Old Testament.

Gentiles come to God through Jesus Christ and they come understanding that the original blessings came to the Israelites, who have been set aside and for whom God has a great plan.

The Bible says in Jer. 31:35-37, *"Thus saith the LORD, which giveth the sun for a light by day, and the ordinances of the moon and of the stars for a light by night, which divideth the sea when the waves thereof roar; The LORD of hosts is his name: If those ordinances depart from before me, saith the LORD, then the seed of Israel also shall cease from being a nation before me for ever. Thus saith the LORD; If heaven above can be measured, and the foundations of the earth searched out beneath, I will also cast off all the seed of Israel for all that they have done, saith the LORD."*

God is saying here that if He does away with the sun, the moon, and the planets, only then would Israel cease to be. Obviously, He is not going to do that.

The basis for our Christian faith is found in the holy Old Testament Scriptures. The Old and New Testaments go side by side, and together they form the very Word of the living God. Many great books have been written throughout history, but none like the Bible, and it states very clearly that God has a plan for the nation of Israel as well as a plan for you and me.

We as Christians must uphold Israel. The United States as a nation is no longer the greatest friend of Israel, but its greatest friends are those Christians who understand the teachings of the Bible and know how important Israel is.

God said it to Abraham on multiple occasions, beginning in Gen. 12:3. *"And I will bless them that bless thee, and curse him that curseth thee: and in thee shall all families of the earth be blessed."* It doesn't get any plainer than that, and there is a Judeo-Christian ethic that we must understand.

When Christ came to this earth, He did not come to Italy or Spain or any other country. He came to a town called Bethlehem that was located in Israel. That was God's choice.

The fourth witness, in verses 16-24, is made up of the patriarchs. The *"firstfruit"* cited in verse 16 is a common Biblical reference to the first or the best. This verse also cites the illustration of the lump of dough as seen in Numbers 15, where the first part of the dough is offered to God as the best, much like our tithe is given today. When God accepts the first part, He is accepting the whole.

God accepted Abraham because He chose him. The patriarchs who followed, such as Isaac and Jacob, were chosen in spite of their sins and their failings, and God made a covenant with them that He will fulfill.

One of the most common symbols in the Bible is the olive tree, which represents a nation. This symbol is mentioned several times in verses 16-24.

These verses are not speaking about the salvation of individuals but of a nation. The Gentiles have been grafted in by the power of God. The part of the tree referred to as the "*natural branches*" is Israel. One day the olive tree of Israel will flourish again, and when you become a child of God, you become a part of the blessings of the covenant of Abraham as we saw in Gen. 12:3.

When my brother was alive he did a tremendous amount of work on our family tree. Like most of you, I have some family members that make me very proud. It is always interesting to learn about where you came from and even the origin of your family name. My last name was originally known as Pedone (pronounced "Pe-DON-ay"), which means pedestrian. If you go today to Rome you will see many "Pedone" signs all over the city.

My uncle Tony (every Italian has an Uncle Tony) came through Ellis Island many years ago and decided that he would change the last name to Pedrone, which means boss or landowner. I like it very much and have no intention of changing it back.

As Christians you should be able to follow your family tree. We all come together in Christ, but before Him there were many promises given that are being fulfilled.

That brings us to the fifth and final witness, in verses 25-36 – the testimony of God Himself. I think we would all agree that His testimony is the most important of all.

Verse 25 shows us God's timetable, as the Gentiles are coming to Christ and this is causing jealousy among the Jewish people. It leads to the very next event on the heavenly calendar, the coming of Jesus Christ. He could come at any time.

Some people may ask, "What signs remain to be fulfilled before Jesus can come?" I don't believe there are any such signs. There are those who wish for His coming very soon, while others may want to wait for a little while. When I was about to be married I wanted the Lord to tarry so I could enjoy our marriage. After all four of our children arrived there were days that I prayed, "Lord, come quickly." The expense and responsibility were huge.

Our desires have no effect on God's timetable, but we are commanded to be looking for His coming at all times. Christ is coming because He said He would.

Verse 26 shows us God's promise, talking about Israel's salvation and return to the promised land. God's covenant is addressed in verses 27-28, while verse 29 displays the very nature of God, as it says His promises are "*without repentance,*" or irrevocable.

We should always remember the words of Mal. 3:6. "*For I am the LORD, I change not.*" God never changes; what He says will always come to pass.

Verses 30-32 replay a familiar and wonderful theme of the book of Romans – the grace of God – as they convey the sinful state of Israel and His subsequent mercy shown to them. But it could scarcely be written more beautifully than in verse 33: *O the depth of the riches both of the wisdom and knowledge of God! how unsearchable are his judgments, and his ways past finding out!*"

You may be going through a miserable time in your life as a Christian, going through trials and wondering what is happening or why. God is working out His plan for your life by His grace, and He is always in control of whatever is taking place, so we should not go through our lives in constant worry.

We have all been the person identified in verses 34-35. All of us have wanted to tell God our own plans for life at some point, but He has no need for our counsel or advice. God is described well in the final verse of the chapter: "*For of him, and through him, and to him, are all things: to whom be glory for ever. Amen.*"

One writer said that the theology of this chapter leads to doxology. God has a plan for Israel, and He has a plan for you.

We must surrender our understanding to God's plan for the nation of Israel. He has chosen them, and we as God's people should support them. The Bible says in Ps. 122:6, *"Pray for the peace of Jerusalem."* We have that admonition because one day the Prince of Peace will return to rule and reign.

It is interesting that every time we take that trip to Israel and we ride up the hill to Jerusalem, I look around the bus and see people weeping. They feel as though they are coming home even though they have never been there before.

When you take a tour of the White House or some castle in England, you can't help but strain your neck and look around every corner because you think you might see the president or the queen. One day the King of Kings and Lord of Lords will be here, and we will be able to see Him.

Chapter 24

RELATIONAL THEOLOGY

> *"I beseech you therefore, brethren, by the mercies of God, that ye present your bodies a living sacrifice, holy, acceptable unto God, which is your reasonable service. And be not conformed to this world: but be ye transformed by the renewing of your mind, that ye may prove what is that good, and acceptable, and perfect, will of God."* **(Rom. 12:1-2)**

If you asked the congregation at your church this Sunday morning what they brought with them, you would get a dozen or more different answers. People will say a Bible, or a coat and tie, or a car, or who knows what else. One of the most critical answers would likely be overlooked – your body.

Every one of us has a body and a living soul. Romans 12 begins a study of what I like to call relational theology, and the first two verses of the chapter – two of the most familiar verses in the entire Bible – deal with the relationship of our bodies to God.

In the life of a Christian doctrine and duty go hand in hand, and what we believe will determine how we behave. The book of Romans is similar to several of Paul other writings in that the first portion of the book deals with what we believe and where we stand, while the latter portion shows us how to live out our faith.

The first two verses in Romans 12 talk about our relationship with God. Verses 3-12 cover our relationship with other believers, and verses 13-21 address our relationship with our enemies. How we relate to government is the subject of Romans 13.

Notice that the fourth word in Rom. 12:1 is *"therefore."* As we have said previously, when you see a "therefore" in the Bible you need to find out what it is "there for." This important word appears four significant times in Romans.

Looking back through this book, we see the "therefore" of condemnation in Rom. 3:20 and the "therefore" of justification in Rom. 5:1. The "therefore" of assurance appears in Rom. 8:1 and now we are at the fourth important "therefore" in Rom. 12:1.

What is it that makes us dedicate our hearts to the Lord?

Many of us are motivated by a challenge. I know I fall into that category. If my wife tells me I can't do something, I want to do it right away just to prove that I can do it. She probably uses that often to get me to do something I really don't want to do.

Napoleon once said, "Men are motivated by trinkets." He meant that if you put a ribbon on someone's jacket or a certificate on the wall, it will often be a great motivator.

I have a collection in print and audio of some of the greatest speeches in recorded history. Many of them were given by former British prime minister Winston Churchill, who often spoke about victory during some of Great Britain's darkest times. He talked about such things as victory at all costs, victory against terror, and victory no matter how long and hard the road may be. These impassioned words often motivated the British people to do great things.

So what it is that motivates us to give our bodies to the Lord? It is found in Rom. 12:1 – *"by the mercies of God."* The mercy of an almighty God is the reason for us to want to give ourselves to Him.

Grace is when God gives us what we do not deserve. Through His mercy He withholds from us what we should be getting, which is His judgment. The word "mercy" comes from a Greek word which means to take pity or be kind. The mercy seat in the Old Testament was known as the *"footstool of our God"* as seen in I Chr. 28:2, and His mercy is the reason we give ourselves to Him.

Wherever you go, you take your body with you. It's the only one you have. You cannot separate from yourself. You may wish you were smarter or better looking, but you have the mind and body that God gave you. You are what you are.

Arthur Pink wrote, "Mercy denotes the ready inclination of God to relieve the misery of fallen creatures."

In his book "Rediscovering Holiness," J.I. Packer wrote these incredible words: "The secular world never understands Christian motivation. Faced with the question of what makes a Christian tick, unbelievers believe and maintain that Christianity is practiced only out of self-serving purposes. They see Christians as fearing the consequences of not being Christians (religion as fire insurance), the need of help and support to achieve their goals (religion as a crutch), or wishing to sustain a social identity (religion as a badge of respectability). No doubt, all of these motivations can be found among the membership of churches, but just as a horse brought into a house is not made human, so a self-seeking motivation brought into a church is not made Christian, neither will holiness ever be the right name for religious routines thus motivated. The only authentic force in Christian living should not be the hope of gain, but a heart of gratitude."

Aren't you thankful for the mercies of God? Now that we see the reason for giving ourselves to Him, let's look at three aspects of this passage.

Verse 1 speaks of the dedicating of your body. Our bodies are, as we are reminded in I Cor. 6:19, the temple of the Holy Spirit. Jesus took on the form of a human body to do His will on earth, and so we are to give our bodies back to Him that we can continue to do His will here.

There are two living sacrifices mentioned in the Bible. The first is Isaac, and the second is our Lord and Saviour Jesus Christ.

Look at Heb. 4:14-16. *"Seeing then that we have a great high priest, that is passed into the heavens, Jesus the Son of God, let us hold fast our profession. For we have not an high priest which cannot be touched with the feeling of our infirmities; but was in all points tempted like as we are, yet without sin. Let us therefore come boldly unto the throne of grace, that we may obtain mercy, and find grace to help in time of need."*

We give our bodies to God because of His mercy, and by doing so we continue to find mercy in Him.

There is a process outlined in Rom. 12:1 as you *"present"* your body; it is from the same word that gives us *"yield"* in Rom. 6:13-16. We all know what it means to yield because of the many road signs we see instructing us to do that (even if most of us don't do it). On the road you give up the priority position in traffic to the oncoming vehicle. Here we are told to give ourselves and make a presentation of ourselves to God – a one-time, total commitment.

The words *"your reasonable service"* at the end of verse 1 are also translated as "your spiritual worship." That concept is at the heart of this passage – our spiritual worship.

We are in a spiritual warfare. When you accept Jesus Christ as your personal Saviour, you will find it all around you. If you think you don't have much spiritual warfare, it's because you are not living very much for Christ.

Think back to the children of Israel's travels to the promised land. You will recall that they encountered a multitude of problems during their journey, beginning with the plagues in Egypt. They crossed the Red Sea and then wandered in the wilderness for 40 years, not getting anywhere.

Eventually Moses got to see the promised land from the top of Mount Nebo, where he is buried. The task of leading the Israelites fell to Joshua, whom God told to take his people into the promised land with strength and courage, and he did so. Then there was the adventure of the spies hidden by Rahab, and the assault on Jericho during which they never laid a hand on the city; they marched around it and blew their trumpets, and the walls came tumbling down. Think about how the Israelites saw the miraculous hand of God in these events.

At the battle of Ai, which should have been easy, they were defeated because of the sin of Achan, and they had to straighten that out before they could resume their march forward. They finally reached the promised land and *"took the whole land,"* according to Jos. 11:23.

But all along the way as Moses and Joshua led the children of Israel, there was a struggle. When we give our bodies to the Lord we have to understand that there will be a spiritual battle every step of the way, because the devil doesn't want us to serve God. If you have it easy right now you'd better check your faith and your walk with God, because when you start walking with God the devil will try to get into your mind and your heart anywhere he can. When that happens you need to reaffirm that you are trusting God and tell the devil to go back where he came from.

I remember a kid in our neighborhood when I was growing up. He was a nice kid, but he was a huge guy and a weightlifter on top of that. Another guy said one day, "I think I can take him."

"Don't even try it," I warned. "He'll destroy you."

He tried anyway and was destroyed. He should never have tested him.

If you don't think the devil is real or is out to hurt you, my warning to you is this: Don't test him. The Bible commands us to resist him and flee from him. The devil is out to get you, but *"greater is he that is in you than he that is in the world"* (I John 4:4). God is all-powerful, and He is always worthy of our best.

A number of years ago a group of missionaries went to minister to the Auca Indians and lost their lives. It's a very familiar story. Jim Elliot was one of those missionaries who was told not to go, that he would waste his life. After he was killed, it was discovered that he had written these words: "He is no fool who gives what he cannot keep to gain what he cannot lose."

William Borden was a very wealthy, privileged man. An heir to the Borden dairy fortune, he was educated at Yale and destined for a life of power and prestige. Instead he went to China as a missionary, and his family and friends told him he was absolutely wasting his life. When he died from disease while still in his 20s, those naysayers thought their presumption was confirmed. But these handwritten words were found in the pages of his Bible: "No reserves; no retreat; no regrets."

You and I will find that, regardless of what seems to be an enormous earthly sacrifice on our part, a life of service to Jesus Christ is entirely reasonable. Your body belongs to God.

The second thought I want to give you is the transforming of our mind as mentioned in verse 2. The word *"conformed"* refers to being shaped or formed like a certain thing – in this case, the world. It all goes back to our worship; as we worship God our minds become transformed, but as we think about the world and the culture around us we become conformed to its likeness.

The word *"transformed"* here is the same word translated as *"transfigured"* in the account of Christ's transfiguration. As Matt. 17:2 reports, *"His face did shine as the sun, and his raiment was white as the light."* This is defined as a metamorphosis, a change from within.

The world loves to control our thinking and make us conformers. If God controls your mind you will be a transformer. That transformation comes from meditating upon the Word of God as well as the people we meet, the places we go and the books we read.

The third thought in this passage is the giving of your will to God. I'm not talking about will power. The culture in which we live today wants us to think like it does. Turn on your television and it will tell you where you should go, what you should buy and what you should think.

While you are living in this world and its culture, you have to make certain you are listening to the substance of truth. In our society today if someone is attractive, charming, charismatic or talented, people want to follow that person. You can be easily led down the wrong path by someone like that if you do not consider the message carefully. You can't just look at the form; you must also look at the substance.

I remember when I was a teenager watching the first-ever televised presidential debate, in 1960 between John F. Kennedy and Richard Nixon. Most pundits and political experts believe that Kennedy won the election on the basis of the debate.

I listened to the debate on the radio, and if you had asked me who won the debate I would have said Nixon. Nearly everyone who listened on the radio agreed with that assessment. But those who watched on television thought Kennedy won. This was largely because Nixon was ill at the time and looked pale on camera, while Kennedy was made up and looked very good. Appearances made a huge difference in this case. Interestingly, Kennedy was recently voted in a Harris poll as one of the top 10 leaders in American history, despite being in the Oval Office less than three years.

There is a huge difference between form and substance. Make sure what you are listening to has the right kind of substance and is based upon the Word of God.

The devil is after your mind, and once he gets it he can make you believe anything, even things you know are not true. This is why it is vital to give your will over to God.

Look at how Paul described his own battle with his will in Rom. 7:15-20. *"For that which I do I allow not: for what I would, that do I not; but what I hate, that do I. If then I do that which I would not, I consent unto the law that it is good. Now then it is no more I that do it, but sin that dwelleth in me. For I know that in me (that is, in my flesh,) dwelleth no good thing: for to will is present with me; but how to perform that which is good I find not. For the good that I would I do not: but the evil which I would not, that I do. Now if I do that I would not, it is no more I that do it, but sin that dwelleth in me."*

The Christian mind is not about mind over matter; it is about learning and following what God says. Henry Blamires wrote a book titled "The Christian Mind: How Should A Christian Think?" In it he concluded that there are relatively few Christian minds left because too many of us have allowed the world to tell us how and what to think.

Verse 2 of Romans 12 talks about the *"renewing of your mind."* Several Greek scholars have said that the word *"renewing"* as it appears here is not found in classical Greek texts, but only in Scripture. It refers to being made new on the inside and then working its way out. This allows you to properly do what the latter part of that verse suggests: *"that ye may prove what is that good, and acceptable, and perfect, will of God."*

Most people, when talking about the will of God, look at it as a place. They talk about God calling them to Africa, or Florida, or wherever. That is sometimes the case, but in this section of the Bible it has nothing to do with that. It is simply doing what God wants us to do right now. The subsequent verses and chapters in Romans expound further upon this matter of submitting our will to God in areas of our spiritual gifts and our relationship with government and authority.

Robert Muldane wrote it this way: "The will of God is here distinguished as good, because however much the mind may be opposed to it and how much we may think it curtails our pleasures and mars our enjoyment, obedience to God is conducive to our happiness."

The word "*perfect*" in verse 2 is the Greek word *telias*, which means attaining a full and complete destiny and having maturity in our lives by following the will of God.

When you give God your body, you are also giving Him your mind. By giving Him your mind, you are following what He has in store for you in your life.

I have learned from experience that following God's will is never easy in the beginning. So many things in the world seem easy and attractive and we just want to jump right on board. The will of God is not that way initially, but at the end of the day you know it is the best thing you could have done.

You are responsible for the person you see in the mirror every morning. Have you ever noticed how easy it is to tell other people how to live their lives and what they are doing wrong? Your ultimate responsibility is to commit your own mind and body to God and do His will – to make a presentation of yourself to the Lord.

By looking ahead to the end of the book of Romans we can bring this into slightly better focus. Rom. 16:25-27 says, "*Now to him that is of power to stablish you according to my gospel, and the preaching of Jesus Christ, according to the revelation of the mystery, which was kept secret since the world began, But now is made manifest, and by the scriptures of the prophets, according to the commandment of the everlasting God, made known to all nations for the obedience of faith: To God only wise, be glory through Jesus Christ for ever. Amen.*"

The reason we give ourselves to God is to bring honor and glory to Him. The devil does not like that – he doesn't even like you, for that matter – and he will mount a daily assault on your mind. How we respond to those attacks will dictate how effectively we live out our faith. We need to worship the Lord our God in spirit and in truth.

Make yours a life of worship, and by giving yourself over to Him you will see how He can do a marvelous work in your life.

Chapter 25

PARTICIPATING WITH OTHER CHRISTIANS

"For I say, through the grace given unto me, to every man that is among you, not to think of himself more highly than he ought to think; but to think soberly, according as God hath dealt to every man the measure of faith. For as we have many members in one body, and all members have not the same office: So we, being many, are one body in Christ, and every one members one of another. Having then gifts differing according to the grace that is given to us, whether prophecy, let us prophesy according to the proportion of faith; Or ministry, let us wait on our ministering: or he that teacheth, on teaching; Or he that exhorteth, on exhortation: he that giveth, let him do it with simplicity; he that ruleth, with diligence; he that sheweth mercy, with cheerfulness. Let love be without dissimulation. Abhor that which is evil; cleave to that which is good. Be kindly affectioned one to another with brotherly love; in honour preferring one another; Not slothful in business; fervent in spirit; serving the Lord; Rejoicing in hope; patient in tribulation; continuing instant in prayer; Distributing to the necessity of saints; given to hospitality. Bless them which persecute you: bless, and curse not. Rejoice with them that do rejoice, and weep with them that weep. Be of the same mind one toward another. Mind

not high things, but condescend to men of low estate. Be not wise in your own conceits." (**Rom. 12:3-16**)

Why are you a part of a church? What is church all about to you?

A church cannot help but grow spiritually and numerically if its members do what the Bible says to do. When we accept Christ, we immediately belong to each other and to the family of God.

It is easy for us to say that the family of God is all over the world, and that is a correct statement. If we were to travel to another country and meet with other believers, it wouldn't take long until we felt as though we had known them a long time because of the bond that ties us together.

The church as stated in the New Testament is the Greek word *ecclesia* that means a gathering. It's the idea of a called-out body that is assembling together. So when we think about participation, it is important to understand that in the Bible it is described as a local body of believers.

What many families do today is look for a church based on a particular aspect, such as great preaching or worship or an excellent program for children or teens. It is a "salad bar" approach that causes people to miss out on what the church is really all about.

The Apostle Paul's epistles in the New Testament were letters written mostly to churches. You can tell from the title of the epistle to whom it was written – the book of Romans was to the church in Rome.

As we saw in the first two verses of Romans 12, our bodies belong to God first and foremost. But when we are born again, we also belong to one another within the family of God, which is one body of believers. We also belong to one another within our own local body of believers.

When you are a member of a church, you have a responsibility to the other members of that church. The church I am privileged to pastor has two locations in South Florida, and some people do not have the opportunity to meet those at other campuses. But we all are doing the work of God together and we have a responsibility to each other.

So I will ask once again: Why do you come to church? Is it so you can walk in carrying your Bibles and compliment each other on your appearance? There is much more to it than that. If I continually tell my wife at home how nice she looks and she tells me to take out the garbage but I don't, things are not getting done. The garbage still has to go out.

God has called every one of us to do something in the local church. You may think that you cannot figure out what that something is in your life, but a study of Rom. 12:3-16 may give you a better understanding of how God has equipped you to minister to others.

Look in verse 3 at the **honest evaluation**. The grace we receive is not just for salvation, but also that we can see our proper position within the family of God and not think more highly of ourselves than we should, as the verse indicates. The source of this grace is the Holy Spirit.

When you accept Christ, the Holy Spirit comes to live within you and He gives to you certain spiritual gifts to follow through on. It is not wrong to recognize the gifts in your life and in other people's lives, but you cannot use your own gifts to put yourself over other people.

For example, someone with the gift of teaching might adopt the attitude that they are better than others because of superior knowledge. That is not the way to build the body of Christ.

Notice that this passage speaks about the spiritual ability that we have. Since the gifts are from God, we cannot take credit for them. Whatever He has given us is for the purpose of building and edifying the body of Christ. There is great danger when we as believers are not doing this.

Think about all of the things you did this past week during your busy life. Who did you edify in the body of Christ? To whom were you a blessing or a help? There is a responsibility for each of us to have an honest evaluation and edify one another.

In verses 4-8 we see the process of **harmonious cooperation**. Verse 6 points out that there are different gifts given by God, and we are told in verse 7 to use whatever gifts we have been given in conjunction with others who are using different gifts. God is saying to us here that if we have the Holy Spirit in our lives, there should be harmony in the way we serve Him together and work with each other.

As one writer defined it, "A spiritual gift is an extraordinary endowment bestowed by the Holy Spirit sovereignly and undeservedly upon believers as instruments for Christian service and church edification."

When you accept Christ as your Saviour, there is something that God wants you to do. A big part of that is what you do within the body of Christ and the local church, that assembly of people God has called together. We don't go to church just to be entertained or to see what the pastor looks like; we go to be equipped so we can edify others.

When you consider the definition of a spiritual gift in the preceding paragraph, you must remember that no single gift is more important than any of the others.

Look at I Cor. 12:29-31. "*Are all apostles? are all prophets? are all teachers? are all workers of miracles? Have all the gifts of healing? do all speak with tongues? do all interpret? But covet earnestly the best gifts: and yet show I unto you a more excellent way.*"

Those verses conclude that chapter, and the "*more excellent way*" Paul is referred to in the final verse is the love that is so eloquently spoken of in I Cor. 13.

I Cor. 12:7 says, "*But the manifestation of the Spirit is given to every man to profit withal.*" When you start functioning within the gifts God has given to you, you feel good about yourself. You think, "Wow, this is what I was meant to do." When that happens, church becomes a better place and you are less critical and judgmental about others because you are serving God as He meant you to serve. This is real New Testament Christianity, and it is how the body of Christ was meant to be put together.

God also tells us that if you don't use your gift, you could lose it. If you are a golfer, you know that when you haven't played in a long time you want to go out on the course by yourself so no one can see you hit the ball, since you have no idea where it will land. The same goes for any other athletic endeavor or discipline, and it is also true in the family of God.

You are not meant to use your gifts as an end unto themselves, but rather a means to God's end and with the right spirit as expressed in Gal. 5:22-23. *"But the fruit of the Spirit is love, joy, peace, longsuffering, gentleness, goodness, faith, Meekness, temperance: against such there is no law."*

When you stop and think of how God has ordained the local church, it is a masterpiece of organization. A church can be too overly organized and consumed with structure to the point of missing out on the Spirit. It is more important to have the power of the Holy Spirit at the expense of structure, but it's really good with both things can work hand in hand.

In my church, I feel that my job as senior pastor is to lead, feed and cast vision for the church. We have a pastoral staff of people who all have important roles as well. A lot of people think about ministry as pastors and worship leaders and administrators on a church staff, but ministry is a responsibility of every single child of God.

Spiritual gifts are important, but it is even more important to be a part of a local body. As Rom. 12:4 points out, not every member has the same function, and verse 5 shows us that there is unity in the midst of diversity.

Have you been in a meeting while someone is doing or talking about something and thought to yourself that you know a better way of doing that? You probably thought that because you are gifted in that particular area and your way may indeed be a better one. I tend to make those kinds of comments, much to the dismay of my wife, who has told me on more than one occasion to keep quiet. But being a leader myself I can't help it sometimes.

A fantastic book on this subject is "19 Gifts of the Spirit" by Leslie Flynn. Here is a humorous excerpt from that book:

"Someone has imagined the carpenter's tools holding a conference. Mr. Hammer is presiding. Several suggested he leave the meeting because he's too noisy.

Replied the hammer, "If I have to leave this shop, then Mr. Screw must go also. You have to turn him around again and again to get anything accomplished."

Mr. Screw spoke up and said, "If you wish, I'll leave, but Mr. Plane must leave also. All of his work is on the surface; his efforts have no depth."

Mr. Plane then said, "Mr. Rule will have to withdraw, because he is always measuring folks as if he is the only one who is right."

Mr. Rule then complained about Mr. Sandpaper. "You're too rough and always rubbing people the wrong way."

In the midst of the discussion, in walked the carpenter from Nazareth to start His day. Putting on His apron, He went to the bench to make a pulpit from which He proclaimed the Gospel. And everybody had their place."

You also have your place, and I have my place. What is our place? Each of us has a function, and we function individually as well as collectively.

Verses 6-8 mention some of the gifts of the Spirit. Verse 6 says, *"Having then gifts differing according to the grace that is given to us, whether prophecy, let us prophesy according to the proportion of faith."* The word *"prophesy"* refers to a spokesman for God, and these people often had great faith. Sometimes a group of people will see an impossible situation and one person will stand up and say, "Yes, we can do this." That person may have the gift of prophecy.

With regard to ministry, verse 7 talks about being a servant. Every Christian is called to be a servant, but the particular word in this verse talks about a behind-the-scenes servant for God.

Years ago I was walking to the platform at a conference in upstate New York, and a woman came up to me and asked, "How do you like your water?" I thought it was a strange question, but she was as serious as she could be. One of her ministries at the church was to bring water in and put it on the platform for the speaker. I told her to bring cold water, but I was impressed at how important she felt this task was. She was ministering to others in the body of Christ.

Teaching is also mentioned in verse 7, as in someone applying the Word of God. A good teacher is not necessarily a spiritual teacher. A person who uses the spiritual gift of teaching properly will take the Bible and teach it in such a way that those who hear it can apply it to their lives.

Exhortation is the next gift named in the passage, and it means to encourage and come alongside to help. It is the same word used to refer to the Holy Spirit when He calls people unto Himself and is known as the "great encourager."

Next is the gift of giving – the ability to make money and to give freely and liberally of one's resources. Everyone is supposed to give, but there are some who are especially gifted in this area.

In verse 8 we see "*he that ruleth,*" which is an overseer much like a coach, plugging people in where they need to be. Next is mercy, or showing pity and gracious favor, but I especially like the phrase "*with cheerfulness.*" That trait is so important, because no matter what you or I may be going through, God is still on the throne.

Many churches have specific programs to help people find their gifts and where they can be utilize them in the local congregation. It's not necessarily because the church needs more workers, although it might, but because every Christian needs a place to serve and church leaders would be remiss if they did not teach their members how to find their place.

That brings us to the next step, a **healthy participation**, discussed in verses 9-16. What is healthy participation in the body of Christ? It is serving Christ but understanding that when you do, as Warren Wiersbe pointed out, there will be satanic opposition and days of discouragement.

Look at verse 9. "*Let love be without dissimulation. Abhor that which is evil; cleave to that which is good.*" The love that is spoken of here, one writer has said, is "the circulatory system of the body of Christ that enables us to function in a healthy and harmonious way."

This is an honest love. When you get to know people and love them, you are honest with them. We need to be honest with each other.

When you speak about someone, say only what you would say if that person were present. The Bible talks a great deal about gossip, and we need to be very careful because love is the basis for healthy participation in the body of Christ and we cannot damage that.

When the unsaved world looks at a church and sees people really connecting, and wants to find out what's going on – that's when the greatest evangelism takes place.

Verse 10 talks about respect for one another and verse 11 refers to the idea of doing your best as unto the Lord. Respect and passion go together well here. The diligence cited in verse 11 is an earnestness and zeal, a haste to do something and do it right.

When you go to a ball game, you want to see passion on the field or on the court. You want the teams to give everything they've got and leave it all on the playing field. You especially desire that if you are a coach. God wants the same from us in our service to Him.

A key phrase begins verse 12: *"Rejoicing in hope."* The word *"rejoicing"* is the grounds for the Gospel, while *"hope"* is a word found many times in Romans, meaning a confident expectation. The next phrase, *"patient in tribulation,"* refers to our spiritual growth amid affliction. It is understood that there are afflictions for the child of God. The early church grew so fast not because of their zeal for soul winning (although they definitely had that), but the persecution of the church that scattered the people everywhere.

The final words of that verse, *"continuing instant in prayer,"* are really the key to everything. We are to be constantly spending time with God and asking Him what He would have us do in service to Him.

We see in verse 13 the priority God places on meeting the physical needs of others. It is amazing to see how many needs there are in the typical local church. You and I have a responsibility to give to the needs of people, and we should all have our finances in order so that we can do that. As economic times in the United States grow worse for some people, we need to be asking how we can be a blessing to others more than ever.

Look at verses 14-15. *"Bless them which persecute you: bless, and curse not. Rejoice with them that do rejoice, and weep with them that weep.*" How we do that is a fair gauge of how we are fulfilling all of the responsibilities laid out in Romans 12.

It is not too hard to weep with those who are weeping. When we see someone in a moment of sadness, we connect with them quickly most of the time. But what about when someone is rejoicing? You hear of a friend who got a huge raise at work and you say, "Great." But inside you are thinking, "I'm smarter than he is. I'll be lucky if I don't get laid off. Why can't I get a raise like that?" It's harder to rejoice with others than to weep with them.

Verse 16 talks about living by God's agenda. *"Be of the same mind one toward another. Mind not high things, but condescend to men of low estate. Be not wise in your own conceits."* That verse can really be an entire message in itself.

When a church decides it only wants a certain class of people, it departs from the Christian command to ministry. Every congregation should have rich and poor sitting in the same pew. Those who were saved as children and in church their entire lives should be next to those who were just saved and delivered out of decades of sinful living. All are welcomed into the body of Christ.

That final phrase of verse 16 is a tough one. I like to think I'm right most of the time, and so do most of you. However, our churches are not to be led by our opinions. The true leader is God the Holy Spirit.

When a church family starts functioning as we are instructed in Romans 12, there is a new zeal to come to church. You want to do more than just sit and listen; you want to find your spot so you can do what God has called you to do.

During my first year of Little League baseball I sat on the bench most of the time. There were no rules about every kid playing back then. As I sat there I often thought about what the team was doing wrong (at least, my opinion of it) and which players were not doing well. But when I got in the game, although I wasn't very good, my attitude changed. People want to be involved. You sit in the stands at a college or professional game and it's easy to criticize. But we all have a more positive outlook when we are playing.

When we all take part as we should, our church grows numerically as well as spiritually. Find your place and get involved, because God wants His kingdom to grow through every local body of believers.

Chapter 26

THE PLACE OF GOVERNMENT

"Let every soul be subject unto the higher powers. For there is no power but of God: the powers that be are ordained of God. Whosoever therefore resisteth the power, resisteth the ordinance of God: and they that resist shall receive to themselves damnation. For rulers are not a terror to good works, but to the evil. Wilt thou then not be afraid of the power? do that which is good, and thou shalt have praise of the same: For he is the minister of God to thee for good. But if thou do that which is evil, be afraid; for he beareth not the sword in vain: for he is the minister of God, a revenger to execute wrath upon him that doeth evil. Wherefore ye must needs be subject, not only for wrath, but also for conscience sake. For for this cause pay ye tribute also: for they are God's ministers, attending continually upon this very thing. Render therefore to all their dues: tribute to whom tribute is due; custom to whom custom; fear to whom fear; honour to whom honour." **(Rom. 13:1-7)**

God has ordained three institutions.

First is the home or the family, begun when He placed Adam and Eve in the Garden of Eden. He intended for them to reproduce that so families could continue down through the years. It is the most important institution of the three.

Second is the government, established in Genesis 9 after the Flood. Its purpose is to protect people, and God says a great deal about government throughout the Bible.

Third is the church. Jesus spoke of it when He was on earth, saying that He would build His church *"and the gates of hell shall not prevail against it"* (Matt. 16:18). We find the beginning the church in Acts 2, and we are now living in what is known as the church age.

We must remember that God is preparing a far greater world for us than what we live in now, but while we are here we have these institutions in which to build our lives.

It is important to note that these words written by Paul in Romans 13 were written during the Roman Empire. Great persecution had not yet started for Christians, but it was on the way. Christianity was looked upon as a Jewish sect, and the Jewish religion was approved by the Roman government. But the day would come when Christians could not be loyal to Rome because they were expected to declare that Caesar was God and put incense on an altar to Caesar. Through that persecution the church of Jesus Christ began to grow, and this time of crisis turned into a glorious part of church history. The devil cannot stop the work of God.

So the timing of this passage in Romans 13 makes it especially interesting, as Christians were beginning to ask questions about what they should do regarding the various authorities around them.

Let's look first at the role of government. Beginning in verse 1, we see repeated references to the fact that all levels of authority are ordained by God. There are 15 Greek words used in the Bible that translate as "appointed" or "ordained," and the one used here means "to place in order, to arrange, to appoint."

Think of that. God appoints the people who are placed in these positions. When you and I go into the voting booth our prayer should be this: "God, who do You want in this position of authority?" That should dictate how we cast our ballots.

On a typical Sunday at my church in south Florida, the congregation includes people from dozens of countries. Many of those people have moved here and gained U.S. citizenship. I was privileged to be born in the United States and receive citizenship at birth. I am very thankful and happy to be an American.

Voting is one of the privileges we have as Americans. A lot of people sit around and say, "There's no one to vote for." If that is your belief, perhaps you should find an elected office and make a run for it yourself. We need good people in every elected office. But when it comes time to vote, do not neglect your duty. Americans need to vote; it is a responsibility God has given to us. Regardless of whether we respect a person in a specific office, we must respect the office because it was ordained by God.

Verses 3-4 indicate that the governmental authorities' main concern should be good works. The story in Acts 16 is a familiar one, beginning with Paul and Silas delivering a young girl from an evil spirit. Some people in that city who made money from this girl's fortune-telling saw their money train disappear and they took Paul and Silas to the authorities.

Look at Acts 16:19-22. *"And when her masters saw that the hope of their gains was gone, they caught Paul and Silas, and drew them into the marketplace unto the rulers, And brought them to the magistrates, saying, These men, being Jews, do exceedingly trouble our city, And teach customs, which are not lawful for us to receive, neither to observe, being Romans. And the multitude rose up together against them: and the magistrates rent off their clothes, and commanded to beat them."*

The magistrates in this case thought they were doing right by the law. In the later verses Paul and Silas escape prison when God sends an earthquake, and the jailer fears he will lose his life before they tell him how to be saved in Acts 16:31. The magistrates and the jailer were all part of the government structure, and all were doing their duty according to the law.

Sometimes God puts you in unusual circumstances that look rather difficult, but in doing so He is getting ready to perform a miracle in your life. When Paul and Silas are sitting in prison, they are singing praises to God despite their situation, and before they leave they are able to see the jailer and his entire family come to Christ.

We need to be praying for our leaders in the United States because God has commanded us to do so, and because they need to be making the proper laws and decisions. Many of the earliest settlers in our country believed in the authority of the Bible and of God, and they had an idea that religious freedom and a government based upon morality could be found in the New World. If you go to Washington D.C. today and visit many of the historic buildings you will find Scriptures on the walls, because the men who built those buildings so many years ago believed in the authority of the Word of God.

The charge of those in authority over us is to protect citizens. I believe that one of the judgments of God on this nation will be over the matter or abortion – the killing of the helpless unborn. If you have had an abortion, I want you to know that God loves you and will forgive you. But as a nation we have done serious harm and God will not overlook it.

There is a financial responsibility upon us to support our government, and that is why we pay taxes. We are also to support our leaders with prayer. I Tim. 2:1-2 says, *"I exhort therefore, that, first of all, supplications, prayers, intercessions, and giving of thanks, be made for all men; For kings, and for all that are in authority; that we may lead a quiet and peaceable life in all godliness and honesty."*

Some churches will provide prayer lists with the names of various government leaders. If you have one, take it out and start praying. Make your own list if necessary.

It is not only important to look at the role of government in this passage, but also the role of citizens. There are two separate warnings here about resisting the authority in place over you. That resistance can be defined as "leaving persistent evildoers to pursue their self-determined course and eventual retribution."

Simply put, we should not break the law. Of course, there are exceptional cases where man's law contradicts God's law, such as Daniel's decision to pray in defiance of the king's decree. Peter said in Acts 5:29, *"We ought to obey God rather than men."* But a manmade law should not be broken unless it is a direct reversal of the Bible.

Verse 5 of Romans 13 says, *"Wherefore ye must needs be subject, not only for wrath, but also for conscience sake."* We obey authority because of our conscience, which is defined as the faculty by which we apprehend the will of God. The Bible has many things to say about the conscience, and whatever your conscience dictates to you should always be from the Word of God.

Verses 6-7 are pretty clear about the subject of taxes. *"For this cause pay ye tribute also: for they are God's ministers, attending continually upon this very thing. Render therefore to all their dues: tribute to whom tribute is due; custom to whom custom; fear to whom fear; honour to whom honour."* The reference to government leaders being ministers reinforces the notion that their offices are ordained by God.

One of our greatest struggles today is with the god of materialism. There's nothing wrong with having money or even a lot of money, but be careful that your money does not become your god.

Look at I Tim. 6:17-19. *"Charge them that are rich in this world, that they be not highminded, nor trust in uncertain riches, but in the living God, who giveth us richly all things to enjoy; That they do good, that they be rich in good works, ready to distribute, willing to communicate; Laying up in store for themselves a good foundation against the time to come, that they may lay hold on eternal life."* Those are good principles to follow for those who have been blessed with an abundance of material wealth.

Our country is a great country with a great system of government, and I am very thankful for that. But this world is not our ultimate destination; we are headed for another kingdom. In the meantime, we must support our authority figures as God has commanded us to do. But we must never lose sight of that other world that is our home.

Chapter 27

RELATIONAL THEOLOGY: WHAT DO I OWE?

"Owe no man any thing, but to love one another: for he that loveth another hath fulfilled the law. For this, Thou shalt not commit adultery, Thou shalt not kill, Thou shalt not steal, Thou shalt not bear false witness, Thou shalt not covet; and if there be any other commandment, it is briefly compre-hended in this saying, namely, Thou shalt love thy neighbour as thyself. Love worketh no ill to his neighbour: therefore love is the fulfilling of the law. And that, knowing the time, that now it is high time to awake out of sleep: for now is our salvation nearer than when we believed. The night is far spent, the day is at hand: let us therefore cast off the works of darkness, and let us put on the armour of light. Let us walk honestly, as in the day; not in rioting and drunkenness, not in chambering and wantonness, not in strife and envying. But put ye on the Lord Jesus Christ, and make not provision for the flesh, to fulfil the lusts thereof." **(Rom. 13:8-14)**

Notice the phrases *"owe no man any thing"* and *"now it is high time to awake out of sleep."*

Every spring, for students and teachers alike, the days are counted down until the end of the school year. The summer break is a time all of them await with joyful anticipation.

271

I remember well my school years growing up in upstate New York. For me the summer was a time that I would be able to sleep late, until 10 a.m. or even noon sometimes. That was a great feeling.

We all have bills to pay every month. My normal routine is to sit down on Saturday morning, when things are a bit relaxed, and pay the bills. My electric bill, for instance, has several columns with numbers representing how much electricity we use. The two most important columns for me are the ones that show how much I owe and when that amount is due.

You know what that is like. If you have a bill, you should pay it. If you don't, you get a phone call or some other form of communication to remind you.

God is telling us two important things in this passage: Wake up, and think of what you owe. An alarm clock is going off in your life and you need to listen to it.

Many people over the years have taken the words of verse 8 as an admonition to avoid owing money to anyone. Legendary missionary J. Hudson Taylor and renowned preacher Charles Haddon Spurgeon were two such people, following that verse to the letter and not incurring debts. I must say that neither of those men lived in the south Florida housing market.

This verse does not forbid borrowing or legal financial transaction involving interest. Matthew 25 and Luke 19 tell us that it is right and good to bank and invest your money in the proper way, although there are warnings in the Bible against charging too much interest or failing to pay debts. It is a stretch to apply Rom. 13:8 to all financial dealings, but God is saying something important here about what we owe and how much time we have.

This portion of Scripture is a clear reminder to us that the coming of Jesus Christ could be today. Think of that. The Bible tells us that Christ is coming again, and with every passing day we are getting closer to that time.

With that in mind, let's look at what you and I really owe the Lord. Verses 8-10 especially tell us that we owe love back to God as well as to others. We see at the end of verse 8 that "*he that loveth another hath fulfilled the law.*" After that there is a partial listing of the commandments, and they are summarized in one phrase: *"Thou shalt love thy neighbor as thyself."*

When you are saved and your life is changed by Christ, you understand not only that God loves you but also that you are to fulfill His law through love. Consider the story of Zaccheus, that "wee little man" who sat in a tree until Jesus came by and brought him unto Himself. A tax collector by trade, Zaccheus decided that all of those people he had overcharged and essentially robbed over the years would be paid back fourfold. He was not saved because of this financial correction, but he wanted to put his house in order and do the right thing because he had become a follower of Christ.

Look at I John 3:22-23. *"And whatsoever we ask, we receive of him, because we keep his commandments, and do those things that are pleasing in his sight. And this is his commandment, That we should believe on the name of his Son Jesus Christ, and love one another, as he gave us commandment."* Love fulfills the law, but it also fulfills relationships. God's commandments are to believe in Christ and love one another.

Some people are hard to love. You may have family members who are difficult to love. But that is what we are to do.

The 10 Commandments are divided into two sections – those that are God-ward and those directed toward others. The five commandments listed in Rom. 13:8-10 are all commandments that have to do with relationships with other people.

Jesus later condenses all 10 of them, in effect, into two commandments. This is expressed in Matt. 22:37-40. *"Jesus said unto him, Thou shalt love the Lord thy God with all thy heart, and with all thy soul, and with all thy mind. This is the first and great commandment. And the second is like unto it, Thou shalt love thy neighbour as thyself. On these two commandments hang all the law and the prophets."*

So with regard to what we owe, we must consider our relationship with God as well as our relationships with others.

Now we see the second half of this passage. Verse 11 says that it is *"high time to awake out of sleep."* Our salvation is nearer than it has ever been.

There is a line of teaching throughout the Bible regarding what is called the imminence of the Lord. God gets things done in His time, and when it is time for something to happen God makes it happen.

He spoke and the world came into existence. For all of eternity before that there was nothing, but one day God began the process of creation with a word.

When evil ran rampant upon the earth, He told Noah to build an ark. Noah worked on this project for 120 years, but one day God told him to get the animals aboard and when he turned to close the door, God had closed it for him. It was time for the Flood.

There was a day when God promised over and over again that a Messiah would come. For centuries people waited. Then a peasant woman named Mary met her future husband, a carpenter named Joseph, and God said, "Now it is time." When the time came, God made it happen.

Just as all of these events came to pass, there will come a day when Jesus Christ returns. When He comes, it will be imminent and immediate. As I John 3:3 says, "*And every man that hath this hope in him purifieth himself, even as he is pure.*" The coming of Christ is drawing near.

We are closer today to His coming than we have ever been before. If He doesn't come today and we wake up here tomorrow, we will then be closer to His coming than we have ever been before.

The phrase "*now our salvation is nearer than when we believed*" in verse 11 is an interesting one. There are three tenses to your salvation.

The first is the past tense. When you were saved you were delivered from the penalty of your sin, which Jesus did away with when He died on the cross.

The second is the present tense. This deals with the power of sin and the fact that you and I don't have to live in sin today because Christ has delivered us from it.

The third is the future tense. This is the wonderful knowledge that one day we will be with the Lord to life forever.

For generations Christians have been looking for the coming of the Lord. This is known as the "blessed hope," which the Apostle

Paul wrote about in the New Testament. Even when he knew he would probably die at the hands of his captors in Rome, he wrote in II Timothy 4 about how he looked forward to Christ's return right up until the moment of his death.

As His coming has been anticipated for the past several centuries, it looms even larger today. At the time of this writing – with the explosion of the Islamic faith in the United States and elsewhere, the growing unity in Europe, nuclear power in Iran, and terrorism around the globe – the coming of Jesus is nearer than ever.

But even without all of this, I believe His coming is near simply because He said, "I am coming again." You might say, "But we have been waiting for years." If He said He would come, then it will happen.

I believe in the pre-tribulation rapture of the church. That means that after Christ gathers His children and they leave this world, there will be seven years of tribulation unlike anything that has ever been seen. In the middle of that period the world will be thrown into chaos and ultimately there will be a gathering of people near Megiddo for the battle of Armageddon.

If you are left behind when Jesus comes, you are left to face tribulation. There are many reasons to be saved, most importantly because you need Christ to deliver you from your sinful state. But there is a time of great tribulation coming and you need to be prepared to escape it. Knowing Jesus Christ as your Saviour is the only escape.

Robert Sumner is a long-time evangelist who for years has published a magazine called the Biblical Evangelist. He told a story about a crusade he held where many people came to Christ. A woman came and prayed for several nights that her husband would be saved. He was not coming to the meetings, but one night he finally did. Sumner preached about the coming of the Lord and described the tribulation period while this man sat in the audience and listened. He did not come forward.

After the service they drove home, the man and his wife in the front seat and a child in the back. The little boy asked, "Mommy, if Jesus comes, will Daddy be left behind?" The mother was embarrassed and told the boy not to talk about it.

When they got home and put the child to bed, the parents sat downstairs having a bite to eat. The boy appeared at the foot of the stairs, walked into the room and asked the same question about his dad. She scooped him up and took him back to bed, telling him that if they talked about it in front of Dad he might never come back to church. They prayed together and the boy went to sleep.

That night the man could not sleep, and he couldn't concentrate on his work the next day. He took the afternoon off and went home to see his wife.

"I've got to know," he told her. "If Jesus comes, I don't want my little boy's daddy to be left behind. Show me how to be saved."

That is how serious this matter is. Christ could come today or at any time, and we must be ready for His return. Ask yourself if your family is ready. Don't hope so; know so!

Look at verse 12. *"The night is far spent, the day is at hand: let us therefore cast off the works of darkness, and let us put on the armour of light."*

There are 18 verbs in the Greek text that could be rendered *"cast off."* This one means to put off or lay aside. It is definite and emphatic.

When you get up in the morning and look up in the sky, you may see the sun. Daylight has arrived and darkness is gone. Darkness lends itself to things being done quietly and secretly that should not be done. My father used to tell me not to stay out past 10 p.m. because nothing good happened after that hour. God wants us to wake up to the light, not the darkness.

This brings us to the final two verses that show us how we should give our very best to Christ. Bible scholar John Phillips put it this way: "The believer is to walk virtuously, slaying with the Spirit's shining sword the very thought of sin."

We are being instructed to get ourselves prepared. When I tell my wife that someone is coming over to see us, she immediately tells me to make sure the house is ready. If someone drops in to see us, she worries about the state of the house. We want it to look nice when company is planned so they think it always looks that good. Most people think that way about their homes.

That is the type of preparation God is talking about here. Being ready for His coming is about more than just salvation. He wants us to have our lives in order, and verse 13 lists several things to lay aside. "*Let us walk honestly, as in the day; not in rioting and drunkenness, not in chambering and wantonness, not in strife and envying.*"

So as you get ready for Christ's coming, how are you living? Someone once said, "If Jesus came to your house, what would He find?" That is a reference not so much to the brick-and-mortar structure you live in as it is to your body.

I think sometimes as Christians we still don't get it. God wants us to always be His and living for Him as we await His Son's return. He wants us to live every day of our lives thinking, "This could be the day. This could be the hour. This could be the moment."

Every decade, every generation we find out new and wonderful things about the Lord. In recent years scholars have developed a rich new area of study in what is called the Hebrew roots of our faith and the "Jewishness" of our Lord. For example, Jesus was known as the Son of the Covenant. Just as people have their favorite preachers or speakers, the Jews in Jesus' day tended to gravitate to one rabbi over another. To attract followers a rabbi would develop his own style that set him apart.

Jesus was often spoken of as "Rabbi." In this era, the second temple period, He excelled at telling stories and people swarmed to hear public discourses He made. They also thought of Him as the miracle worker who made the lame walk and the blind see. Some rabbis had healing ministries nearby but none like His.

Christ was also unique in the sense that He spoke with authority. A rabbi would exude authority if he quoted another rabbi, but Jesus did not quote other rabbis. He told people about God the Father and was known as the Rabbi of Rabbis.

Verse 14 says, "*But put ye on the Lord Jesus Christ, and make not provision for the flesh, to fulfil the lusts thereof.*" That is an admonition to remember what this great teacher, the Rabbi of Rabbis, has taught us. Let me give you two things He has taught us.

When He was going to be crucified and His disciples were gathered around Him, He took a basin of water and a towel and went around teaching them how to be servants. One might imagine that when they saw His resurrected body, they remembered how He had washed their feet just a few days earlier.

Not only did He do that, but during the Last Supper the custom of dipping bread from the person on the left suggests that Jesus even shared it with Judas Iscariot, giving perhaps an outside chance that Judas would come into the Kingdom (which, of course, he did not). He gave him every possible chance to accept Him.

Let's allow the greatest Teacher the world has ever known to show us how to *"put ye on the Lord Jesus Christ."* We need to adjust our lives and our attitudes so we can see what we owe and what time it is, and our lives will show that to a lost world as we await the coming of Christ.

Chapter 28

GETTING ALONG WITH DIFFICULT FAMILY MEMBERS

"Him that is weak in the faith receive ye, but not to doubtful disputations. For one believeth that he may eat all things: another, who is weak, eateth herbs. Let not him that eateth despise him that eateth not; and let not him which eateth not judge him that eateth: for God hath received him. Who art thou that judgest another man's servant? to his own master he standeth or falleth. Yea, he shall be holden up: for God is able to make him stand. One man esteemeth one day above another: another esteemeth every day alike. Let every man be fully persuaded in his own mind. He that regardeth the day, regardeth it unto the Lord; and he that regardeth not the day, to the Lord he doth not regard it. He that eateth, eateth to the Lord, for he giveth God thanks; and he that eateth not, to the Lord he eateth not, and giveth God thanks. For none of us liveth to himself, and no man dieth to himself. For whether we live, we live unto the Lord; and whether we die, we die unto the Lord: whether we live therefore, or die, we are the Lord's. For to this end Christ both died, and rose, and revived, that he might be Lord both of the dead and living. But why dost thou judge thy brother? or why dost thou set at nought thy brother? for we shall all stand before the judgment seat of Christ. For it is written, As I live, saith the Lord,

every knee shall bow to me, and every tongue shall confess to God. So then every one of us shall give account of himself to God. Let us not therefore judge one another any more: but judge this rather, that no man put a stumblingblock or an occasion to fall in his brother's way." **(Rom. 14:1-13)**

Most of you, when you read the title of this chapter, probably thought it referred to blood relatives or those family members who live with you. But we are actually talking about those who make up the body of Christ and are in the family of God.

When you accept Christ as your Saviour the very next steps usually include following Him in believer's baptism and becoming part of a local church. Among its many descriptions, the church is often known as a family of sorts.

During the 2008 presidential campaign, Democratic candidate Barack Obama found himself in a controversial situation due to some remarks made by his pastor in Chicago, Rev. Jeremiah Wright. One newscaster made a very telling comment when she said that the reason so much was being made of Wright's statements in relation to Obama was because the church is like a family. She was right. Even in my home community in south Florida and other places where people move so often, there is still a family dynamic in most Bible-believing churches.

Have you ever been a part of a large family reunion? Some people say that the best thing about a family reunion is all the relatives showing up, and the worst thing about a family reunion is all the relatives showing up. There are always a few people in the family you're just not sure about.

When the church family gets together initially, everyone gets along great because everything is new and nice. We like it. It's the same as if you come over to my house for breakfast, and my wife and I smile as we serve you whatever you like to eat. We are on our best behavior for our guests. If it's just my wife and me at breakfast, we may not act the same way. Just as biological families have squabbles, so do church families.

Just before Christ went to the cross, one of His prayers to the Father was on behalf of believers in Him throughout the world. Here is a portion of that prayer as recorded in John 17:21. *"That they all may be one; as thou, Father, art in me, and I in thee, that they also may be one in us: that the world may believe that thou hast sent me."*

It is our responsibility as Christians to keep unity in our churches. Ps. 133:1 says, *"Behold, how good and how pleasant it is for brethren to dwell together in unity."*

The Bible is a very honest book and it gives many accounts of Christians not getting along. Ephesians 5 talks about people in the church who were at each other's throats; we see in I Corinthians 1 that there were disputes over human leadership; and Philippians 4 shows us two women who were at odds with each other and causing a church split. It doesn't take long to realize that these kinds of things happen within the body of Christ after we have gotten to know each other for a while.

I have been in the ministry for more than 40 years and a pastor for almost that entire time. One thing I have found in my life is that Christians fight. There are battles over the version of the Bible, and I have seen people who don't even know their subject almost come to blows over this. I have watched people fight over how everyone should dress. Recently I preached on a Sunday morning in my church without a tie, and I did it purposely to illustrate my point. I asked for a show of hands, and a few people preferred to see me with a tie or without one, but the vast majority did not care in the slightest.

People argue over the weekly schedule of services and the decorations in the sanctuary – and don't get me started about styles of worship music. People have these unbelievable debates on this subject as if they know what kind of music God Himself listens to.

In Romans 14 the church members had their own squabbles that were just as important to them. The first one was over special diets. Some of the Jewish people subscribed to a very legalistic eating regimen, shunning meats that were offered to idols or just going completely over to a vegetarian diet. I suppose this might be a better nutritional choice, but it had nothing to do with theology and the Gentiles who had never heard of this type of practice did not agree with it, which led to arguments.

There were also debates over special days. The Jews considered the Sabbath a sacred time of the week. Christ rose on the first day of the week, and Christians thought that was when they should gather. Suddenly there was a small war breaking out over special diets, special days, and the law.

When you and I accept Jesus Christ as Saviour, we know that He is the only way to salvation and to the Father. There is no dispute about it. But we often fail to realize that there are many gray areas in the church beyond that.

Our church has 12 pastors on two campuses. It is natural for people to prefer a certain pastor depending upon which services they attend, and they may not even know another pastor at all. If we are not careful, we can become as those in I Cor. 1:12 who broke into factions: *"Now this I say, that every one of you saith, I am of Paul; and I of Apollos; and I of Cephas; and I of Christ."*

You may think that your Sunday school class is the best one in your church, and you should believe that. But opinions can sometimes lead to divisions and even to carnality. We must understand that at the end of the day, our honor and worship and glory go to God, the King of Kings and Lord of Lords.

There are three principles that Paul says we should consider. We are to receive one another, edify one another, and please one another. The church is not just for me. It is for all of us who are born again.

The first principle is found in Rom. 14:1. *"Him that is weak in the faith receive ye, but not to doubtful disputations."* Many immature Christians in that day put too much emphasis on legalistic guidelines regarding what they ate and other issues. Romans 14 shows us that the judgmental Christian is the weaker Christian. We must receive one another because God has received us.

I don't belong in the family of God and neither do you. We are accepted there by grace through faith. Augustine put it this way: "In essentials, unity; in non-essentials, liberty; in all things, charity." The weak must not condemn the strong, and the strong must not despise the weak.

I know all of my pastoral staff very well. I know their strengths and weaknesses. All of them are used by God in a special way. None of us are completely alike, but God can use all of us. He commands to us take those who are weak in the faith, disciple them and bring them along.

Years ago when I was a young pastor I saw a minor-league pitcher in the Baltimore Orioles organization accept Christ. He was saved in our church and realized that he would likely have to change the course of his life fairly soon, partly because of injuries. He came to see me after he had been saved about three weeks. We did not have a youth pastor at that time, and he told me, "I believe God wants me to be your youth pastor."

His passion and desire were right, but he was not equipped to do that at the time. So what do you do in a situation like that? You don't tell him that he's nuts or ask what he was thinking. You start training him so he can be better used of God in the future.

There is a man in my church today who has been saved three or four years. Before he was saved every third or fourth word out of his mouth was a curse word. After he accepted Christ every 19th or 20th word he uttered was a curse word. People complained to me about him, but I was encouraged because he was getting better. You don't change something like that overnight.

Have you ever noticed that when someone is on fire for God, there are always people shooting darts at that person? They feel bad because another person is doing so well. The strong should help the weak, and the weak should respect the strong.

Look at verses 4-5. *"Who art thou that judgest another man's servant? to his own master he standeth or falleth. Yea, he shall be holden up: for God is able to make him stand. One man esteemeth one day above another: another esteemeth every day alike. Let every man be fully persuaded in his own mind."*

This is another instance of a strong Christian being condemned by a weak Christian, and this passage suggests that we should just be busy serving the Lord. If you and I are busy serving God, we will not have the time to investigate everyone else's life.

Church history has always included traditions. There is nothing wrong with that, but too often we worship traditions and don't notice when something better comes along. For instance, many years ago when radio was a relatively new invention and gaining mainstream acceptance, there were many Christians who said, "Radio is of the devil." One writer even espoused that no one should have a radio because "Satan is the prince of the power of the air." I don't know a single Christian alive today who believes that radio is inherently evil. When we insist on attacking every new thing that comes along we are missing out on what God is trying to teach us.

Notice that in verses 5-9 the word "*Lord*" is used eight times. It is from the Greek word *kurios* meaning "Master." So when we consider such things as special diets and special days, what makes any of them special? The answer comes from this passage – it is when we do it as unto the Lord.

When you have a meal, do you bow and give thanks in recognition that this meal has come from God? Do you go to church acknowledging that it is the Lord's day and you want to hear from God so you can learn what He would have you know to live for Him? Or are you just passing time?

Verse 5 says, "*Let every man be fully persuaded in his own mind.*" That means to be sure that you are doing what you are doing for the Lord's sake and not just on the basis of opinion.

There is a great story about this in the Bible. Jesus is about to ascend into Heaven, and He tells Peter to feed His sheep. Peter looks over at John and asked Jesus, "What about him?" Jesus repeats His command to Peter two more times, gently reminding him to mind his own business. If he concentrates on what he is supposed to do and leaves others alone, everyone will be better off.

The devil loves to get into your mind and give you the idea that you are better than others because of what you do or don't do, and that causes you to miss out on what God has for you in life.

Another reason we are to receive one another is because Christ is the true judge, not us. Verse 10 says, "*But why dost thou judge thy brother? or why dost thou set at nought thy brother? for we shall all stand before the judgment seat of Christ.*"

The judgment for your sins is taken care of when you accept Christ as your Saviour. You will never have to stand before God in your sin because Jesus took care of that when He died on the cross. You will, however, stand at the Judgment Seat of Christ one day to give an account of what you have done in your life with your works for the Lord. You prepare for this by daily making Him the Lord of your life and obeying Him.

Look at Heb. 13:17. *"Obey them that have the rule over you, and submit yourselves: for they watch for your souls, as they that must give account, that they may do it with joy, and not with grief: for that is unprofitable for you."*

I John 2:28 says, *"And now, little children, abide in him; that, when he shall appear, we may have confidence, and not be ashamed before him at his coming."*

I will have to give an account one day to God for what I do as a pastor of my church. You will give an account regarding your faithfulness to the Lord Jesus Christ. It can be with grief, but it doesn't have to be. It could be with joy. God wants to say to you, "Well done, good and faithful servant."

But we look at other people, how they live and act, and we become very judgmental. I don't have to stand in judgment for you, nor you for me. Each of us stands individually.

In the Victorian era of England there were some powerful preachers in London. One of them was Joseph Parker, who had a great ministry. One of his friends was Charles Spurgeon, perhaps the best-known preacher of that era. These two men spoke from behind each other's pulpits, dined together and enjoyed one another's friendship.

One day Spurgeon became very angry at Parker because of his attendance at outdoor theater productions. He said publicly that Parker should not be doing that. Parker reacted by condemning Spurgeon's practice of smoking cigars. These two great leaders of the faith in their century came apart because one went to the theater and the other smoked cigars.

As you read this, you have probably taken sides already in the Parker-Spurgeon dispute, reasoning that one practice is worse than the other. It's just human nature. Now consider what Paul Harvey would call "the rest of the story."

Spurgeon had several orphanages. When one of them burned to the ground, Parker heard about it and told his congregation, "I want you to forgive me. I have spoken out publicly about Spurgeon, and now he is in distress. We must come to their aid." Parker's church took up a massive offering and sent it to Spurgeon.

When Spurgeon received it, he asked his own congregation for forgiveness as well. "Joseph Parker has shown much greater Christianity than I," he said. At this time Spurgeon eventually decided to give up his cigars. These two men had walked away from each other over issues that should never have divided them.

Consider three principles from this passage.

First, would you be doing what you are doing if the Lord were sitting right next to you? (Keep in mind that he promises in His Word never to leave you or forsake you.)

Second, if you are offending a weaker brother or placing a stumbling block to that person's growth, stop it.

Third, if you are always judging others, I challenge you to stop that practice as well.

The issues Paul wrote about in Romans 14 are very similar to the issues that can divide the church of Jesus Christ today. These matters are far removed from what real Christianity is all about.

We are not in church for ourselves. We are there for one another. When we start to live our lives with that in mind and learn to receive one another, it will make a huge difference for all of us.

Chapter 29

TO EDIFY: IT'S NOT ABOUT ME

"I know, and am persuaded by the Lord Jesus, that there is nothing unclean of itself: but to him that esteemeth any thing to be unclean, to him it is unclean. But if thy brother be grieved with thy meat, now walkest thou not charitably. Destroy not him with thy meat, for whom Christ died. Let not then your good be evil spoken of: For the kingdom of God is not meat and drink; but righteousness, and peace, and joy in the Holy Ghost. For he that in these things serveth Christ is acceptable to God, and approved of men. Let us therefore follow after the things which make for peace, and things wherewith one may edify another. For meat destroy not the work of God. All things indeed are pure; but it is evil for that man who eateth with offence. It is good neither to eat flesh, nor to drink wine, nor any thing whereby thy brother stumbleth, or is offended, or is made weak. Hast thou faith? have it to thyself before God. Happy is he that condemneth not himself in that thing which he alloweth. And he that doubteth is damned if he eat, because he eateth not of faith: for whatsoever is not of faith is sin." **(Rom. 14:14-23)**

Most of us remember the famous Shakespearean line, "To be or not to be: that is the question." Those words are from the third act of "Hamlet." An appropriate way to sum up this passage in Romans might be to say, "To do or not to do: that is the question."

The beginning of Romans 14 told us how to get along with difficult family matters and difficult family members. Now we are going to look at how we should edify one another.

We have regular meetings at our church with the pastoral staff, during which we discuss the various programs that are ongoing or in the works. But we always say – and the entire staff is in full agreement on this – that we must put people above programs. This passage is saying the same thing. When we relate to other people, we must be careful not to put a stumbling block in someone else's way.

When Paul wrote the book of Romans, the Jewish people believed that they could eat kosher food according to their traditions and dietary laws of that day. The Gentiles, knowing that they were in Christ and had been grafted into the family of God, said that they could eat their pork with a clear conscience and told the Jews, in essence, "Leave us alone." A major battle arose over this controversy, which brings to mind the words of Rom. 14:5, which says, *"Let every man be fully persuaded in his own mind."*

On a recent trip to Israel I sat next to a woman from another group and we spent a couple of hours in conversation. She tried to convince me of the importance of keeping the Sabbath according to the law, while I told her there were many days we could keep, although I respected her view.

Christians often get into fights and feuds over relatively minor issues and bring the work of God's Kingdom to a halt, allowing lost people to slip away into Hell. We split into two sides – the legalists on one side who say, "Touch not, taste not, etc.," and the libertarians on the other side who say, "We can do whatever we want; it doesn't matter."

For the most part we don't deal with dietary laws as they did in Paul's day, but we have our own issues that can divide the body of Christ if we are not careful.

Go to your local Blockbuster store and spread out the latest DVDs on the counter. You will instantly see some that make you think, "No one should be watching that." That's fine. But Christians will separate from one another over which videos some of them might be watching.

The same goes for the music you listen to. Worship wars in the church are front-page news in the Christian world. Too many Christians think to themselves, "God listens to the same music I listen to."

Some of you may believe in drinking wine, and others probably do not. I do not touch alcoholic beverages, but it is a fact that Christians will separate over this issue as well. Any of these matters, when they cause divisions in the body of Christ, become our "dietary laws."

If any of these topics were brought up in your church service this Sunday, people all over the auditorium would become intensely interested in a matter of seconds. Many would want to start a discussion that would lead to a debate and perhaps a war, all for the chance to prove that they are right and everyone else is wrong.

When the Apostle Paul was writing about this in Romans 14, church members were choosing sides in battles like this while lost people stood on the outside watching. Nothing was getting done for the Kingdom of God.

There are three principles to be learned from this passage, the first of which is the need to be **convinced**. Verse 14 begins, "*I know, and am persuaded by the Lord Jesus, that there is nothing unclean of itself.*" The word "*know*" means "to see from an observation." Paul is saying here that he has been watching the situation and is convinced, or "*persuaded*," about his stance on this matter, just as he was convinced in Rom. 4:21 about God in that "*what he had promised, he was able also to perform.*"

So what had God convinced Paul in this case? He was convinced that nothing is unclean. Eat what you want, do it in moderation, no problem. But the second part of verse 14 says, "*but to him that esteemeth any thing to be unclean, to him it is unclean.*" Wait a minute. That sounds like a contradiction of the first half of the verse. What is he talking about?

It becomes clearer in verse 15: "*But if thy brother be grieved with thy meat, now walkest thou not charitably. Destroy not him with thy meat, for whom Christ died.*" The word "*grieved*" here means offended. He is saying that we must be careful how we treat other people and influence young Christians.

Apologetics is the practice of telling people what we believe and what we stand for. But if we just use apologetics without walking in love, we forfeit relationships and lose the very people we are trying to reach. We can destroy others and cause divisions by how we handle these issues, and God is telling us here not to destroy those for whom Christ died.

If you are hurting someone because of something you are doing, even if that practice in and of itself is not wrong, the spiritual response would be to give it up.

Many years ago my wife and I knew a woman who had been a great missionary, and she was trying to win one of her friends to Christ. The unsaved woman was very difficult. One day she told the missionary, "I believe it is a sin for Christians to chew gum, and you chew gum all the time."

What would you do? You might say, "That's silly. I'm not giving up chewing gum because she said that." But the missionary gave it up.

When I was in Israel in 2008 I had the privilege of meeting with a reformed rabbi who invited our group to go to his synagogue for their service. I was given the opportunity to give a brief greeting in the service, and our people even were able to sing a song or two. This kind of invitation is unheard of for a synagogue like this.

The service began with the congregation reading prayers, as the Jewish people do, and some songs accompanied by the rabbi on the guitar. Our group then sang "The Days of Elijah" and the audience came alive, clapping and encouraging us.

I got up and said, "We are evangelical Christians who do not compromise our beliefs. We believe that Yeshua is the Messiah. But we love you unconditionally." The congregation applauded, not because of me but the fact that we had showed them love that day.

Many sincere Christians would have suggested that I not even accept the rabbi's invitation to attend that service. How you choose to deal with that situation should be based upon the principles of Romans 14, and you must do what you feel in your heart is appropriate. I thought that our group should go, and we were glad we did.

If we are going to reach people like these, we will have to build relationships with them. I don't mean we should compromise on the essentials of our faith, but there are relationships that must be built.

Jesus always went out looking for the lost, not for the religious. We don't have to be like the lost to reach them, but we need avenue or bridges to reach them.

Go back to Rom. 14:13. *"Let us not therefore judge one another any more: but judge this rather, that no man put a stumblingblock or an occasion to fall in his brother's way."* The spirit of accepting a weaker brother is given over and over again in the Bible.

Do we have to take a stand at times? Absolutely. As Rom. 16:17 says, *"Now I beseech you, brethren, mark them which cause divisions and offences contrary to the doctrine which ye have learned; and avoid them."* There are those will always be looking to cause trouble, and those are situations we need to avoid.

Once we are convinced, it leads to conviction. Look at verse 17 of Romans 14. *"For the kingdom of God is not meat and drink; but righteousness, and peace, and joy in the Holy Ghost."*

Our top priority must always be the kingdom of God. It's not about what you eat or what you listen to. It's much more than that.

The word *"kingdom"* here is the Greek word *basilea*, an abstract noun that refers to sovereignty, royal power and absolute dominion. As this verse plainly shows, spiritual development is built upon relationships. People don't need a religion of DOs and DON'Ts; they need one built upon relationships – most importantly, how to have a relationship with God and walk with Him.

In your church congregation this Sunday morning, every row of seats will have someone with a broken heart. That person needs God. You may not be one of those people with a broken heart right now, but one day you will be.

So if we serve God as instructed in verse 17, look at what happens to us in verse 18: *"For he that in these things serveth Christ is acceptable to God, and approved of men."* The word *"acceptable"* means it is pleasing to God.

When I was in college I met a young woman who was going to one of the state universities in the area, and we had a discussion that turned into a debate about what we believed. I went for the jugular at the outset and thought I won the debate, but afterward I felt as though I could never win her to Christ.

It's not about a debate; the Holy Spirit has already won the debate. It's about relating to people so we can bring them into the family of God.

Rick Warren said that if people in the church loved one another as they should, you would have to lock the doors to keep people from coming in. How are we doing in that regard?

That takes us to the third principle, which deals with our conscience. Verse 19 says, "*Let us therefore follow after the things which make for peace, and things wherewith one may edify another.*" Our goal should not be divisiveness, but peace. As I stated earlier, it is your responsibility, and that of every member of your church, to work toward unity in the church.

The church is not about me or you, but about Him. When we are consumed with how the church can help us or meet our needs, we are missing the mark. We are to be glorifying Him and building up one another.

I remember one day I was cutting up in my fifth-grade class and the teacher caught me. We went for a private conversation, and I prayed nonstop that my teacher would not tell my mother I was in trouble.

When we sat down, my teacher said, "I know you're going to be a fine young man. You've got a lot of ability. I need you to be my helper in this class. Let's stop fooling around so you can help me."

What was she doing? She was building me up. That's what the Apostle Paul is talking about here. Think about how good it feels when someone puts an arm around you and says, "Hey, you're all right. You're going to make it. Everything's going to be OK." That is edification. We all need correction and discipline at times, but everyone needs someone to come alongside and offer encouragement.

Let me show you three verses in I Corinthians 14 that go to the heart of this matter. Look at verse 5. "*I would that ye all spake with tongues but rather that ye prophesied: for greater is he that proph-*

esieth than he that speaketh with tongues, except he interpret, that the church may receive edifying."

Verse 12: *"Even so ye, forasmuch as ye are zealous of spiritual gifts, seek that ye may excel to the edifying of the church."*

Verse 26: *"How is it then, brethren? when ye come together, every one of you hath a psalm, hath a doctrine, hath a tongue, hath a revelation, hath an interpretation. Let all things be done unto edifying."*

Each of those verses talks about edification. That is the most important thing. It's not about how you can dazzle the audience at church or elsewhere with your spiritual gifts. It's about edifying those who are worshipping with you. We must build up the body of Christ and never hurt God's work.

Look at the emphasis on faith in verses 22-23 of Romans 14. *"Hast thou faith? have it to thyself before God. Happy is he that condemneth not himself in that thing which he alloweth. And he that doubteth is damned if he eat, because he eateth not of faith: for whatsoever is not of faith is sin."*

God is reminding us here of the importance of living a life of faith. To violate our conscience would lead us to a place of doubt and guilt where we don't need to be.

Everyone needs three people in their lives. Paul was a mentor to his disciple Timothy, while Barnabas was an encourager to Paul. All of us need to be mentoring someone, while we are still being mentored by someone else, and we all need people to encourage us. When all of us are living like that, it builds up the body of Christ and we will understand the importance of not offending weaker brothers and sisters.

Can you imagine Christ ever saying, "I'm going to do such-and-such because I want to do it," without ever considering others? Jesus lived His entire life in service to others. As the old poem goes, "Others, Lord, yes, others; let this my motto be: Help me to live for others, that I might be like thee."

There will always be people who take advantage of us, and even some Christians will not be in agreement with what has been discussed in this chapter. But if we are truly seeking after spiritual things, God forbid that we put up any kind of stumbling block to others that might prevent them from coming into the family of God.

We need to be thinking day and night about the things of the kingdom of God – righteousness, peace and joy. It is in those areas that God truly comes to meet us. The kingdom of God is about people, and it is people whom Jesus loves and for whom He died.

Chapter 30

BEARING OTHERS' BURDENS

"We then that are strong ought to bear the infirmities of the weak, and not to please ourselves. Let every one of us please his neighbour for his good to edification. For even Christ pleased not himself; but, as it is written, The reproaches of them that reproached thee fell on me. For whatsoever things were written aforetime were written for our learning, that we through patience and comfort of the scriptures might have hope. Now the God of patience and consolation grant you to be likeminded one toward another according to Christ Jesus: That ye may with one mind and one mouth glorify God, even the Father of our Lord Jesus Christ. Wherefore receive ye one another, as Christ also received us to the glory of God." **(Rom. 15:1-7)**

A parent tells a child to eat his breakfast, then tells him again five minutes later. This goes on throughout the meal. The same thing happens when the parent tells the son or daughter to make the bed or do any of a number of other tasks around the house.

What do you call this? For a parent, it is frustration. But it is also repetition, which many people still consider the key to learning.

If you want to remember a portion of Scripture, you will usually have to memorize it by reciting it over and over again. But when you do that, you will often find that in the darkest times of your life you remember the right verse at just the right time.

This the same method God is using in Romans 14 and 15 through the Apostle Paul. The issue He is dealing with here is selfishness. We are by nature a very selfish people, and God is showing us the example of Jesus Christ, letting us compare potential sacrifices in our own lives with those that Christ made.

A primary thought begun in Romans 14 and continuing into the opening verses of Romans 15 is our responsibility to help weaker brothers and sisters in Christ. The truths found in these verses will show you if you are truly fulfilling this responsibility and maturing as a Christian, rather than constantly portraying yourself as a victim and wanting blessings for yourself.

Also in these verses we find something very interesting about the local church. What makes a great local church? To some people it is a megachurch with thousands of people in attendance, while for others it is a small congregation that does things in a certain way. But this passage tells us that the two key elements of a great local church are the Word of God and prayer.

There is a great story in the Old Testament relating to this. In Genesis 13 we see how the herdsmen of Abram and Lot had a disagreement over where each man's herd would graze. It is a familiar story, and Abram eventually allows Lot to choose the best land. Consider his words in verse 8: *"And Abram said unto Lot, Let there be no strife, I pray thee, between me and thee, and between my herdmen and thy herdmen; for we be brethren."*

This is a picture of how we are responsible for keeping unity in the local church, as we have previously discussed. Even though he was in a far stronger position, Abram showed no selfishness or determination to have his own way.

In Romans 14 we looked at how to receive people and how to edify people. Now we will see how to please people, and by doing so also please God.

Our church in south Florida has two locations, and I am constantly mindful of making sure each congregation knows what is happening on the other campuses. But I also know that if we love one another as we should, it will be impossible to keep lost people away from any of the three campuses because they will be pouring in to see what we have that they need.

There are four principles in verses 1-7 that we need to know about bearing others' burdens. The first one, in verse 1, is the admonition that the strong help the weak. There will always be stronger Christians and weaker Christians, and we need to come alongside those who need our help.

In a commentary on Romans by James Montgomery Boice is a story from Donald Gray Barnhouse about a man who came to see him with grave concerns about problems in a mission. Barnhouse asked the man to list the problems, and they included an unforgiving and self-serving spirit, legalism, hypocrisy, lack of patience and sympathy for others, evil speaking, assuming others are at fault, a domineering and rebellious spirit, snobbery, hatred, grumbling, arrogance, murmuring, maliciousness, greed, bitterness, laziness, resentment, and the list goes on. And this was among missionaries.

When asked about the missionaries who were doing well, the list was quite different. These people were considerate, willing to be in subjection, not insisting on their own way, full of faith and joy, with a gentle and quiet spirit as well as an intimate relationship with God. That is a huge difference.

The end of verse 1 tells us *"not to please ourselves"* while the beginning of verse 2 instructs everyone to *"please his neighbour."* There are several Greek words that translate in the Bible as *"please,"* and this one means to be acceptable. It is the same word used in the book of Genesis to describe how Enoch pleased God.

We who are stronger have a responsibility to please others and help them through their walk of life. As I mentioned previously, each of us needs a mentor to help us, a pupil that we can mentor, and someone to encourage us. (We all need to be encouragers as well.) When we are doing all of that, we are living as God teaches us to live in Romans 15.

We are instructed in verse 2 to please others for edification, and in verse 3 we see these words: *"For even Christ pleased not himself."* Jesus is our Saviour, but He is also our example. We can learn from the lives of men like Paul and Peter, but ultimately we have the example of Christ throughout the Bible to show us how we should live.

You cannot be the help to a weaker brother or sister that you need to be unless you are growing in the Word of God. Throughout Romans 15 Paul makes reference to other passages, such as this phrase in verse 3: *"The reproaches of them that reproached thee fell on me."* Those words are originally found in Psalm 69. Verses 9-12 refer to passages in Psalms, Deuteronomy and Isaiah. The Old and New Testaments go hand in hand.

I encourage you to get into regular Bible study so you can let it be your guide as you grow in the Lord. So much of what you hear about the Bible on radio and television is false, and we need sound teaching straight from the Word of God more than ever. I Tim. 5:22 says, *"Lay hands suddenly on no man,"* which means those who are called into the ministry are not to be sent out too quickly and without the proper knowledge and understanding that can only be gained through the Bible. God will give you opportunities when you are properly preparing yourself.

That leads directly to the process we see outlined in verse 4. *"For whatsoever things were written aforetime were written for our learning, that we through patience and comfort of the scriptures might have hope."* The Bible gives us hope – a confident expectation of what is yet to come.

The saddest words on the face of the earth are the words, "No hope." But I am thrilled to tell you today that we have hope through Jesus Christ and what He means to us. We need to be busy going about the Father's business and telling others about this hope they can have through the Gospel of Christ.

I made a phone call one day to one of our church members upon the death of her brother. The sister was in tears as she spoke to me, but she said, "Now he is in the presence of the Lord." When you think about the immediacy of that you can't help but be excited. On the other hand, for those without Christ there is no hope after death.

In verse 5 Paul builds upon this thought to encourage us to be *"likeminded"* and in verse 6 to glorify God *"with one mind and one mouth."* These are yet more examples of the need for unity that we have been focusing on in Romans 14 and 15. Also used is the phrase *"one another,"* which we see all through the Bible to promote unity. This unity is not gained by organization or conformity, but is based upon our relationship with God.

The opening verses of Ephesians 4 talk about unity. Look at verses 7-8. *"But unto every one of us is given grace according to the measure of the gift of Christ. Wherefore he saith, When he ascended up on high, he led captivity captive, and gave gifts unto men."*

Verses 11-13: *"And he gave some, apostles; and some, prophets; and some, evangelists; and some, pastors and teachers; For the perfecting of the saints, for the work of the ministry, for the edifying of the body of Christ: Till we all come in the unity of the faith, and of the knowledge of the Son of God, unto a perfect man, unto the measure of the stature of the fulness of Christ."*

Unity is our family relationship with God. We are saved to live out our Christian lives and serve the Lord together. It is also a fellowship, as several New Testament passages point out. It is the Greek word *koinonia*, which means the gathering together of the body of Christ. Unity is a family, a fellowship, and a body.

What does it exactly mean to bear one another's burdens? We have talked about the theology of it, but what about the practical aspects? Consider this story from our church.

A man was saved after a life as a hopeless drunkard. His life was dramatically changed after he accepted Christ, and a man came along to mentor him in the things of God while also helping him find a job. This new Christian's life went along wonderfully for a few years.

One day he got a call from an ex, and it so upset him that he went backward. No one could reach him, and his mentor went to his house to see if he was there. He knocked on the door and the man appeared, completely drunk.

His friend came inside and surveyed the wreck that was his home. He stooped down and cleaned the vomit off his living room floor and then cleaned his bathroom as well. He got the man to sleep and stayed with him at the house until the next morning.

When he called the drunk man's employer to explain the situation, he was told that the man need not come back to work. He called back that afternoon to ask that his friend be given another chance but was rejected again. He tried a third time that night, calling the boss at home, and was told not to call anymore.

He didn't call again, but the next morning he showed up at the man's business. Walking into his office, he sat down and with tears in his eyes said, "Please give this man another chance. He had a setback; we all have them. He needs this job."

The boss was puzzled. "Why are you doing this?" he asked.

"Because I'm bearing his burden," the drunk man's friend replied.

The man got his job back. He has stumbled once or twice since then but he still has the job, not because the boss wanted him back, but perhaps because the boss didn't want to put up with the persistence of his friend who bore his burden.

That brings us to the purpose of this, which is displayed in verses 6-7. It is, quite simply, the glory of God. There is a miraculous cycle that is played out when you are I are glorifying God and bearing one another's burdens.

We are far better people if we understand that this life is not about what we can get out of it, but rather what we can give to other people. Perhaps the best illustration in the Bible is that of the Good Samaritan, who came to someone of a different race and religion and did all he could to help him. That is how you bear another's burden.

Look at Gal. 6:1-2. "*Brethren, if a man be overtaken in a fault, ye which are spiritual, restore such an one in the spirit of meekness; considering thyself, lest thou also be tempted. Bear ye one another's burdens, and so fulfil the law of Christ.*" We must help our weaker brethren with gentleness, not being judgmental but always keeping in mind that it could happen to us.

Skip down to verse 5, which says, "*For every man shall bear his own burden.*" If you can't mature and get to where you need to be, you can't help someone else. We must avoid always being victims and wanting others to tend to our needs. Instead, go through every day asking who may need you to be a blessing and an encouragement to them.

The verb *"bear"* used in these passages is defined that we should move out of our comfort zones and support someone else's burdens. Our example for this is not Paul, the writer of Romans, but the Lord Jesus Christ.

We saw in the early chapters of Romans what wonderful things God has done for us. Now we are seeing how He wants us to live out our faith, and one of the ways we do this is by bearing one another's burdens. It sweetly breaks us, as the song says, and does something in our hearts when we do this.

These thoughts are concluded succinctly and clearly in Rom. 15:7. *"Wherefore receive ye one another, as Christ also received us to the glory of God."* This is a challenge to the Christian and to the church.

There is a scenario that we see played out far too often. Someone gets saved and is so excited at this new life. The new convert begins with a feeling of great love for fellow Christians until one of them disappoints him. He backs up a bit, and it happens again so he backs up some more. This is not the time to back up, but a mature Christian needs to come by and say, "This is part of the Christian's growth experience."

We have all been disappointed by other believers. It is easy for some people to lump all Christians in the same group like politicians or lawyers. But God says we go through these experiences so we can bear another's burdens at a later time. Older Christians who have been down their road for a long time realize that the troubles they have gone through brought them to the level where God wants them to be.

Our faith is not in people, but in Him. But we can thank God for the many people who are doing their best to live out their faith according to His guidelines. Bearing one another's burdens is one way to know that we are living out our faith.

Chapter 31

LIVING A FULL LIFE

"Now I say that Jesus Christ was a minister of the circumcision for the truth of God, to confirm the promises made unto the fathers: And that the Gentiles might glorify God for his mercy; as it is written, For this cause I will confess to thee among the Gentiles, and sing unto thy name. And again he saith, Rejoice, ye Gentiles, with his people. And again, Praise the Lord, all ye Gentiles; and laud him, all ye people. And again, Esaias saith, There shall be a root of Jesse, and he that shall rise to reign over the Gentiles; in him shall the Gentiles trust. Now the God of hope fill you with all joy and peace in believing, that ye may abound in hope, through the power of the Holy Ghost. And I myself also am persuaded of you, my brethren, that ye also are full of goodness, filled with all knowledge, able also to admonish one another. Nevertheless, brethren, I have written the more boldly unto you in some sort, as putting you in mind, because of the grace that is given to me of God, That I should be the minister of Jesus Christ to the Gentiles, ministering the gospel of God, that the offering up of the Gentiles might be acceptable, being sanctified by the Holy Ghost. I have therefore whereof I may glory through Jesus Christ in those things which pertain to God. For I will not dare to speak of any of those things which Christ hath not wrought by me,

to make the Gentiles obedient, by word and deed, Through mighty signs and wonders, by the power of the Spirit of God; so that from Jerusalem, and round about unto Illyricum, I have fully preached the gospel of Christ. Yea, so have I strived to preach the gospel, not where Christ was named, lest I should build upon another man's foundation: But as it is written, To whom he was not spoken of, they shall see: and they that have not heard shall understand. For which cause also I have been much hindered from coming to you. But now having no more place in these parts, and having a great desire these many years to come unto you; Whensoever I take my journey into Spain, I will come to you: for I trust to see you in my journey, and to be brought on my way thitherward by you, if first I be somewhat filled with your company. But now I go unto Jerusalem to minister unto the saints. For it hath pleased them of Macedonia and Achaia to make a certain contribution for the poor saints which are at Jerusalem. It hath pleased them verily; and their debtors they are. For if the Gentiles have been made partakers of their spiritual things, their duty is also to minister unto them in carnal things. When therefore I have performed this, and have sealed to them this fruit, I will come by you into Spain. And I am sure that, when I come unto you, I shall come in the fulness of the blessing of the gospel of Christ. Now I beseech you, brethren, for the Lord Jesus Christ's sake, and for the love of the Spirit, that ye strive together with me in your prayers to God for me; That I may be delivered from them that do not believe in Judaea; and that my service which I have for Jerusalem may be accepted of the saints; That I may come unto you with joy by the will of God, and may with you be refreshed. Now the God of peace be with you all. Amen." **(Rom. 15:8-33)**

If you go to a cemetery, you will see on nearly every tombstone a couple of dates with a dash in between. It is easy to see the dash and wonder what happened in the dash, or what kind of life that person lived.

According to the Centers for Disease Control, the average life span in the United States is now about 78 years of age – 75 for men and 81 for women. Where are you on that scale? If you are 40 years old, you are halfway there. Of course, any of us could die at any time, but these numbers are a good way for you to gauge whether you are living a full life.

We know that you can only live a full life by being born again, so you should also consider how old you were when you were saved and look at your life since then. Are you living a full life?

The key verse in this passage is verse 14: *"And I myself also am persuaded of you, my brethren, that ye also are full of goodness, filled with all knowledge, able also to admonish one another."* There are also some key words in this passage that help illustrate what we are talking about regarding a full life.

The word *"minister"* in verse 8 and 25 come from a Greek word that depicts a common servant. Some English translations use the word *"servant"* in verse 8, where Paul is referring to Jesus Christ. Verses 16 and 27 also contain *"minister"* and *"ministering"* but in those cases the original Greek word suggests a public servant such as one in elected office. The word *"service"* in verse 31 actually means to perform sacred rites or perform in a priestly capacity.

From all of these references, it is logical to assume that living a full life must include some degree of service to others. Most people are consumed with what they can do or get for themselves, but you cannot live a full life until you become a servant.

Verse 14 contains several references to being full or filled. The word *"fulness"* in verse 29 is defined as actually being filled with service. A full life means that you have given yourself over to others.

There are several ingredients in this passage that are necessary for a full life. Verse 8 indicates that one needs an understanding of the Person of Jesus Christ, as He is the example of a servant depicted in that verse. He said in Luke 22:27, *"I am among you as he that serveth."*

Jesus has a purpose during His ministry on this earth, and there was a sequence to what He did. When He began to send out the disciples, we see His instructions to them in Matt. 10:5-6. *"These twelve Jesus sent forth, and commanded them, saying, Go not into the way of the Gentiles, and into any city of the Samaritans enter ye not: But go rather to the lost sheep of the house of Israel."*

After Christ ascended into Heaven, the book of Acts describes the ministry of the Holy Spirit descending first upon the Jewish people, and there was the phenomenon of the various languages spoken there and some 3,000 people saved. From there the Gospel went to the Samaritans (Acts 8), the Gentiles (Acts 10) and eventually the entire Roman Empire (Acts 13).

Why did the Gospel have to go to the Jews first? You have to understand God's calling of the Jews. He gave them the Torah and the sacred covenants, making them the first to receive His Word. God used them to begin the process of sharing His truth with the world.

The Bible is a life-changing Book for everyone who possesses it. I usually open my Bible when I am on an airplane, and recently a woman sitting next to me on a flight to Atlanta noticed it. "I've often wondered what the Bible is all about," she said.

What an opportunity! I asked if I could share with her from the Bible and she said yes. A few moments later I led her to Christ on that airplane. It's all because of God's Word.

In verses 9-12 Paul speaks about his mission to take the Gospel to the Gentiles, and several phrases in those verses are actually quotes from Old Testament verses, showing how the Old and New Testaments are tied together. These verses also emphasize praise and glory being given to God through Paul's work with the Gentiles, *"that in all things he might have the preeminence"* (Col. 1:18).

You must include the Person of Christ and the Word of God together to have a full life. When you accept Christ you have the potential for a full life, but to do it properly you must have the right understanding of the authority and the promises found in the Bible.

Go back to verse 14 and see how the fullness of God produces a reason to live. Remember that Paul, when he was known as Saul, was a man who persecuted Christians wherever he could find them. Now he is writing to the Romans about his confidence in the goodness of God and how that goodness and knowledge of who God is will allow his brethren to carry forth His Word.

I hear people say from time to time, "I need more of God." They say that in sincerity, but the fact of the matter is that God needs more of us, not the other way around. When you are saved you receive all of God that you will ever need.

I was at a restaurant with my family on a Saturday and sat next to my granddaughter. We had a good time with crayons and paper for 15 minutes or so, but then she decided she wanted out of her chair. The meal had not yet arrived, so I took her for a walk around the restaurant, and as she saw many people she didn't know she began to cling to me. Once she got bored and more familiar with her surroundings, however, she did everything she could to wriggle out of my arms and I finally took her back to her father so he could deal with her.

That's how we are sometimes with God. At times we get close to Him because we want to or because of circumstances in life that worry us, but at other times we voluntarily get away from Him and desire to get out on our own. When you do that, you are missing out on the fullness of God and the best life you can have.

Jesus said in John 10:10, "*I am come that they might have life, and that they might have it more abundantly.*" God wants you to have an abundant life and to enjoy your life. This life is one that comes from within and affects others.

The word translated as "*admonishing*" in verse 14 means the Word being put into someone else's mind or training a mind. This is to emphasize how the Word of God changes our lives.

Verse 15 shows that a full life evolves from the grace of God. The religions of the world do not fulfill us, but the grace of God does.

In verses 17-19 Paul talks about the mighty things God had done in his ministry, and you see his desire for results and a fruitful work. He specifically mentioned Illyricum, which was 1,400 miles from Rome, so you get an idea of the scope his missionary journeys.

People were always attracted to the apostle because of the great signs and wonders being performed, but the Gospel was the great divide. In Acts 14 Paul and Barnabas were referred to as gods, but when Paul gave the Gospel he was stoned and left for dead at Lystra.

If you plan to tell the wonderful story of Jesus and be a proponent of the Gospel, you will undoubtedly have some hard times. But a full life includes giving out the Gospel to a lost and dying world.

In verses 22-25 we see that the fullness of God includes a plan. No matter who you are, God has a plan for your life. Paul was a very busy man, and he had a tremendous desire to travel and serve. He wrote of his need to see his friends during a future trip while on his way to Spain.

Your church has an important ministry in your community, but it also has a job to do that affects other parts of the world. God is at work all over the globe, and we as a church must understand that. As I've gone to the Holy Land and on mission trips over the years I have recognized the vastness and variety in the world as well as its need for the Gospel.

Are you living a "status quo" life? Are you living in the joys of the past or the things of the present, or are you thinking about what's ahead for you? It may be hard for you to have a vision of the future sometimes because you're worried about just paying this month's bills. But God has a plan for you, and to have a full life you must have a vision and sense of where you are going.

Paul went from place to place without planes, trains or automobiles and yet he managed to cover an incredible amount of ground. He even spent some of time raising funds for the ministry, as he noted in verses 25-27. *"But now I go unto Jerusalem to minister unto the saints. For it hath pleased them of Macedonia and Achaia to make a certain contribution for the poor saints which are at Jerusalem. It hath pleased them verily; and their debtors they are. For if the Gentiles have been made partakers of their spiritual things, their duty is also to minister unto them in carnal things."*

Historians tell us that thousands of people probably attended the church in Jerusalem. As persecution increased and the apostles spread out over the region, Paul took it upon himself to raise support abroad for the mother church in Jerusalem that had fallen on hard financial times. That is how we support missions today, and we need to always be thinking about what is going on in other communities aside from our own.

In the latter verses of Romans 15 Paul encourages his brethren concerning prayer. Verse 30 says, *"Now I beseech you, brethren, for the Lord Jesus Christ's sake, and for the love of the Spirit, that ye strive together with me in your prayers to God for me."* The word *"strive"* denotes someone giving their all much like an athlete would in competition.

There is a concept known as quantum thinking, which challenges assumptions and mental models while rearranging cognition. It goes back to the Romans who always asked, "How much?" They were always thinking of how much more was really possible.

When Rick Warren wrote "The Purpose-Driven Life," many who read it thought that it was mostly ideas that everyone already knew. But Warren put them together in a way that took it to a different level and helped millions around the world.

Max Anders wrote in one of his books that when he hires someone, he is "buying vision." He once said, "God wants us all to have wealth, but be careful not to settle just for money."

We need to constantly be thinking about what else is out there. When God plants a seed of vision in your heart and you take off in pursuit of it, God will change it many times as you travel down the road. That's how you remember that it is actually God's vision, not yours.

The concept of quantum thinking actually has its roots in the Bible, where Paul wrote in Eph. 3:20, *"Now unto him that is able to do exceeding abundantly above all that we ask or think, according to the power that worketh in us."*

Think about where God is leading you, and go back to that dash in between the dates of your life. There are a lot of problems in there, but as you go on you realize that the things you worried about so much last year aren't problems at all this year. No matter your age, a full life consists of advancing your life beyond where it is today.

One day we will leave this world for eternity, but there is much living to be done before that. Living a full life encompasses an understanding of Christ and the Bible, knowing that God has a plan and realizing what kind of effect each of us can have on the entire world for the Gospel. In the midst of that we must never lose our joy in Christ. If anyone should be happy in life, it is the child of God.

Chapter 32

THE BEST OF FRIENDS

"I commend unto you Phebe our sister, which is a servant of the church which is at Cenchrea: That ye receive her in the Lord, as becometh saints, and that ye assist her in whatsoever business she hath need of you: for she hath been a succourer of many, and of myself also. Greet Priscilla and Aquila my helpers in Christ Jesus: Who have for my life laid down their own necks: unto whom not only I give thanks, but also all the churches of the Gentiles. Likewise greet the church that is in their house. Salute my well-beloved Epaenetus, who is the firstfruits of Achaia unto Christ. Greet Mary, who bestowed much labour on us. Salute Andronicus and Junia, my kinsmen, and my fellow-prisoners, who are of note among the apostles, who also were in Christ before me. Greet Amplias my beloved in the Lord. Salute Urbane, our helper in Christ, and Stachys my beloved. Salute Apelles approved in Christ. Salute them which are of Aristobulus' household. Salute Herodion my kinsman. Greet them that be of the household of Narcissus, which are in the Lord. Salute Tryphena and Tryphosa, who labour in the Lord. Salute the beloved Persis, which laboured much in the Lord. Salute Rufus chosen in the Lord, and his mother and mine. Salute Asyncritus, Phlegon, Hermas, Patrobas, Hermes, and the brethren which are with them. Salute Philologus, and Julia,

Nereus, and his sister, and Olympas, and all the saints which are with them. Salute one another with an holy kiss. The churches of Christ salute you. Now I beseech you, brethren, mark them which cause divisions and offences contrary to the doctrine which ye have learned; and avoid them. For they that are such serve not our Lord Jesus Christ, but their own belly; and by good words and fair speeches deceive the hearts of the simple. For your obedience is come abroad unto all men. I am glad therefore on your behalf: but yet I would have you wise unto that which is good, and simple concerning evil. And the God of peace shall bruise Satan under your feet shortly. The grace of our Lord Jesus Christ be with you. Amen. Timotheus my workfellow, and Lucius, and Jason, and Sosipater, my kinsmen, salute you. I Tertius, who wrote this epistle, salute you in the Lord. Gaius mine host, and of the whole church, saluteth you. Erastus the chamberlain of the city saluteth you, and Quartus a brother. The grace of our Lord Jesus Christ be with you all. Amen. Now to him that is of power to stablish you according to my gospel, and the preaching of Jesus Christ, according to the revelation of the mystery, which was kept secret since the world began, But now is made manifest, and by the scriptures of the prophets, according to the commandment of the everlasting God, made known to all nations for the obedience of faith: To God only wise, be glory through Jesus Christ for ever. Amen." **(Rom. 16:1-27)**

Think for a moment about the friends your have. Someone once said, "A friend walks in the front door of your life when you are in trouble."

Friends are extremely important to all of us. Nearly every parent is concerned about the friends of their children. Husbands and wives wonder about each other's friends.

The family of God is a big family. It is amazing how Paul takes the time in the final chapter of his remarkable letter to the Romans that he greets so many of his friends personally. He mentions by name nine friends from Corinth who were special to him.

How did Paul get so many friends? Well, he was a soul winner. Some of his best friends were people he had led to Christ and discipled.

As we look at Paul's friends it might be a good time to ask yourself what kind of friend you are and what kind of friends you have.

Have you ever had a friend who you caught talking about you behind your back? It changed the way you felt about that person, didn't it? On the other hand, you may have had a friend call you during a difficult period in your life and simply say, "I don't know what's going on, but I'm here for you." That made a difference as well.

Paul had many good friends in Romans 16, and one thing about them is that they were all in the Gospel. Just as he began the book of Romans by talking about the Gospel, he wraps it up the same way.

There are a lot of good programs and conferences that a church can take part in, but some of them can take a church away from an emphasis on the Gospel if we are not careful. We must always remember that. The message of the book of Romans is the message of the Gospel.

In verse 1 Paul cites Phebe, whom he calls "*a servant of the church*" at a port city in Corinth. The word "*servant*" here means deaconess, and a deaconess was usually a person who visited the sick, assisted young women and helped the poor. This woman was very involved in the church, and Paul called her a helper in verse 2. She was the kind of person you could pour your heart out to, and she would pray with you and keep it all between the two of you. She was a true friend, and as Paul wrote this letter from his prison cell he wanted others to tell her how important she was.

The next two names are Aquilla and Priscilla, who are mentioned in Acts, I Corinthians and II Timothy as well. As this passage notes, they risked their own lives to help Paul and are known and respected by several churches in the region. Paul speaks of them fondly as "*my helpers in Christ Jesus.*" We don't exactly know what they did that was dangerous but it was certainly important.

You've probably heard someone say, "I've got your back." Sometimes the person who says that is nowhere to be found when trouble starts brewing. But Aquilla and Priscilla had Paul's back, and they were there when it counted.

Paul probably met Aquilla when they were in the tent-making business and began having church services in the couple's home. In this time it was common to worship this way. Paul told the Romans that whenever they had the chance they should tell Aquilla and Priscilla of his appreciation for them.

These were vital instructions, because most communication at this time was still by word of mouth. There were no cell phones, e-mail messages or postal service. In fact, many scholars believe that Phebe delivered Paul's letter to the Romans herself.

Paul was an interesting person. He went from city to city, and each time he landed somewhere he began preaching. Sometimes there was revival, and other times there were riots. He needed some people who would stand by him, and the ones mentioned in Romans 16 are some who did just that.

The person listed is in verse 5. *"Salute my well-beloved Epaenetus, who is the firstfruits of Achaia unto Christ."* This was the first person Paul led to Christ in that region of Asia.

Think about the first person you led to Christ. Can you remember who it was? When you lead someone to Jesus Christ there is an affinity between you and that person that is often similar to that of a parent and a child. It is something special.

Paul mentioned someone named Mary in verse 6 and comments on how much she has labored. It is likely that she is an older woman who has been in the church for many years, and one commentator dubbed her "Mary the toiler." She was a laborer.

One day in the summer of 2008 I was preaching at the First Presbyterian Church of Binghamton, New York, in my capacity at president of Davis College. During the service I asked all of the Davis College students in attendance to stand, and when they did an older woman stood and said, "I am 72 years old. I am the oldest student at Davis College."

That is something. You might have a little bit of gray hair, but your life isn't over until God says it is. We can all learn from Mary in this passage and other people like this college student. I under-stand those who wish to retire from their careers, but no one should ever retire from service to God. Don't retire; transition to something else.

Paul referred to the next two people, Andronicus and Junia, as "*my kinsmen*," meaning that they were fellow Jews and possibly even relatives. More importantly, they spent time in prison with Paul for the sake of the Gospel.

Often when we hear of friends or family members who are in jail, we think about how they probably belong there and will learn some kind of lesson, then we forget about them. But some of the greatest things in a person's life can happen even in prison.

Most of you have heard of Chuck Colson, who was in the Nixon administration and sent to prison with others in the wake of the Watergate scandal. He found Christ in prison and now has a far-reaching ministry. He might never have become a believer had he not reached that low point in his life.

You may have a past that you aren't particularly proud of, but if you are redeemed in Jesus Christ you are truly redeemed. You can forget about the past and move forward.

Andronicus and Junia were longtime believers, having been saved before Paul, and probably husband and wife. Author John Crososta wrote this about Junia: "How great is the devotion of this woman that she should be counted worthy of the appellation of the apostles." This couple was well-thought of and greatly used of God.

It is interesting to see the many godly women in this passage. Women often come to the forefront, even today, in the church of Jesus Christ. We need both men and women to step up for God. Men should never sit in the background, but they should be the leaders that God meant for them to be.

Notice Amplias in verse 8. According to historians, in the early catacombs there was an elaborate tomb called the cemetery of Domatila. Apparently Domatila was related to Amplias, meaning that Christianity had penetrated the higher ranks of society.

In verses 9-11, Paul calls Stachys "my beloved" and speaks of Apelles as a relative or someone of the Jewish faith who has come to the Lord. Herodian is called "my kinsman." But Paul mentions the households of Aristobulus and Narcissus because he has something to say to all who live in their houses, including the slaves.

It was commonly known that Aristobulus was the grandson of the Jewish king Herod the Great, and when the king died his slaves were passed down through the family. Narcissus was a wealthy man who was prominent under Claudius but put to death when Nero took the throne. There were many believers in these two households and Paul made certain to send his greetings to all of them.

Tryphena and Tryphosa, both women, are named in verse 12. It is interesting that their names mean the same thing – delicately in touch. But the Bible says here that they worked very hard at what they did. Next was another woman, Persis, who *"laboured much in the Lord."* She was also a hard worker.

In verse 13 Paul calls Rufus "chosen in the Lord" and sends a greeting to *"his mother and mine."* Who is Rufus? For the answer to that question look at Mark 15:21. *"And they compel one Simon a Cyrenian, who passed by, coming out of the country, the father of Alexander and Rufus, to bear his cross."*

Several Bible scholars have said that this is the same Rufus mentioned in Romans 16. His father Simon, when compelled to carry the cross, had no love for the Romans but did it anyway. Then he probably saw Christ being crucified, which undoubtedly changed his life. We know from Acts 11:20 that men from Cyrene came to Antioch during the time of the early church, and Rufus likely had a role in that, having heard from his father the story of the crucifixion and coming in contact with the Gospel that way. When you give the Gospel to someone you have no idea whose lives will ultimately be touched.

Many commentators say that the men mentioned in verse 14 made up a group of businessmen who gathered to study the Bible and were influenced by Paul's teaching. Verse 15 names family members and others to illustrate how the Gospel was spreading all over the city of Rome.

Stop for moment and think about a question we mentioned earlier. Who are your friends? With whom do you have the best relationships? We have already pointed out that Paul's friends in Romans 16 were all in the Gospel and co-laborers with him.

After the general greeting in verse 16, Paul shifts gears and leaves these friends of his with a series of warnings. Verse 17 is a warning about division in the church that is similar to the theme in previous chapters of Romans regarding every Christian's responsibility to maintain unity. This verse specifically addresses those who would come into a church with a certain doctrine and divide that church over whether they believe that doctrine. Paul's instruction is clear about avoiding those people, and the word "offense" is translated as a kind of trap like one would use to catch an animal. Paul wanted to keep his friends from being trapped by these situations.

Those who would divide in this way are categorized in verse 18 by their motivations (they are doing it for themselves, not Christ) and their methods (they are smooth talkers who deceive those around them).

If all Christians in the United States would agree on the essentials of the faith and live their lives as the book of Romans teaches, there might be a sweeping revival across the country. We need to heed Paul's advice here and avoid pointless and dangerous confrontations.

The apostle concludes this final chapter of Romans with a tribute to some true heroes. We should all give careful consideration to who our heroes are.

In verse 21 Paul mentions Timothy and cites him as a fellow worker. If anyone was close to Paul during his ministry it was Timothy. The others in that verse, being named with Timothy, were certainly close to Paul as well.

Tertius, in verse 22, actually wrote down the words of Paul for this epistle. Verse 23 brings us Gaius, a man Paul led to Christ in Corinth and referred to as *"mine host,"* along with Erastus, who held a high office in the city. All of these people are being displayed by Paul as heroes and heroines of the faith.

Verse 24 begins the benediction of Romans. Notice in particular verses 25-26. *"Now to him that is of power to stablish you according to my gospel, and the preaching of Jesus Christ, according to the revelation of the mystery, which was kept secret since the world began, But now is made manifest, and by the scriptures of the prophets, according to the commandment of the everlasting God, made known to all nations for the obedience of faith."*

As we saw earlier, Paul began the book of Romans with the Gospel and ended it with the Gospel. He showed here how it is to be given – by preaching – and that it is to be taken to every nation on the face of the earth.

When our churches cease to give out the Gospel, we become no different than any other well-meaning secular organizations in our communities. The distinctive mark of any Bible-believing church must always be the Gospel.

Let me close this study with three things to remember from Romans:

- We are saved by grace and live by grace. The law should be preached and taught, but it saves no one; it drives us to Christ.
- Life is full of potentially life-changing friendships.
- The world is the parish for every church, as John Wesley once said, but it begins with the local church.

When we understand what we are and what we have in Christ, it is an awesome thing. As the book of Romans reminds us, we should never forget what He has done for us. Put Jesus Christ first and foremost in your life, and you will begin to live the kind of life He wants you to live.

This is what God is doing in the world.

Breinigsville, PA USA
25 March 2010

234857BV00002B/1/P